Solicitors' Accounts

Solicitors' Accounts

A Student's Guide

Fourth edition

Janet Baker LLB (Hons), Solicitor

BLACKSTONE PRESS LIMITED

This edition published in Great Britain 1992 by Blackstone Press Limited, 9-15 Aldine Street, London W12 8AW. Telephone: 081-740 1173

Previously published by Financial Training Publications Ltd

© Janet Baker 1984
First edition 1984
Second edition 1985
Third edition 1989
Fourth edition 1992

ISBN: 1 85431 238 3

British Library cataloguing in Publication Data
A CIP catalogue record for this book is available from the British Library

Typeset by Murdoch Evans Partnership, Tonbridge, Kent
Printed in Great Britain by Redwood Press Ltd, Melksham, Wiltshire

Contents

1.1 Introduction   1.2 Double-entry bookkeeping   1.3 Class-
ification of accounts   1.4 Worked example on double entry
1.5 The trial balance   1.6 Exercises on double-entry bookkeeping and trial balance   1.7 Suggested answers to exercises
on double-entry bookkeeping and trial balance   1.8 Test on
double-entry bookkeeping and trial balance   1.9 Suggested
answers to test on double-entry bookkeeping and trial balance

2.1 Introduction   2.2 Closing the accounts   2.3 Presentation
of final accounts   2.4 Exercise on basic final accounts   2.5
Suggested answer to exercise on basic final accounts   2.6 The
need for adjustments   2.7 Outstanding expenses adjustment
2.8 Payments in advance   2.9 Closing stocks   2.10 Work in
progress   2.11 Bad debts and doubtful debts adjustments
2.12 Depreciation   2.13 Sale of assets   2.14 Exercises on
adjustments and final accounts   2.15 Suggested solutions to
exercises on adjustments and final accounts   2.16 Test on final
accounts of a sole practitioner   2.17 Suggested answer to test
on final accounts of a sole practitioner

Preface

Unlike many traditional law subjects which are passive at an academic level, accounts is an active subject in which the student must participate. It is not enough to read and absorb. The basic accounting principles which are learned must be applied by translating the principles into worked examples. Thus to gain maximum use from this book the student must use it first as a reader from which to learn the basic principles and then as a workbook from which to learn the skill of applying those principles. To assist, numerous examples, exercises and past examination questions have been provided. It has been necessary in some cases to amend questions to reflect changes which have occurred since the question was set.

The principles which are stated in this book are in the main universal accounting principles which could apply as easily to a shopkeeper's accounts as to a solicitor's but because the book is specifically designed for law students and solicitors, nearly all the examples in it relate to a solicitor's practice.

The student using this book must methodically work through all chapters in the order in which they appear in the book. At the end of each chapter there are exercises which you should work through at your own pace, without first looking at the suggested answer. If you are not confident that you can do the exercises, work through the chapter again. When you are confident that you understand all the principles in a chapter and that you can do the exercises you should proceed to do the test set out at the end of the chapter. The test must be completed in the time stipulated and must be attempted under examination conditions. *Do not cheat* by looking at the suggested answer before or during the test. Remember the only person you are cheating is yourself!

Only when you are satisfied that you have truly mastered the principles in a chapter and have demonstrated your ability to apply them by completing the exercises and test should you go on to the next chapter.

At the end of the book you will find seven specimen examination papers. These papers should not be attempted until you have worked through the book. The test papers should be completed in the time stipulated and under examination conditions. It is essential from the outset that your accounts are neat and that you show all your workings. Untidy presentation is likely to lead to error as well as resulting in deduction of marks in the examination. In all cases the details column of the accounts should clearly show the account of double entry.

If you complete the work programme which this book provides, using the method suggested you should approach the examination with confidence. You have prepared thoroughly for it.

Acknowledgements

I should like to express my thanks to my erstwhile colleagues Maria Tighe and Penny Dickson for their help in developing the accounts teaching material used at Leeds Polytechnic which has formed the basis of this book and to all my former students who have unwittingly provided the inspiration for this book. To the publishers and their staff, in particular Heather Saward who has displayed a remarkable degree of tolerance and efficiency. Last but not least to my husband Peter and our children Richard and Matthew without whose help and understanding this book would never have been possible.

I should like to acknowledge with thanks the cooperation of the Law Society in agreeing to the use of past examination questions and to point out that the suggested answers given to those questions are my own.

1 Introduction to Solicitors' Accounts

1.1 INTRODUCTION

Solicitors' accounts are the written record of the financial transactions in which the firm engages. In a solicitors' practice there are really two sets of accounts:

(a) Those which record the day-to-day business transactions, for example the payment of a business expense, and which are largely the same as the accounts kept by any other business.

(b) Those which record transactions in which the practice handles money belonging to its clients, for example the receipts of sale proceeds on behalf of a client for whom the firm acts on the sale of a house.

1.1.1 Types of accounts kept by a solicitor

A solicitor must keep separate accounts for:

(a) Each person, firm or company with whom he has business dealings, for example if he buys office equipment on credit from Office Supplies Ltd he will open an account in the name of Office Supplies Ltd to record his indebtedness to that company.

(b) Each source of income, for example he will open an account called the 'costs account' to record costs charged to his clients.

(c) Each type of business expenditure, for example if he pays rent for his office he will open a rent account.

(d) Each type of asset, for example he will open a motor cars account to record the purchase of cars for use by the firm.

(e) Each client on whose behalf money is handled.

1.1.2 The purpose of keeping accounts

Accounts provide information about the firm which will be of interest to the following:

(a) The solicitors running the practice.
(b) A prospective purchaser of the practice.
(c) A prospective partner.
(d) A creditor or prospective creditor.
(e) HM Inspector of Taxes.
(f) Customs and Excise.
(g) The Law Society.

1.1.3 Duty to keep accounts

A solicitor has a duty to keep accounts to record transactions involving clients' money. The accounts and all bank statements must be preserved for a minimum period of six years from the date of the last entry in the case of accounts, or from the date of issue by the bank in the case of bank statements (rule 11(4) Solicitors' Accounts Rules 1991). Where a computerised system is used the solicitor must ensure that a hard copy can be produced within a reasonable time and remains capable of reproduction for at least six years.

In addition all paid cheques and copies of authorities must be retained for at least two years. To avoid the practical problems associated with storage, there is provision in the rules for the solicitor to obtain confirmation from the bank that it will retain cheques for the required two-year period.

A solicitor who comes within the provisions of the Accountant's Report Rules 1991 must have his client accounts inspected by an accountant 'qualified' within the meaning of the rules, and must submit an accountant's report to the Law Society annually. All solicitors must now comply with rule 7 of the Accountant's Report Rules 1991 unless they come within the three exemptions specified in the rules, which are:

(a) where the solicitor did not hold or receive clients' money at any time during the previous practice year.

(b) where the solicitor, having held clients' money during the previous year, has ceased to do so and an accountant's report has been delivered confirming this.

(c) where the solicitor is a public officer or employed by a local authority.

The Law Society has the power to appoint an accountant to investigate a solicitor's practice.

1.1.4 The layout of an account

There are several methods of drawing an account. The one method adopted in this book is as follows.

NAME OF ACCOUNT

Date	Details	Dr	Cr	Balance

The following points should be noted:

(a) This layout has five columns.

(b) There is one column each for date and details. The details column must indicate clearly the name of the account which forms the other part of the double entry.

(c) The column headed 'Dr' (abbreviation of debit) is always on the left. Debit entries, the meaning of which will be explained later in the chapter, are made in this column.

(d) The column headed 'Cr' (abbreviation of credit) is always on the right. Credit entries are made in this column.

(e) There is a balance column which gives a running balance on the account after each transaction is completed.

Rule 11(1) Solicitors' Accounts Rules 1991 now imposes an obligation to show the current balance on each client's ledger.

1.2 DOUBLE-ENTRY BOOKKEEPING

1.2.1 The principle

The system of double-entry bookkeeping operates on the basis that when the firm is involved in a transaction there are two sides to the transaction:

(a)   The firm receives value from the transaction.
(b)   The firm gives consideration for the value received.

The double-entry system records both sides of the transaction so that somewhere in the accounts both parts of the transaction will be shown — the double entry.

Example

On 1 March the firm buys a car for £3,000 and pays by cheque drawn on the firm's bank account. The two sides to this transaction are:

(a)   The receipt of value in the form of an asset acquired by the firm, i.e., the car.
(b)   The giving of consideration, i.e., reducing the firm's bank balance by £3,000.

To record this transaction the firm will use two accounts:

(a)   The motor cars account.
(b)   The cash account.

MOTOR CARS ACCOUNT

Date	Details	Dr	Cr	Balance
March 1	Cash purchase of car	£ 3,000	£	£ 3,000 Dr

CASH ACCOUNT

Date	Details	Dr (Received)	Cr (Paid)	Balance
March 1	Motor cars	£	£ 3,000	£

The following is of vital importance and must be committed to memory:

A debit represents:

(a) An increase in the value of an asset; or
(b) A reduction in the amount of a liability; or
(c) An item of expenditure.

A credit represents:

(a) A reduction in the value of an asset; or
(b) An increase in the amount of a liability; or
(c) An item of income.

The principle of double-entry bookkeeping is therefore: FOR EVERY DEBIT ENTRY IN ONE ACCOUNT THERE MUST BE A CORRESPONDING CREDIT ENTRY IN ANOTHER ACCOUNT.

1.2.2 The cash account in the double-entry system

The cash account records all money, cash and cheques, paid into the firm's bank account and all payments made by cheque (NB: a separate account is kept to record cash payments – the petty cash account). So in all transactions involving the receipt of money/cheques paid into the bank or payments by cheque the cash account will be one account of double entry.

Example

Jack Jones starts up in business as a painter and decorator. He borrows £1,000 from his brother Fred Jones and spends £300 on wallpaper and paint and £600 on a second-hand van. He does a job for £125 and pays the cheque he receives in payment into the bank.

At this stage Jack's cash account will look like this:

CASH ACCOUNT

Date	Details	Dr	Cr	Balance
		(Received) £	(Paid) £	£
	Fred Jones' loan	1,000		
	Decorating materials		300	
	Motor van		600	
	Income	125		225 Dr

The cash account tells Jack how much money he has in the bank but it does not tell him the whole story about his business:

(a)   It does not show that he owes Fred £1,000.
(b)   It does not show that he has spent his money on decorating materials which he will use to earn his income.
(c)   It does not show that he has acquired an asset, the van.
(d)   It does not show that he has earned an income of £125.00.

To complete the picture, Jack will have to open accounts to show the other side of each transaction:

FRED JONES: LOAN ACCOUNT

Date	Details	Dr	Cr	Balance
	Cash loan	£	£ 1,000	£ 1,000 Cr

DECORATING MATERIALS ACCOUNT

Date	Details	Dr	Cr	Balance
	Cash — wallpaper and paint	£ 300	£	£ 300 Dr

MOTOR VEHICLES ACCOUNT

Date	Details	Dr	Cr	Balance
	Cash — van	£ 600	£	£ 600 Dr

INCOME ACCOUNT

Date	Details	Dr	Cr	Balance
	Cash	£	£ 125	£ 125 Cr

Of course not all transactions will involve money being paid into or out of the bank, i.e., where the firm buys or sells goods on credit. By looking at the cash account Jack will not be able to tell how much he owes to others (his creditors) or how much is owed to him (his debtors). To record credit transactions two accounts other than the cash account will be used.

Suppose in the above example the following had occurred:

(a) Instead of paying £600 cash for the van Jack bought it on credit from Kwiksales. He will still use the motor cars account to show that he owns a van value £600 but now instead of the double entry being in the cash account he will open an account to show that he owes £600 to Kwiksales (a creditors account).

MOTOR VEHICLE ACCOUNT

Date	Details	Dr	Cr	Balance
	Kwiksales — van bought on credit	£ 600	£	£ 600 Dr

KWIKSALES ACCOUNT

Date	Details	Dr	Cr	Balance
	Motor vehicles — van on credit	£	£ 600	£ 600 Cr

(b)   As well as receiving a cheque for £125 for work done, Jack did £250 worth of work for Brown and agreed with Brown that he could pay at the end of the month. Jack needs to show in his income account that he has earned £250, but as he has not been paid yet, the double entry will not be in the cash account. He must open another account in the name of Brown to show that Brown is indebted to him to the tune of £250 (a debtors account).

INCOME ACCOUNT

Date	Details	Dr	Cr	Balance
		£	£	£
	Cash		125	
	Brown		250	375 Cr

BROWN ACCOUNT

Date	Details	Dr	Cr	Balance
		£	£	£
	Income – work done on credit	250		250 Dr

1.3   CLASSIFICATION OF ACCOUNTS

1.3.1   Personal accounts

The following should be noted with regard to personal accounts:

(a)   They record transactions involving individuals, firms or companies.

(b)   A separate account must be kept for each person, firm or company with which the firm has dealings, for example each debtor and creditor.

The rule for making entries in a personal account is:

DEBIT THE ACCOUNT OF THE PERSON, FIRM OR COMPANY WHICH RECEIVES VALUE FROM THE TRANSACTION.

Thus in the example above Brown's personal account is debited with £250 because he has received credit from the firm.

CREDIT THE ACCOUNT OF THE PERSON, FIRM OR COMPANY GIVING VALUE TO THE FIRM.

Thus in the example above (involving Kwiksales) their personal account is credited because they have given credit to the firm.

1.3.2 The personal accounts of the business proprietor

The accounts look at a transaction from the point of view of the business. For accounting purposes the business and its owner are treated as separate entities. This principle holds good for a solicitor's practice. The accounts which record transactions between the business and its owner are personal accounts. These accounts are:

Capital account

When a solicitor sets up in practice he will introduce assets, e.g., money, premises, car and equipment. When this happens:

(a)   The business receives assets, the value of which must be recorded in the appropriate account.
(b)   The business incurs a liability to the proprietor for the assets introduced – this is the proprietor's capital and is shown in his capital account.

Example

On 1 January Harry starts up in practice as a sole practitioner. He introduces £8,000 cash, a car valued at £5,000 and office equipment worth £2,000. These opening entries will be recorded as follows:

CASH ACCOUNT

Date	Details	Dr	Cr	Balance
		(Received)	(Paid)	
Jan 1	**Capital introduced by Harry**	£ 8,000	£	£

MOTOR CARS ACCOUNT

Date	Details	Dr	Cr	Balance
		£	£	£
Jan 1	Capital introduced by Harry	5,000		5,000 Dr

OFFICE EQUIPMENT ACCOUNT

Date	Details	Dr	Cr	Balance
		£	£	£
Jan 1	Capital introduced by Harry	2,000		2,000 Dr

CAPITAL ACCOUNT

Date	Details	Dr	Cr	Balance
		£	£	£
Jan 1	Cash and assets introduced		15,000	15,000 Cr

Drawings account

From time to time the proprietor will take money out of the business either in cash or by paying private expenses, for example a home gas bill. These are called drawings and are usually recorded in a personal account, the drawings account.

Example

On 31 January Harry draws £1,000 out of the firm's bank account for his own use and pays his personal poll tax of £500. The entries to record these transactions are as follows:

DRAWINGS ACCOUNT

Date	Details	Dr	Cr	Balance
		£	£	£
Jan 31	Cash — drawings	1,000		
Jan 31	Cash — personal poll tax	500		1,500 Dr

CASH ACCOUNT

Date	Details	Dr	Cr	Balance
		£	£	£
Jan 31	Drawings — cash		1,000	
	Drawings — personal poll tax		500	1,500 Cr

The credit balance on the capital account shows the amount which the business owes to its proprietor, i.e., the amount he has invested. The debit balance on the drawings account shows the amount the proprietor owes the business. You will see later that when the final accounts are prepared the firm's profit is calculated in the profit and loss account and where the business is run by a sole proprietor this profit belongs to him. The amount which the proprietor has invested in the business (i.e., the amount which the business owes to him) is calculated by taking the drawings from the profit and adding the resulting figure to the balance on the capital account.

1.3.3 Real accounts

The following should be noted with regard to real accounts:

(a)   They record the cost price of the firm's assets.

(b)   To decide whether a purchase is an asset, consider its degree of permanence. A typewriter, for example, has a relatively long working life and its purchase is the acquisition of an asset. A ball-point pen on the other hand has a relatively short working life and its purchase is a business expense recorded in a nominal expense account not in a real account.

(c)   The cash account is a real account as it records the value of money in the bank. The cash account is also sometimes treated as the personal account of the banker.

(d)   Real accounts usually have a debit balance. An exception to this general rule is the cash account which will have a credit balance if the firm has a bank overdraft.

(e)   The rule for making entries in real accounts is:

DEBIT A REAL ACCOUNT WITH THE VALUE OF AN ASSET ACQUIRED BY THE PRACTICE.

Thus in the example about Jack Jones, the decorator, his motor vehicles account was debited with £600 when he purchased the van.

CREDIT AN ASSET ACCOUNT WHEN THE STOCK OF ASSETS IS REDUCED

Either by sale or depreciation. A credit entry will be made in the cash account when cheques are drawn against the firm's bank account.

1.3.4   Nominal accounts

The following should be noted with regard to nominal accounts:

(a)   Some nominal accounts are income accounts. Nominal income accounts record the receipt of income by the firm. The following are examples of nominal income accounts kept by a solicitor:

(i)   Costs account. This account records details of profit costs charged to clients.

(ii)   Interest receivable account. This account records interest received by the firm on money held in a deposit account.

(iii)   Rent receivable account. This account records rent received by the firm if it leases off its surplus office accommodation.

Nominal income accounts are credited with income received and will therefore always have credit balances.

Example

A firm lets its surplus office premises for which it receives rent of £300 per month. On 1 January the firm receives the first month's rent.

RENT RECEIVABLE ACCOUNT

Date	Details	Dr	Cr	Balance
		£	£	£
Jan 1	Cash		300	300 Cr

CASH ACCOUNT

Date	Details	Dr	Cr	Balance
		£	£	£
Jan 1	Rent receivable	300		300 Dr

(b)   Some nominal accounts are expense accounts. Nominal expense accounts record the payment of business expenses.

(c)   A separate nominal expense account is opened for each type of expense which the firm has; for example, most firms will have rent, rates, electricity, telephone and salaries accounts.

(d)   A nominal expense account is debited each time the firm pays a business expense.

Example

On 30 November the firm pays an office electricity bill of £500.

ELECTRICITY ACCOUNT

Date	Details	Dr	Cr	Balance
Nov 30	Cash	£ 500	£	£ 500 Dr

CASH ACCOUNT

Date	Details	Dr	Cr	Balance
		(Received) £	(Paid) £	£
Nov 30	Electricity		500	500 Cr

   (e)   If goods are acquired under leasing or rental agreements under which the firm does not acquire ownership of the goods, the goods are not assets and their acquisition will not be recorded in a real account. Payments made under the leasing or rental agreement are business expenses and are recorded in a nominal expense account.

Example

A firm leases a word processor from Computor Supplies Ltd. The quarterly rental is £100. On 1 April the first instalment is paid.

RENTALS ACCOUNT

Date	Details	Dr	Cr	Balance
Apr 1	Cash (word processor)	£ 100	£	£ 100 Dr

CASH ACCOUNT

Date	Details	Dr	Cr	Balance
		£	£	£
Apr 1	Rentals (word processor)		100	100 Cr

Nominal expense accounts will always have debit balances.

1.4 WORKED EXAMPLE ON DOUBLE ENTRY

Fergus, a sole practitioner sets up his practice on 1 February with £5,000 cash, office equipment worth £1,000 and premises valued at £40,000.

During the month of February the practice engages in the following transactions:

    (a)   It buys a copier costing £2,000 on credit from Office Aids Ltd.
    (b)   It pays his home telephone bill of £80.
    (c)   It pays his secretary's salary of £300.
    (d)   It receives one month's rent from the tenant occupying part of the office premises – £200.
    (e)   It buys a desk for £500 in cash.
    (f)   It buys a car on credit from Karsales Ltd for £5,000.
    (g)   It pays the first instalment of £125 to Karsales Ltd under the credit agreement.
    (h)   Fergus draws £200 out of the bank for his own use.
    (i)   It buys a bookcase for £200 cash.

OFFICE EQUIPMENT ACCOUNT

Date	Details	Dr	Cr	Balance
		£	£	£
Feb 1	Capital introduced Office Aids Ltd (copier)	1,000 2,000		3,000 Dr

A real account.

PREMISES ACCOUNT

Date	Details	Dr	Cr	Balance
Feb 1	Capital introduced	£ 40,000	£	£ 40,000 Dr

A real account.

OFFICE AIDS LTD ACCOUNT

Date	Details	Dr	Cr	Balance
Feb	Office equipment	£	£ 2,000	£ 2,000 Cr

A personal account.

DRAWINGS ACCOUNT

Date	Details	Dr	Cr	Balance
Feb	Cash (home telephone bill) Cash (drawings)	£ 80 200	£	£ 80 Dr 280 Dr

A personal account.

SALARIES ACCOUNT

Date	Details	Dr	Cr	Balance
Feb	Cash (secretary)	£ 300	£	£ 300 Dr

A nominal expense account.

RENT RECEIVABLE ACCOUNT

Date	Details	Dr	Cr	Balance
Feb	Cash	£	£ 200	£ 200 Cr

A nominal income account.

OFFICE FURNITURE ACCOUNT

Date	Details	Dr	Cr	Balance
		£	£	£
Feb	Cash (desk)	500		500 Dr
	Cash (bookcase)	200		700 Dr

A real account.

MOTOR VEHICLES ACCOUNT

Date	Details	Dr	Cr	Balance
		£	£	£
Feb	Karsales Ltd (car)	5,000		5,000 Dr

A real account.

KARSALES LTD ACCOUNT

Date	Details	Dr	Cr	Balance
		£	£	£
Feb	Motor vehicles (car)		5,000	
	Cash (HP instalment)	125		4,875 Cr

A personal account.

CAPITAL ACCOUNT

Date	Details	Dr	Cr	Balance
		£	£	£
Feb	Cash and assets introduced		46,000	46,000 Cr

A personal account.

CASH ACCOUNT

Date	Details	Dr	Cr	Balance
		£	£	£
Feb	Capital introduced	5,000		5,000 Dr
	Drawings (telephone)		80	4,920 Dr
	Salaries		300	4,620 Dr
	Rent receivable	200		4,820 Dr
	Office Furniture		500	4,320 Dr
	Karsales Ltd		125	4,195 Dr
	Drawings (cash)		200	3,995 Dr
	Office furniture (bookcase)		200	3,795 Dr

1.5   THE TRIAL BALANCE

1.5.1   Purpose of the trial balance

The trial balance is a technique for ensuring the accuracy of the double-entry system and for assembling the balances on the accounts in a form convenient for the preparation of final accounts.

1.5.2   Preparation of the trial balance

We have seen earlier in this chapter that every transaction is recorded by means of two entries in the accounts, a debit entry in one account and a credit entry in another. It follows therefore that at any given time the total of the debit balances and the total of the credit balances should agree.

The trial balance is prepared by listing all the debit balances in one column and all the credit balances in another column. The two columns are totalled and should agree.

Example

On 31 October the bookkeeper extracts the following balances from the accounts of A.Solicitor:

	£
Capital account	1,500
Motor cars account	2,000
Office furniture account	500
Rent account	30
General expenses account	20
Rates account	125
Postages account	10
Stationary account	8
Salaries account	60
Drawings account	80
Cash account	650 Dr
Petty cash account	17
Loan account	2,000

The following trial balance is then prepared.

A. SOLICITOR: TRIAL BALANCE AS AT 31 OCTOBER

Name of account	Dr	Cr
	£	£
Capital		1,500
Motor cars	2,000	
Office furniture	500	
Rent	30	
General expenses	20	
Rates	125	
Postage	10	
Stationery	8	
Salaries	60	
Drawings	80	
Cash	650	
Petty cash	17	
Loan		2,000
	3,500	3,500

1.5.3   Errors not revealed by the trial balance

The fact that the total debit and total credit balances agree does not mean that the bookkeeper has not made any mistakes. There are some errors which will not be revealed by the trial balance, for example:

(a)   Errors of entry — the same incorrect entry is made in both accounts used to record the transaction.

Example

The firm buys a typewriter for £500. The bookkeeper inadvertently makes a debit entry in the office equipment account of £50 and a credit entry of £50 in the cash account.

(b)   Compensating errors — the bookkeeper makes two separate errors which cancel each other out.

Example

The bookkeeper incorrectly totals one account by £100 too much on the credit side and another by £100 too much on the debit side.

(c)   Errors of omission — the bookkeeper omits both parts of the double-entry from the accounts.

(d)   Errors of commission — the bookkeeper makes the correct entry but in the wrong account.

Example

The firm buys office equipment costing £1,000. Instead of debiting the office equipment account with £1,000 the bookkeeper debits the office furniture account.

(e)   Errors of principle — the bookkeeper makes an entry in the wrong type of account.

Example

The purchase of office equipment is shown in the general expenses account, i.e., a nominal instead of a real account. If this error remains undetected at the time the firm's final accounts are prepared the business expenses will be overstated in the profit and loss account and the value of the assets will be understated in the balance sheet.

1.6 EXERCISES ON DOUBLE-ENTRY BOOKKEEPING AND TRIAL BALANCE

1 Complete the following:

	Account to be debited	Account to be credited
(a) Buys office equipment for cash.		
(b) Buys office equipment on credit from Brown.		
(c) Buys a new car for use by the firm and pays cash.		
(d) Pays an employee's salary.		
(e) Buys stationery for cash.		
(f) Pays insurance premium.		
(g) Draws cash for own use.		
(h) Pays office telephone bill.		
(i) Pays private electricity bill.		

2 Peter starts in practice as a solicitor on 1 July with cash of £1,000, a car worth £6,000 and premises worth £28,000. During the month of July the following transactions occur:

 1 July   Pays water rates £90.
 3 July   Buys office furniture £180. Pays by cheque.
 8 July   Pays part-time secretary's salary £25.
10 July   Receives £2,500 as a loan from his brother-in-law Ted, to be
           repaid in three years without interest.
12 July   Pays home telephone bill £40.
13 July   Pays office cleaner £10.
14 July   Draws £50 for his own use.
15 July   Pays assistant solicitor's salary £150.
17 July   Buys stationery £50.
19 July   Leases a photocopier from Supplies Ltd for £50 per month
           and pays the first month's instalment.
20 July   Buys a typewriter on credit from Supplies Ltd for £800.
21 July   Pays office electricity bill £75.
27 July   Pays instalment of £20 to Supplies Ltd.

   Prepare accounts to record the above transactions and prepare a trial
balance as at 31 July.

3   The bookkeeper has extracted the following balances from the
accounts of Sam, a sole practitioner, on 30 September. From the balances
you are asked to prepare a trial balance.

	£
Salaries	1,000
Travelling expenses	400
Furniture	600
Leasehold property	1,500
Capital	12,500
Drawings	2,000
Loan account	1,000
Petty cash	100
Rates	150
Rent	750
Administration expenses	4,000
Motor cars	2,500
Cash account	500 Dr

4 The bookkeeper has extracted the following balances from the accounts of Sally Jones, a sole practitioner, on 31 January. From the balances you are asked to prepare a trial balance.

	£
Salaries	3,000
Office equipment	5,000
Freehold property	35,000
Capital	20,000
Drawings	13,200
Midshire Bank — loan account	10,000
Cash — office	1,000 Dr
Cash — client	125,000 Dr
Rates	900
General expenses	1,400
Debtors	2,000
Creditors	1,500
Rent received	2,000
Costs	30,000
Due to clients	125,000
Bank interest paid	2,000

5 From the following information, extracted as at 30 June, prepare a trial balance for Timothy, a sole practitioner.

	£
General expenses	200
Salaries	1,200
Drawings	4,000
Rent	250
Rates	150
Electricity	800
Creditors	2,500
Office furniture	7,000
Bank overdraft	1,300
Loan account	3,000
Car	1,700
Capital	8,500

1.7   SUGGESTED ANSWERS TO EXERCISES ON DOUBLE-ENTRY BOOKKEEPING AND TRIAL BALANCE

1	Account to be debited	Account to be credited
(a) Buys office equipment for cash	Office equipment account (real account)	Cash account (real account)
(b) Buys office equipment on credit from Brown	Office equipment account	Brown's Account (personal account)
(c) Buys a new car for use by the firm and pays cash	Cars account (real account)	Cash account
(d) Pays an employee's salary	Salaries account (nominal expense account)	Cash account
(e) Buys stationery for cash	Stationery account (nominal expense account)	Cash account
(f) Pays insurance premium	Insurance account (nominal expense account)	Cash account
(g) Draws cash for own use	Drawings account (personal account)	Cash account
(h) Pays office telephone bill	Telephone account (nominal expense account)	Cash account
(i) Pays private electricity bill	Drawings account	Cash account

2 CAPITAL ACCOUNT

Date	Details	Dr	Cr	Balance
		£	£	£
July 1	Sundry assets and cash introduced		35,000	35,000 Cr

MOTOR CARS ACCOUNT

Date	Details	Dr	Cr	Balance
		£	£	£
July 1	Capital	6,000		6,000 Dr

PREMISES ACCOUNT

Date	Details	Dr	Cr	Balance
		£	£	£
July 1	Capital	28,000		28,000 Dr

RATES ACCOUNT

Date	Details	Dr	Cr	Balance
		£	£	£
July 1	Cash (water rates)	90		90 Dr

OFFICE FURNITURE ACCOUNT

Date	Details	Dr	Cr	Balance
		£	£	£
July 3	Cash	180		180 Dr

SALARIES ACCOUNT

Date	Details	Dr	Cr	Balance
		£	£	£
July 8	Cash (secretary)	25		25 Dr
July 13	Cash (office cleaner)	10		35 Dr
July 15	Cash (assistant solicitor)	150		185 Dr

LOAN ACCOUNT: TED

Date	Details	Dr	Cr	Balance
		£	£	£
July 10	Cash		2,500	2,500 Cr

DRAWINGS ACCOUNT

Date	Details	Dr	Cr	Balance
		£	£	£
July 12	Cash (telephone bill)	40		40 Dr
July 14	Cash	50		90 Dr

STATIONERY ACCOUNT

Date	Details	Dr	Cr	Balance
		£	£	£
July 17	Cash	50		50 Dr

RENTALS ACCOUNT

Date	Details	Dr	Cr	Balance
		£	£	£
July 19	Cash (photocopier)	50		50 Dr

OFFICE EQUIPMENT ACCOUNT

Date	Details	Dr	Cr	Balance
		£	£	£
July 20	Supplies Ltd (typewriter)	800		800 Dr

SUPPLIES LTD

Date	Details	Dr	Cr	Balance
		£	£	£
July 20	Office equipment (typewriter)		800	800 Cr
July 27	Cash	20		780 Cr

ELECTRICITY ACCOUNT

Date	Details	Dr	Cr	Balance
		£	£	£
July 21	Cash	75		75 Dr

CASH ACCOUNT

Date	Details	Dr	Cr	Balance
		£	£	£
July 1	Capital	1,000		1,000 Dr
	Rates		90	910 Dr
July 3	Office furniture		180	730 Dr
July 8	Salary		25	705 Dr
July 10	Loan: Ted	2,500		3,205 Dr
July 12	Drawings		40	3,165 Dr
July 13	Salary		10	3,155 Dr
July 14	Drawings		50	3,105 Dr
July 15	Salary		150	2,955 Dr
July 17	Stationery		50	2,905 Dr
July 19	Rentals		50	2,855 Dr
July 21	Electricity		75	2,780 Dr
July 27	Supplies Ltd		20	2,760 Dr

PETER: TRIAL BALANCE AS AT 31 JULY

Name of account	Dr	Cr
	£	£
Capital		35,000
Motor cars	6,000	
Premises	28,000	
Rates	90	
Office furniture	180	
Salaries	185	
Loan accounts		2,500
Drawings	90	
Stationery	50	
Rentals	50	
Office equipment	800	
Supplies Ltd		780
Electricity	75	
Cash	2,760	
	38,280	38,280

3   SAM: TRIAL BALANCE AS AT 30 SEPTEMBER

Name of account	Dr	Cr
	£	£
Salaries	1,000	
Travelling expenses	400	
Furniture	600	
Leasehold property	1,500	
Capital		12,500
Drawings	2,000	
Loan account		1,000
Petty cash	100	
Rates	150	
Rent	750	
Administration expenses	4,000	
Motor cars	2,500	
Cash account	500	
	13,500	13,500

4   SALLY JONES: TRIAL BALANCE AS AT 31 JANUARY

Name of account	Dr	Cr
	£	£
Salaries	3,000	
Office equipment	5,000	
Freehold property	35,000	
Capital		20,000
Drawings	13,200	
Loan account		10,000
Cash (office)	1,000	
Cash (client)	125,000	
Rates	900	
General expenses	1,400	
Debtors	2,000	
Creditors		1,500
Rent receivable		2,000
Costs		30,000
Due to clients		125,000
Bank interest	2,000	
	188,500	188,500

5   TIMOTHY: TRIAL BALANCE AS AT 30 JUNE

Name of account	Dr	Cr
General expenses	200	
Salaries	1,200	
Drawings	4,000	
Rent	250	
Rates	150	
Electricity	800	
Creditors		2,500
Office furniture	7,000	
Cash		1,300
Loan account		3,000
Car	1,700	
Capital		8,500
	15,300	15,300

1.8   TEST ON DOUBLE-ENTRY BOOKKEEPING AND TRIAL BALANCE

Allow a maximum of 45 minutes to complete this test.

James starts in practice as a solicitor on 1 January. He introduces £2,000 into the firm's bank account and a car worth £1,200. He leases his office premises and pays rent of £50 per month. During the month of January the following transactions take place:

4 January	Pays first month's rent.
5 January	Pays salary £40 to secretary.
6 January	Buys a secondhand typewriter costing £250 on credit from Wylie Ltd.
9 January	Pays office telephone bill £25.
11 January	Pays rates £150.
18 January	Pays legal executive's salary £60.
19 January	Pays home electricity bill £20.
21 January	Buys car on credit from Motors Ltd. The car costs £2,000.
22 January	Buys stationery for £30.
23 January	Pays office electricity bill £45.

24 January   Pays instalment of £40 to Wylie Ltd.
25 January   Draws £80 for his own use.

Prepare accounts to record the above transactions, and prepare a trial balance as at 31 January.

1.9   SUGGESTED ANSWERS TO TEST ON DOUBLE ENTRY BOOKKEEPING AND TRIAL BALANCE

CAPITAL ACCOUNT

Date	Details	Dr	Cr	Balance
Jan 1	Sundry assets and cash introduced	£	£ 3,200	£ 3,200 Cr

MOTOR CARS ACCOUNT

Date	Details	Dr	Cr	Balance
Jan 1	Capital	£ 1,200	£	£ 1,200 Dr
Jan 21	Motors Ltd	2,000		3,200 Dr

RENT ACCOUNT

Date	Details	Dr	Cr	Balance
Jan 4	Cash	£ 50	£	£ 50 Dr

SALARIES ACCOUNT

Date	Details	Dr	Cr	Balance
		£	£	£
Jan 5	Cash (secretary)	40		40 Dr
Jan 18	Cash (legal executive)	60		100 Dr

OFFICE EQUIPMENT ACCOUNT

Date	Details	Dr	Cr	Balance
		£	£	£
Jan 6	Wylie Ltd (typewriter)	250		250 Dr

WYLIE LTD

Date	Details	Dr	Cr	Balance
		£	£	£
Jan 6	Office equipment		250	250 Cr
Jan 24	Cash	40		210 Cr

TELEPHONE ACCOUNT

Date	Details	Dr	Cr	Balance
		£	£	£
Jan 9	Cash	25		25 Dr

RATES ACCOUNT

Date	Details	Dr	Cr	Balance
		£	£	£
Jan 11	Cash	150		150 Dr

DRAWINGS ACCOUNT

Date	Details	Dr	Cr	Balance
		£	£	£
Jan 19	Cash (electricity bill)	20		20 Dr
Jan 25	Cash	80		100 Dr

MOTORS LTD ACCOUNT

Date	Details	Dr	Cr	Balance
		£	£	£
Jan 21	Motor cars		2,000	2,000 Cr

STATIONERY ACCOUNT

Date	Details	Dr	Cr	Balance
		£	£	£
Jan 22	Cash	30		30 Dr

ELECTRICITY ACCOUNT

Date	Details	Dr	Cr	Balance
		£	£	£
Jan 23	Cash	45		45 Dr

CASH ACCOUNT

Date	Details	Dr	Cr	Balance
		£	£	£
Jan 1	Capital	2,000		2,000 Dr
Jan 4	Rent		50	1,950 Dr
Jan 5	Salaries		40	1,910 Dr
Jan 9	Telephones		25	1,885 Dr
Jan 11	Rates		150	1,735 Dr
Jan 18	Salaries		60	1,675 Dr
Jan 19	Drawings		20	1,655 Dr
Jan 22	Stationery		30	1,625 Dr
Jan 23	Electricity		45	1,580 Dr
Jan 24	Wylie Ltd		40	1,540 Dr
Jan 25	Drawings		80	1,460 Dr

JAMES: TRIAL BALANCE AS AT 31 JANUARY

Name of account	Dr	Cr
	£	£
Capital		3,200
Motor cars	3,200	
Rent	50	
Salaries	100	
Office equipment	250	
Wylie Ltd		210
Telephones	25	
Rates	150	
Drawings	100	
Motors Ltd		2,000
Stationery	30	
Electricity	45	
Cash	1,460	
	5,410	5,410

2 Final Accounts

2.1 INTRODUCTION

A solicitor's final accounts consist of:

(a) Profit and loss account; and
(b) Balance sheet.

Final accounts are prepared annually at the end of the firm's financial year.

Immediately before the final accounts are prepared a trial balance is drawn up to assemble the balances on the accounts.

2.1.1 Profit and loss account

The following points should be noted with regard to the profit and loss account:

(a) It is a double-entry account.

(b) Its function is to calculate the net profit or loss made by the practice during the financial year.

(c) The practitioner can use the information in his profit and loss account to calculate the percentage of gross income used in overheads. He can see by comparison with previous years' accounts whether this percentage is increasing. He can use the information thus obtained to reorganise his practice, for example, it may become necessary to make staff redundant or to investigate means of cutting overheads.

(d) A detailed breakdown of the costs figure in the profit and loss account will tell the solicitor whether his income is narrowly or broadly based. For example, he may find that the bulk of his income comes from conveyancing work and that his main conveyancing client is a developer. He may wish to consider whether his practice can diversify.

2.1.2 Balance sheet

The following points should be noted with regard to the balance sheet:

(a) The balance sheet is a statement of the firm's assets and liabilities on a given date, usually the last day of the financial year.

(b) The balance sheet is not an account and is therefore not part of the double-entry system. It is a summary of the balances on the asset and liability accounts.

(c) At any time the assets of the practice should equal its liabilities. This is because each time the practice acquires something of value it gives consideration.

Example

X, a solicitor, commences in practice with £2,000 in cash which he places in the firm's bank account. Immediately X has a balance sheet; it is:

| Capital | £2,000 | | Cash at bank | £2,000 |

X's practice is thus shown to own £2,000 cash (an asset) all of which is owed to X, the owner of the practice (a liability).

(d) An analysis of the information in the balance sheet will tell the solicitor whether his practice is solvent and whether too much of his capital is tied up in fixed assets which will be difficult to realise.

2.2 CLOSING THE ACCOUNTS

(a) Immediately prior to preparing the final accounts the nominal income and expense accounts are closed by transferring the balance on each account to the profit and loss account.

(b) Nominal expense accounts have debit balances and so to effect a transfer from a nominal expense account to the profit and loss account, the bookkeeping entries are:

(i) Credit the nominal expense account.
(ii) Debit the profit and loss account.

Example

At the end of the year the firm's salaries account has a debit balance of £15,000. The balance is transferred to the profit and loss account on 31 December.

SALARIES ACCOUNT

Date	Details	Dr	Cr	Balance
		£	£	£
Dec 31	Balance Profit and loss account: transfer		15,000	15,000 Dr ———

(c)   Nominal income accounts have credit balances and so to effect a transfer from a nominal income account to the profit and loss account, the bookkeeping entries are:
    (i)   Debit the nominal income account.
    (ii) Credit the profit and loss account.

Example

At the end of the year the firm's costs account has a credit balance of £300,000. On 31 December the balance is transferred to the profit and loss account.

COSTS ACCOUNT

Date	Details	Dr	Cr	Balance
		£	£	£
Dec 31	Balance Profit and loss account: transfer	300,000		300,000 Cr ———

(d)   When the transfer entries have been made, the nominal income and expense accounts are closed.

(e)   The balance sheet, unlike the profit and loss account, is not an account of double entry and so the balances on the asset and liability accounts are not transferred to the balance sheet. The asset and liability accounts are ongoing and will be kept open for as long as the asset is owned by the firm or for as long as the liability remains unsettled.

2.3 PRESENTATION OF FINAL ACCOUNTS

2.3.1 Vertical format: profit and loss account

There are two methods of presenting final accounts: the horizontal format and the vertical format. In this book, as in the examination, the vertical format will be used. A vertical format profit and loss account is shown in the following example:

SALLY JONES: PROFIT AND LOSS ACCOUNT FOR THE YEAR ENDED 31 JANUARY 1988

	£	£
INCOME		
Costs	30,000	
Rent received	2,000	32,000
LESS: EXPENDITURE		
Salaries	3,000	
Rates	900	
General expenses	1,400	
Bank interest	2,000	7,300
NET PROFIT		24,700

This is a very simple example of a profit and loss account. You will see later in the chapter when we have dealt with adjustments that a third column is used in the profit and loss account to adjust the nominal income and expense account balances, to show, as accurately as possible, the profit or loss.

2.3.2 Comments on the profit and loss account

(a) Commit the format of the profit and loss account to memory.
(b) Be able to identify the nominal income and expense accounts which make up the profit and loss account.

(c)   At the end of the financial year the nominal accounts are closed. The credit balances from the nominal income accounts are transferred to the income side of the profit and loss account. The debit balances from the nominal expense accounts are transferred to the expenditure side of the profit and loss account.

(d)   The balance left after deducting total expenditure from total income is net profit (or loss). If a profit is made this is credited to the capital account in the case of a sole practitioner. If a loss is made this is debited to the capital account. For the position in the case of a partner-ship see chapter 4.

(e)   Drawings made by the proprietor are appropriations of profit, not business expenses. Thus the balance on the drawings account is not transferred to the profit and loss account.

2.3.3   Vertical format: balance sheet

SALLY JONES: BALANCE SHEET AS AT 31 JANUARY 1988

CAPITAL EMPLOYED	£	£	£
Capital at start of year	20,000		
Add net profit	24,700	44,700	
Less drawings		13,200	31,500
Add long-term liabilities:			
Midshire Bank loan			10,000
			41,500
EMPLOYMENT OF CAPITAL			
FIXED ASSETS			
Freehold property		35,000	
Office equipment		5,000	40,000
CURRENT ASSETS			
Debtors	2,000		
Cash (office account)	1,000	3,000	

LESS CURRENT LIABILITIES
Creditors   1,500
NET CURRENT ASSETS   1,500
CLIENT ACCOUNT
Client bank balance   125,000
Less due to clients   125,000

                                                                   41,500

2.3.4 Comments on the balance sheet

(a) Capital — this is the money owed by the business to its proprietor.

Example

Sprout, a sole practitioner, prepares his final accounts on 30 June each year. On 30 June 1988 his profit and loss account showed a net profit of £15,000. On 1 July 1987 his capital account had a balance of £25,000. Sprout has made drawings during the year to 30 June 1988 totalling £12,000.
  Sprout's capital account will appear as follows:

CAPITAL ACCOUNT

Date	Details	Dr	Cr	Balance
		£	£	£
	Balance			25,000 Cr
	Net profit, from profit and loss account		15,000	40,000
	Drawings	12,000		28,000 Cr

Sprout's drawings account will be closed off as follows:

DRAWINGS ACCOUNT

Date	Details	Dr	Cr	Balance
		£	£	£
	Balance			12,000 Dr
	Capital account		12,000	————

The closing balance figure on the capital account is the relevant figure to be shown on the balance sheet but it is customary to show on the balance sheet the detailed movements in the capital account and not merely the closing balance.

Example

BALANCE SHEET AS AT 30 JUNE 1988

CAPITAL EMPLOYED	£	£	£
Balance at start	25,000		
Add net profit	15,000	40,000	
	————		
Less drawings		12,000	28,000
		————	

(b) Long-term liabilities are added to capital. Mortgages and long-term loans should be included but not short-term loans, for example, bank overdrafts, which are current liabilities. As a general guide, if a liability is to continue for more than twelve months it is usually treated as a long-term liability.

(c) In the example given in section 2.3.3 the assets are listed in order of permanence, i.e., the fixed assets which are most difficult to realise in cash are listed first, followed by the current assets, which are easiest to realise. The fixed assets themselves are also listed in order of permanence so that premises are shown first and motor cars last. An alternative is to list assets in the order of liquidity in which case the order of presentation will be reversed.

(d) When final accounts are presented vertically, it is customary to show current liabilities as a deduction from current assets rather than adding the current liabilities to the liabilities side of the balance sheet.

(e)   The figure which results from deducting current liabilities from current assets is the working capital of the practice. This is the capital which is available to run the practice after fixed assets have been purchased, i.e., the money which is available to meet expenditure.

(f)   The cash in the client bank account is not shown in the balance sheet as it is money which belongs to the individual clients on whose behalf it is held and is not a current asset of the practice.

(g)   The credit balances on clients' personal accounts are not shown as liabilities of the practice because a fund of money — the client account bank balance — is held to discharge this liability.

(h)   The cash at bank on client account and the credit balances on the client accounts (i.e., the firm's liability to its clients) are balanced separately. At any time the two balances should be the same. If they are not, the solicitor has committed a breach of the Solicitors' Accounts Rules 1991.

2.4   EXERCISE ON BASIC FINAL ACCOUNTS

From the following balances extracted from the accounts of Alexander on the 30 November 1988 prepare:

(a)   a trial balance;
(b)   a profit and loss account;
(c)   a balance sheet.

	£
Costs	10,000
Light and heat	360
Drawings	9,300
Creditors	490
Cash at bank (office)	923 Dr
Cash at bank (client)	75,000 Dr
Premises	18,000
Insurance commission	1,300
Rates	1,700
Salaries	2,800
Stationery	700
Capital	10,469
Bank loan	12,000
Debtors	466
Petty cash	10
Due to clients	75,000

2.5   SUGGESTED ANSWER TO EXERCISE ON BASIC FINAL ACCOUNTS

ALEXANDER: TRIAL BALANCE AS AT 30 NOVEMBER 1988

Name of account	Dr	Cr
	£	£
Costs		10,000
Light and heat	360	
Drawings	9,300	
Creditors		490
Cash at bank (office)	923	
Cash at bank (client)	75,000	
Premises	18,000	
Insurance commission		1,300
Rates	1,700	
Salaries	2,800	
Stationery	700	
Capital		10,469
Loan		12,000
Debtors	466	
Petty cash	10	
Due to clients		75,000
	109,259	109,259

PROFIT AND LOSS ACCOUNT FOR THE YEAR ENDED 30 NOVEMBER 1988

	£	£
INCOME		
Costs	10,000	
Insurance commission	1,300	11,300
LESS EXPENDITURE		
Light and heat	360	
Rates	1,700	
Salaries	2,800	
Stationery	700	5,560
NET PROFIT		5,740

BALANCE SHEET AS AT 30 NOVEMBER 1988

CAPITAL EMPLOYED	£	£	£
Capital at start	10,469		
Add net profit	5,740	16,209	
Less drawings		9,300	6,909
Add long-term liabilities:			
Bank loan			12,000
			18,909

EMPLOYMENT OF CAPITAL			
FIXED ASSETS			
Premises			18,000
CURRENT ASSETS			
Debtors	466		
Cash at bank (office)	923		
Petty cash	10	1,399	
LESS CURRENT LIABILITIES			
Creditors		490	
NET CURRENT ASSETS			909
CLIENT ACCOUNT			
Client bank balance		75,000	
Less due to clients		75,000	
			18,909

2.6 THE NEED FOR ADJUSTMENTS

The balances on the nominal income and expense accounts do not show all income earned or all expenditure incurred during the year. Adjustments are made to ensure that income includes all work done during the current year even though it has not yet been billed. They are also made to ensure that expenditure includes expenses incurred in the current year in respect of which bills have not yet been paid, and does not include expenses which although paid in the current year relate to the next financial year.

The adjustments which will be made immediately before the final accounts are prepared are detailed below.

2.7 OUTSTANDING EXPENSES ADJUSTMENT

There are expenses incurred during the current financial year in respect of which payment is not made until the next financial year, for example, gas, electricity and telephone charges.

At the end of the financial year, provision is made for the expense incurred but not paid during the current year. If a bill has not already been received the provision will be an estimate.

The adjustment is shown by making a debit entry in the appropriate nominal expense account. The double entry is a credit in the same nominal expense account at the start of the next financial year.

Example

A solicitor prepares his final accounts on 31 October. At that date his telephone account has a debit balance of £600. He decides to make provision of £200 for telephone charges due but unpaid. His telephone account will appear as follows:

TELEPHONE ACCOUNT

Date	Details	Dr	Cr	Balance
		£	£	£
Oct 31	Balance Provision c/d	200		600 Dr 800 Dr

The balance on the expense account, including the provision made at the end of the financial year is transferred to the profit and loss account and the nominal expense account is closed. Continuing the example:

TELEPHONE ACCOUNT

Date	Details	Dr	Cr	Balance
		£	£	£
	Balance			600 Dr
Oct 31	Provision c/d	200		800 Dr
	Profit and loss account: transfer		800	—

The provision is carried down as a credit entry in the expense account at the start of the next financial year. The provision will be set off against payment of the bill in the next financial year. Continuing the example, on 10 November the bill of £200 is paid.

TELEPHONE ACCOUNT

Date	Details	Dr	Cr	Balance
		£	£	£
	Balance			600 Dr
Oct 31	Provision c/d	200		800 Dr
	Profit and loss account, Transfer		800	—
Nov 1	Provision b/d		200	200 Cr
Nov 10	Cash	200		—

The provision for outstanding expenses is shown on the balance sheet as a current liability because on the date on which the balance sheet is prepared, it is expenditure incurred but not yet paid. Continuing the example:

BALANCE SHEET AS AT 31 OCTOBER

CAPITAL EMPLOYED			XX
EMPLOYMENT OF CAPITAL			
FIXED ASSETS		XX	
CURRENT ASSETS	XX		
LESS CURRENT LIABILITIES			
Outstanding expenses – Telephone	200	XX	XX

2.8   PAYMENTS IN ADVANCE

If a payment is made in the current financial year for a service which will not be used until the next financial year, for example, rates, then, at the end of the financial year, the appropriate expense account is credited with the amount paid in advance. This has the effect of reducing the expenditure and increasing the profit. The corresponding debit entry is made in the same account at the start of the next financial year.

Example

A solicitor pays rates of £400 per annum by two equal instalments, in advance, on 31 March and 30 September each year. He prepares his final accounts on 31 December each year. Thus he is making a payment in advance of £100 for rates because the £200 paid on 30 September is for rates from 1 October to 31 March.

RATES ACCOUNT

Date	Details	Dr	Cr	Balance
		£	£	£
Mar 31	Cash	200		200 Dr
Sept 30	Cash	200		400 Dr
Dec 31	Payment in advance c/d		100	300 Dr

The balance on the expense account is transferred to the profit and loss account at the end of the year. Continuing the example:

RATES ACCOUNT

Date	Details	Dr	Cr	Balance
		£	£	£
Mar 31	Cash	200		200 Dr
Sept 30	Cash	200		400 Dr
Dec 31	Payment in advance c/d		100	300 Dr
	Profit and loss account: transfer		300	——

Note that the firm is charging to the profit and loss account as a business expense only the amount spent on rates from 1 January to 31 December, i.e., in the current financial year.

The payment in advance is brought down as a debit entry on the expense account at the start of the next financial year, which is when the service that has been paid for in the current financial year will be used. Continuing the example:

RATES ACCOUNT

Date	Details	Dr	Cr	Balance
		£	£	£
Mar 31	Cash	200		200 Dr
Sept 30	Cash	200		400 Dr
Dec 31	Payment in advance c/d		100	300 Dr
	Profit and loss account:			
	transfer		300	———
Jan 1	Payment in advance b/d	100		100 Dr

The payment in advance is shown on the balance sheet as a current asset. In theory the person to whom the payment has been made is a debtor of the firm for the service which is to be supplied.

BALANCE SHEET AS AT 31 DECEMBER

	£	£	£
CAPITAL EMPLOYED			XX
			═══
EMPLOYMENT OF CAPITAL			
FIXED ASSETS		XX	
CURRENT ASSETS			
Payments in advance			
Rates	100		

2.9 CLOSING STOCKS

The same principle as for payments in advance applies where the expense was incurred for something tangible such as stationery, stamps, pens, etc. Only the cost of the stationery, etc., actually used during the year should be transferred to the profit and loss account as an expense. When the stationery, etc., was paid for, a debit entry would have been made in the appropriate expense account. At the end of the financial year the stock left over will be valued and the value of this closing stock will be credited to the appropriate expense account. The corresponding debit entry is made in the same account at the start of the next financial year when the closing stock is brought down as opening stock.

Example

During the year the firm pays the following amounts for stationery:

31 March	£40
16 October	£25
8 December	£35

Final accounts are prepared on 31 December. On 31 December the firm has a stock of stationery paid for but unused, valued at £30.

STATIONERY ACCOUNT

Date	Details	Dr	Cr	Balance
		£	£	£
Mar 31	Cash	40		40 Dr
Oct 16	Cash	25		65 Dr
Dec 8	Cash	35		100 Dr
Dec 31	Closing stock c/d		30	70 Dr

At the end of the year the nominal expense account is closed and the balance on it is transferred to the profit and loss account. Continuing the example:

STATIONERY ACCOUNT

Date	Details	Dr	Cr	Balance
		£	£	£
Mar 31	Cash	40		40 Dr
Oct 16	Cash	25		65 Dr
Dec 8	Cash	35		100 Dr
Dec 31	Closing stock c/d		30	70 Dr
	Profit and loss account:			
	transfer		70	——

Note that only the cost of stationery used during the current financial year is transferred to the profit and loss account as a business expense.

The value of the closing stock is brought down as a debit entry in the expense account at the start of the next financial year. Continuing the example:

STATIONERY ACCOUNT

Date	Details	Dr	Cr	Balance
		£	£	£
Mar 31	Cash	40		40 Dr
Oct 16	Cash	25		65 Dr
Dec 8	Cash	35		100 Dr
Dec 31	Closing stock c/d		30	70 Dr
	Profit and loss account:			
	transfer		70	——
Jan 1	Opening stock b/d	30		30 Dr

Note that at the start of the next financial year the closing stock from the previous year becomes opening stock.

On the balance sheet the value of the closing stock is shown as a current asset. Continuing the example:

BALANCE SHEET AS AT 31 DECEMBER

	£	£	£
CAPITAL EMPLOYED			XX
			==
EMPLOYMENT OF CAPITAL			
FIXED ASSETS		XX	
CURRENT ASSETS			
Closing stock of stationery	30		

2.10   WORK IN PROGRESS

Work in progress is work done on behalf of clients during the financial year to which the final accounts relate but in respect of which bills have not been delivered to clients.

If the profit and loss account is to show income earned during the year the value of the work in progress, which must be estimated, must be added to the costs figure.

An adjustment is made on the costs account at the end of the financial year to record the value of work in progress. This is known as the closing work in progress. The adjustment is made by crediting the costs account with the value of closing work in progress. The corresponding debit entry is made in the same account at the start of the next financial year by bringing the old closing work in progress down as opening work in progress.

Example

The firm prepares its final accounts on 31 October each year. On 31 October the costs account has a credit balance of £30,000. Work in progress is valued at £5,000.

COSTS ACCOUNT

Date	Details	Dr	Cr	Balance
		£	£	£
Oct 31	Balance			30,000 Cr
	Closing work in progress c/d		5,000	35,000 Cr

At the end of the financial year the costs account is closed and the balance on the account is transferred to the profit and loss account. At the start of the new financial year the closing work in progress is brought down on the Dr side as opening work in progress. Continuing the example:

COSTS ACCOUNT

Date	Details	Dr	Cr	Balance
		£	£	£
Oct 31	Balance			30,000 Cr
	Closing work in progress c/d		5,000	35,000 Cr
	Profit and loss account: transfer	35,000		————
Nov 1	Opening work in progress b/d	5,000		5,000 Dr

The value of the closing work in progress is shown on the balance sheet as a current asset. Continuing the example:

BALANCE SHEET AS AT 31 OCTOBER

	£	£	£
CAPITAL EMPLOYED			XX
EMPLOYMENT OF CAPITAL			
FIXED ASSETS		XX	
CURRENT ASSETS			
Closing work in progress	5,000		

In the following year the costs account begins with the debit entry for opening work in progress. This reduces the income from costs in that year (as the costs figure includes bills delivered which include costs for work carried out in the previous year). The movement on the costs account will be shown in the profit and loss account.

Example

Work in progress at 1 January 1990	£ 15,000
Costs as at 31 December 1990	£125,000
Work in progress at 31 December 1991	£ 20,000

PROFIT AND LOSS ACCOUNT FOR THE YEAR ENDED
31 DECEMBER 1990

	£	£	£
INCOME			
Costs	125,000		
Add closing work in progress	20,000	145,000	
Deduct opening work in progress		15,000	
			130,000

Note. Only the closing work in progress figure is shown in the balance sheet.

2.10.1   Worked example on closing work in progress adjustment

A firm of solicitors prepares its final accounts on 30 June each year. The firm's costs account shows an opening debit balance on 1 July 1990 of £35,000. During the year ending 30 June 1991, bills have been delivered to clients totalling £175,000. The firm estimates that the value of work done during the year ending 30 June 1991, in respect of which bills have not yet been delivered, is £45,000. The accounts to record the above will appear as follows:

COSTS ACCOUNT

Date	Details	Dr	Cr	Balance
		£	£	£
1990				
July 1	Opening work in progress b/d	35,000		35,000 Dr
1991				
June 30	Sundry costs		175,000	140,000 Cr
	Closing work in progress c/d		45,000	185,000 Cr
	Profit and loss account: transfer	185,000		————
July 1	Opening work in progress b/d	45,000		45,000 Dr

PROFIT AND LOSS ACCOUNT FOR THE YEAR ENDED 30 JUNE 1991

	£	£
INCOME		
Costs	175,000	
Add: Closing work in progress	45,000	
	———	
	220,000	
Less: Opening work in progress	35,000	185,000
	———	———

Note. By convention the detailed movement on the costs account is shown on the profit and loss account.

BALANCE SHEET AS AT 30 JUNE 1991

	£	£	£
CAPITAL EMPLOYED			XX

EMPLOYMENT OF CAPITAL
FIXED ASSETS   XX
CURRENT ASSETS
Closing work in progress   45,000

2.11 BAD DEBTS AND DOUBTFUL DEBTS ADJUSTMENTS

2.11.1 Writing off bad debts

Debts owed to the practice are an asset but it is unlikely that all debts will be recovered. It follows therefore that all income shown in the costs account is unlikely to be actually received. To avoid profit and the asset of debtors being overstated, an adjustment should be made for debts which are known to be bad and those which are considered doubtful.

To write off a debt of a particular client which is known to be irrecoverable make the following entries:

(a) Credit the client's ledger account.
(b) Debit bad debts account.

Example

A bill delivered to Jack two years ago for £115 (including £15 VAT) has not been paid. At the end of the financial year 31 October 1990 the debt is written off.

JACK'S ACCOUNT

Date	Details	Dr	Cr	Balance
1990		£	£	£
	Balance			115 Dr
Oct 31	Bad debt: written off		115	——

Note that the section of Jack's account shown in the example is the office account. Jack's account will also have a separate identical section for recording dealings with clients' money. This will be explained fully in later chapters and you need not be concerned with it at this stage.

BAD DEBTS ACCOUNT

Date	Details	Dr	Cr	Balance
1990 Oct 31	Jack: debt written off	£ 115	£	£ 115 Dr

If the debt is written off in circumstances where the client is bankrupt or a company is in liquidation, Customs and Excise will allow the practice to claim credit for the VAT element of the debt. The entries to write off a bad debt where VAT is recoverable are:

(a)   Credit the client's ledger account with the profit costs and VAT written off (shown as separate entries).
(b)   Debit the Customs and Excise account with VAT.
(c)   Debit the bad debts account with the profit costs written off.

Example

Continuing the above example assume that Jack has been adjudicated bankrupt and that therefore the £15 VAT can be recovered from Customs and Excise.

JACK'S ACCOUNT

Date	Details	Dr	Cr	Balance
1990		£	£	£ 115 Dr
	Balance			
Oct 31	Bad debt: written off		100	
	Customs and Excise: VAT		15	——

CUSTOMS AND EXCISE ACCOUNT

Date	Details	Dr	Cr	Balance
1990 Oct 31	Jack: VAT written off	£ 15	£	£ 15 Dr

BAD DEBTS ACCOUNT

Date	Details	Dr	Cr	Balance
1990 Oct 31	Jack: debt written off	£ 100	£	£ 100 Dr

2.11.2 Recovery of a debt that has been written off

When a debt that has previously been written off as a bad debt is recovered, the following entries will be made in the accounts:

(a) Debit cash account (office).

(b) Credit bad debts account.

Continuing the example, assume that in the year after the debt has been written off, Jack pays his bill.

OFFICE CASH ACCOUNT

Date	Details	Dr	Cr	Balance
1991 Jan 15	Bad debts (recovered from Jack)	£ 115	£	£ 115 Dr

BAD DEBTS ACCOUNT

Date	Details	Dr	Cr	Balance
1991 Jan 15	Cash (debt recovered from Jack)	£	£ 115	£ 115 Cr

No entry is made in Jack's account.

2.11.3   Making a provision for doubtful debts

In addition to writing off debts which are known to be bad the firm may also wish to provide for debts which it anticipates will be irrecoverable. This is done by making an adjustment to the debtor's figure, immediately prior to the preparation of the final accounts. The provision for doubtful debts is usually expressed as a percentage of total debts outstanding at the end of the year. To calculate the provision for doubtful debts, the following steps should be taken:

(a)   Total the balances on the debtors' accounts.

(b)   Deduct from the total any debts which are written off as bad after the balances on the debtors' accounts have been extracted.

(c)   Calculate the appropriate percentage of remaining debtors. The percentage of debts provided for as doubtful will vary from firm to firm and will depend on the debt recovery rate in previous years.

The provision for doubtful debts is like the provisions for outstanding expenses. When the amount of the provision has been calculated it will be entered in the accounts at the end of the financial year as follows:

(a)   Debit the bad debts account with the provision at the end of the current financial year.

(b)   Credit the bad debts account with the provision at the start of the next financial year.

Example

A. Solicitor prepares his final accounts on 31 October. On that date his bad debts account has a debit balance of £1,500 in respect of bad debts written off during the year. Total debts owed to the practice amount to £20,000 and A. Solicitor decides to make a provision for doubtful debts of 5% of the total.

BAD DEBTS ACCOUNT

Date	Details	Dr	Cr	Balance
		£	£	£
	Balance			1,500 Dr
Oct 31	Provision: doubtful			
	debt c/d	1,000		2,500 Dr

2.11.4 Effect of bad debts on final accounts

At the end of the financial year the bad debts account will be closed and the balance will be transferred to the profit and loss account. If, at the end of the financial year, the bad debts account has a debit balance this will be transferred to the profit and loss account as an expense by making the following entries in the accounts:

(a) Credit the bad debts account.
(b) Debit the profit and loss account.

Continuing the example of A. Solicitor:

BAD DEBTS ACCOUNT

Date	Details	Dr	Cr	Balance
		£	£	£
	Balance			1,500 Dr
Oct 31	Provision: doubtful			
	debts c/d	1,000		2,500 Dr
	Profit and loss account:			
	transfer		2,500	———

PROFIT AND LOSS ACCOUNT FOR THE YEAR ENDED 31 OCTOBER 1990

INCOME £

—

EXPENDITURE
Bad and doubtful debts   2,500

At the start of the next financial year the provision will be carried down as a credit entry on the bad debts account. Continuing the example of A. Solicitor:

BAD DEBTS ACCOUNT

Date	Details	Dr	Cr	Balance
1990		£	£	£
	Balance			1,500 Dr
Oct 31	Provision: doubtful debts c/d	1,000		2,500 Dr
	Profit and loss account: transfer		2,500	———
Nov 1	Provision for doubtful debts b/d		1,000	1,000 Cr

The provision for doubtful debts made at the end of the financial year is shown as a deduction from the debtors figure on the current assets side of the balance sheet. The provision for doubtful debts is strictly a current liability but by convention is not shown as such on the balance sheet. Continuing the example of A. Solicitor:

BALANCE SHEET AS AT 31 OCTOBER 1990

	£	£	£
CAPITAL EMPLOYED			XX

		£	£	£
EMPLOYMENT OF CAPITAL				
FIXED ASSETS			XX	
CURRENT ASSETS				
Debtors		20,000		
Less: Provision for doubtful debts		1,000	19,000	

If the bad debts account has a credit balance at the end of the year because the firm has overestimated its provision for doubtful debts in previous years, the credit balance is transferred to the profit and loss account as an income by making the following entries.

(a)   Debit bad debts account.
(b)   Credit profit and loss account.

Example

At the start of the financial year, 1 November 1990, a provision of £800 is brought down from the previous year. During the year bad debts are written off as follows: Black £125, Green £75. At the end of the financial year, 31 October 1991, total debtors amount to £4,000. It is decided to make a provision for doubtful debts of 10%.

BAD DEBTS ACCOUNT

Date	Details	Dr	Cr	Balance
		£	£	£
1990				
Nov 1	Provision b/d		800	800 Cr
	Black	125		
	Green	75		600 Cr
1991				
Oct 31	Provision c/d	400		200 Cr
	Profit and loss account:			
	provision written back	200		——

PROFIT AND LOSS ACCOUNT FOR THE YEAR ENDED 31 OCTOBER 1991

INCOME	£	£
Costs	XX	
Add: Closing work in progress	XX	
	XX	
Less: Opening work in progress	XX	XX
Provision for doubtful debts written back		200

Only one method of providing for bad debts and doubtful debts has been shown in this book. There are other, equally acceptable methods in use.

2.12   DEPRECIATION

2.12.1   Introduction

The real accounts show the cost price of fixed assets. The cost price of an asset is not its true value as most assets will decrease in value through wear and tear or obsolescence. Allowance should be made for this reduction in value of the practice's assets by reducing the profits each year. (The purchase of new assets is thereby provided for.)

2.12.2   Calculating depreciation

To record the reduction in value of an asset, a provision is made for depreciation at the end of each financial year. Depreciation of an asset cannot be assessed accurately until the asset is sold and therefore on the sale of an asset the firm may have to provide for a loss if the provision for depreciation has been underestimated or a profit if the provision has been overestimated.

There are several ways of calculating depreciation. The simplest is the straight-line method. The formula for calculating depreciation by the straight-line method is:

$$\frac{\text{Cost of asset} - \text{value of asset at end of its life}}{\text{life expectancy of asset}}$$

Example

A firm buys a car for £5,500. The car has an estimated life of five years, at the end of which its sale value will be £500. The annual provision for depreciation using the straight-line method of calculating depreciation will be:

$$\frac{£5,500 - £500}{5} = £1,000$$

A separate depreciation account is opened for each class of fixed assets to be depreciated.

2.12.3 Recording depreciation in the accounts

To record depreciation in the accounts at the end of the financial year, the following entries are made:

(a) Credit the appropriate depreciation account with depreciation charged on the fixed asset.

(b) Debit the profit and loss account with the current year's depreciaton, as an expense.

Note that if an asset is bought during the year it is usual to depreciate it for a full year. Do this unless you are told otherwise.

Example

The firm buys a car for £6,000 in December 1988. The estimated life of the car is four years at the end of which it should realise £1,200 on sale.

Annual depreciation on the car using the straight-line method is:

$$\frac{£6,000 - £1,200}{4} = £1,200$$

The firm's financial year ends on 30 November 1989.

DEPRECIATION (MOTOR CARS) ACCOUNT

Date	Details	Dr	Cr	Balance
		£	£	£
1989 Nov 30	Profit and loss		1,200	1,200 Cr

Strictly, depreciation is a current liability but by convention it is shown on the balance sheet as a deduction of accumulated depreciation from the cost price of the asset. Continuing the example:

PROFIT AND LOSS ACCOUNT FOR YEAR ENDED
30 NOVEMBER 1989

INCOME   £
                                                                   —

LESS EXPENDITURE
Depreciation: motor cars   1,200

BALANCE SHEET AS AT 30 NOVEMBER 1989

                                        £   £   £
CAPITAL EMPLOYED   XX
                                                             ══

EMPLOYMENT OF CAPITAL
FIXED ASSETS
Motor cars at cost   6,000
Less: Accumulated depreciation   1,200   4,800

The accounts would be shown as follows at the end of year 2, which is 30 November 1990.

DEPRECIATION (MOTOR CARS) ACCOUNT

Date	Details	Dr	Cr	Balance
		£	£	£
1989				
Nov 30	Profit and loss		1,200	1,200 Cr
1990				
Nov 30	Profit and loss		1,200	2,400 Cr

PROFIT AND LOSS ACCOUNT FOR THE YEAR ENDED
30 NOVEMBER 1990

INCOME   £
                                                                   —

LESS EXPENDITURE
Depreciation: motor cars   1,200

BALANCE SHEET AS AT 30 NOVEMBER 1990

	£	£	£
CAPITAL EMPLOYED			XX

EMPLOYMENT OF CAPITAL
FIXED ASSETS

	£	£
Motor cars at cost	6,000	
Less: Accumulated depreciation	2,400	3,600

2.13 SALE OF ASSETS

When an asset is sold a new account is opened called the asset disposal account. If the asset is sold for more than its book value too much depreciation has been provided for. This 'profit' must be shown as income in the profit and loss account for the year when the asset is sold. If the asset is sold for less than its book value too little depreciation has been provided for. This 'loss' must be shown as an expense in the profit and loss account for the year in which the asset is sold.

The following entries will be made in the accounts when an asset is sold:

(a) Transfer the cost price of the asset from the asset account to the asset disposal account by making the following entries:

(i) Credit the asset account with the cost price of the asset.

(ii) Debit the asset disposal account with the cost price of the asset.

Continuing the example from section 2.12.3, assume that the car is sold in December 1990.

MOTOR CARS ACCOUNT

Date	Details	Dr	Cr	Balance
1988		£	£	£
Dec	Cash	6,000		6,000 Dr
1990				
Dec	Asset disposal		6,000	——

ASSET DISPOSAL ACCOUNT (MOTOR CARS)

Date	Details	Dr	Cr	Balance
1990 Dec	Motor cars	£ 6,000	£	£ 6,000 Dr

(b) Transfer the accumulated depreciation from the depreciation account to the asset disposal account by making the following entries:
  (i) Debit the depreciation account.
  (ii) Credit the asset disposal account.

Continuing the example:

DEPRECIATION (MOTOR CARS) ACCOUNT

Date	Details	Dr	Cr	Balance
1989 Nov 30	Profit and loss	£	£ 1,200	£ 1,200 Cr
1990 Nov 30	Profit and loss		1,200	2,400 Cr
Dec	Asset disposal	2,400		———

ASSET DISPOSAL ACCOUNT (MOTOR CARS)

Date	Details	Dr	Cr	Balance
1990 Dec	Motor cars	£ 6,000	£	£ 6,000 Dr
	Depreciation		2,400	3,600 Dr

(c) Record receipt of sale proceeds by making the following entries:
  (i) Debit the cash account.
  (ii) Credit the asset disposal account.

If the asset is sold on credit a personal account will be opened and the personal account of the buyer is debited with the sale price and *not* the cash account.

Continuing the example, assume that the car is sold for £3,000.

CASH ACCOUNT

Date	Details	Dr	Cr	Balance
1990		£	£	£
Dec	Asset disposal (motor car)	3,000		3,000 Dr

ASSET DISPOSAL ACCOUNT (MOTOR CARS)

Date	Details	Dr	Cr	Balance
1990		£	£	£
Dec	Motor cars	6,000		6,000 Dr
	Depreciation		2,400	3,600 Dr
	Cash		3,000	600 Dr

(d) Transfer the balance on the asset disposal account to the profit and loss account as follows:

(i) If the asset disposal account has a debit balance the firm has made a loss on the sale of the asset and the balance will be transferred to the profit and loss account as an expense. Continuing the example:

ASSET DISPOSAL ACCOUNT (MOTOR CARS)

Date	Details	Dr	Cr	Balance
1990		£	£	£
Dec	Motor cars	6,000		6,000 Dr
	Depreciation		2,400	3,600 Dr
1991	Cash		3,000	600 Dr
Nov 30	Profit and loss: transfer		600	——

PROFIT AND LOSS ACCOUNT FOR THE YEAR ENDED
30 NOVEMBER 1991

	£	£
INCOME		XX
		──
LESS: EXPENDITURE		
Asset disposal: loss on sale of car	600	

(ii)   If the asset disposal account has a credit balance the firm has made a profit on the sale of the asset and the balance on the asset disposal account is transferred to the profit and loss account as income.

Example

In 1987 the firm bought a typewriter for £1,000. Depreciation is charged on the typewriter at the rate of £200 per annum. In 1988 the typewriter was sold for £900 cash. The accounts would appear as follows:

OFFICE EQUIPMENT ACCOUNT

Date	Details	Dr	Cr	Balance
		£	£	£
1987	Cash	1,000		1,000 Dr
1988	Asset disposal		1,000	──────

DEPRECIATION (OFFICE EQUIPMENT) ACCOUNT

Date	Details	Dr	Cr	Balance
		£	£	£
1987	Profit and loss		200	200 Cr
1988	Asset disposal	200		──────

ASSET DISPOSAL ACCOUNT (OFFICE EQUIPMENT)

Date	Details	Dr	Cr	Balance
1988		£	£	£
	Office equipment	1,000		1,000 Dr
	Depreciation (office equipment)		200	800 Dr
	Cash		900	100 Cr
	Profit and loss (profit on sale)	100		——

PROFIT AND LOSS ACCOUNT FOR THE YEAR ENDED 1988

INCOME	£	£
Costs	XX	
Add: Closing work in progress	XX	
	——	
	XX	
Less: Opening work in progress	XX	XX
	——	
Asset disposal: profit on sale of typewriter		100

2.13.1 Disposing of part of an asset

Example

Jones, a solicitor, prepares his final accounts on 31 December each year. The trial balance taken immediately before the preparation of his final accounts for the year ended 1988 shows a figure for motor cars, at cost, of £8,300. Accumulated depreciation on the cars at 31 December 1987 is £1,900. You are told that the trial balance figures include the cost of a car, £4,000, bought on 1 January 1988, and another car being sold by Jones on the same day for £1,350 cash. The second car had been bought by Jones for £2,000 on the 1 January 1987. Depreciation is charged at 25% per annum, of cost price. No provision had been made for the sale and this is done immediately before the final accounts are prepared on 31 December 1988. Jones' accounts to record the above will be as follows:

MOTOR CAR ACCOUNT

Date	Details	Dr	Cr	Balance
1988		£	£	£
	Balance			8,300 Dr
Dec 31	Asset disposal		2,000	6,300 Dr

ASSET DISPOSAL ACCOUNT (MOTOR CARS)

Date	Details	Dr	Cr	Balance
1988		£	£	£
Dec 31	Motor cars	2,000		2,000
	Cash		1,350	650 Dr
	Depreciation		500	150 Dr
	Profit and loss account:			
	Transfer loss on sale		150	———

DEPRECIATION ACCOUNT (MOTOR CARS)

Date	Details	Dr	Cr	Balance
1988		£	£	£
Jan 1	Balance			1,900 Cr
	Asset disposal	500		1,400 Cr
Dec 31	Profit and loss		1,575	2,975 Cr

PROFIT AND LOSS ACCOUNT FOR THE YEAR ENDED
31 DECEMBER 1988

	£	£	£
INCOME		XX	
LESS EXPENDITURE			
Depreciation: motor cars	1,575		
Loss on sale of car	150		XX

BALANCE SHEET AS AT 31 DECEMBER 1988

	£	£	£	£
CAPITAL EMPLOYED				XX
				==
EMPLOYMENT OF CAPITAL				
FIXED ASSETS			XX	
Motor cars	6,300			
Less: accumulated				
depreciation	2,975	3,325		

Note:
The current year's depreciation is calculated by taking the cost price of the car which has been sold (£2,000) from the balance on the motor cars account (£8,300), and finding 25% of the remainder (£6,300) = £1,575.

2.14   EXERCISES ON ADJUSTMENTS AND FINAL ACCOUNTS

1   On 31 October 1988 the firm's light and heat account has a debit balance of £5,000. The firm estimates that a further £250 worth of gas has been used.

Show the state of the light and heat account on 1 November 1988 and the entries which you would make in the final accounts which are prepared on 31 October 1988.

2   The firm pays rates of £1,000 on 1 April and 1 October for the following six months. The firm's final accounts are prepared on 31 December each year.

Show the rates account at 1 January 1989 and the entries you would make in the final accounts.

3   Final accounts are prepared on 30 June each year. On 30 June 1988 the stationery account shows a debit balance of £800. On checking the stationery it is discovered that there is £200 worth left.

Show the stationery account at 1 July 1988 and the entries in the final accounts.

4   At the end of its financial year, 31 December 1987, Grace & Co. had profit costs of £80,000 and its work in progress was valued at £10,000. At the end of its second year, 31 December 1988, the firm had delivered bills totalling £120,000 and its work in progress was valued at £25,000.

Show the costs account and also the final accounts for the year ended 31 December 1988.

5   On 1 July 1987 the balance on the cars account is £25,000 and accumulated depreciation is £7,000. Depreciation on cars is charged at 15% per annum. In December 1987 a car purchased in 1985 for £10,000 is sold for £8,000.

Prepare the ledger accounts to record the above events and show the final accounts as at 30 June 1988.

6   Smith, a sole practitioner, prepares his final accounts on 31 December each year. Immediately prior to 31 December 1987 an inspection of Smith's accounts reveals the following:

(a)   Debts due from Brown, Jones and Green of £124, £86 and £26, respectively, are irrecoverable and are to be written off.

(b)   Black owes £230 (including £30 VAT). He has been made bankrupt and there are no assets available. It is decided to write off his debt.

(c)   The total amount of debts before any adjustments have been made for the above is £5,936.

(d)   It is decided to provide for doubtful debts at 10% of total debtors.

During the year to December 1988 the following events take place:

(a)   Green has been traced and has paid in full.
(b)   It is decided to reduce the provision for doubtful debts to 5%.

At the end of 1988 total debtors amount to £4,000.

You are required to show the bad debts account for both years, together with the necessary entries in the final accounts.

7 The trial balance of Henry Smythe, prepared on 31 December 1988, is as follows:

TRIAL BALANCE AS AT 31 DECEMBER 1988

Name of account	Dr	Cr
	£	£
Drawings	19,000	
Fixtures and fittings	5,200	
Cars	10,600	
Depreciation (cars)		2,120
Depreciation (fixtures and fittings)		1,300
Premises	32,000	
Capital		40,000
Telephone/Postage	1,300	
Rates	2,950	
Light and heat	1,550	
Salaries	5,270	
Cash at bank:		
Office account	14,190	
Client account	115,000	
Petty cash	123	
Debtors	1,422	
Due to creditors		1,763
Due to clients		115,000
Costs		48,422
	208,605	208,605

In addition:

(a) Depreciation at 10% and 5% is to be charged against cars and fixtures and fittings respectively.

(b) At 31 December 1988 electricity and telephone bills outstanding amount to £551 and £505 respectively.

(c) Included in the amount for debtors is £122 which is to be written off. A provision for doubtful debts of 5% of remaining debtors is to be made.

(d)   Work in progress at 31 December 1988 is valued at £4,569.

Prepare final accounts for the year ended 31 December 1988.

8   The following balances were taken from the accounts of C. Hop, solicitor, on 31 December 1988.

Capital	£10,059
Work in progress at 1 January 1988	£36,582
Petty cash	£55
Bank overdraft on office account	£2,552
Bank client account	£150,000
Debtors	£7,009
Creditors	£6,735
Car: cost price	£2,000
Depreciation: car	£500
Drawings	£2,459
Fixtures and fittings at cost	£4,000
Depreciation: fixtures and fittings	£200
Costs	£50,021
Rent and rates	£626
Salaries	£5,226
General expenses	£1,735
Interest on overdraft	£56
Insurance commission	£59
Freehold premises	£10,300
Bad debts (including provision)	£78

C. Hop provides the following additional information about his practice:

(a)   Work in progress was valued at £4,270 on 31 December 1988.
(b)   Salaries outstanding on 31 December 1988 were £426.
(c)   Rates paid in advance on 31 December 1988 amounted to £100.
(d)   The provision for doubtful debts is to be increased to £260, from £162.
(e)   Depreciation is to be charged at 25% per annum on cost of cars and 5% per annum on cost of fixtures and fittings.
(f)   The balance due to clients is £150,000.

Prepare a profit and loss account and balance sheet for the year ended 31 December 1988.

2.15 SUGGESTED SOLUTIONS TO EXERCISES ON ADJUSTMENTS AND FINAL ACCOUNTS

1 LIGHT AND HEAT ACCOUNT

Date	Details	Dr	Cr	Balance
1988		£	£	£
Oct 31	Balance			5,000 Dr
	Provision: Gas c/d	250		5,250 Dr
	Profit and loss:			
	transfer		5,250	
Nov 1	Provision: Gas b/d		250	250 Cr

PROFIT AND LOSS ACCOUNT FOR THE YEAR ENDED
31 OCTOBER 1988

	£	£	£
INCOME			XX
LESS EXPENDITURE			
Light and heat	5,000		
Add provision	250	5,250	

BALANCE SHEET AS AT 31 OCTOBER 1988

	£	£	£
CAPITAL EMPLOYED			XX
EMPLOYMENT OF CAPITAL			
FIXED ASSETS		XX	
CURRENT ASSETS	XX		
Less current liabilities			
Provision for light and heat	250	—	XX

2   RATES ACCOUNT

Date	Details	Dr	Cr	Balance
1988		£	£	£
Apr 1	Cash	1,000		1,000 Dr
Oct 1	Cash	1,000		2,000 Dr
Dec 31	Payment in advance c/d		500	1,500 Dr
	Profit and loss: transfer		1,500	——
1989				
Jan 1	Payment in advance b/d	500		500 Dr

PROFIT AND LOSS ACCOUNT FOR YEAR ENDED
31 DECEMBER 1988

	£	£	£
INCOME			XX
LESS EXPENDITURE			
Rates	2,000		
Less paid in advance	500	1,500	

BALANCE SHEET AS AT 31 DECEMBER 1988

	£	£
CAPITAL EMPLOYED		XX
		=
EMPLOYMENT OF CAPITAL		
FIXED ASSETS	XX	
CURRENT ASSETS		
Rates paid in advance	500	XX

3   STATIONERY ACCOUNT

Date	Details	Dr	Cr	Balance
1988		£	£	£
June 30	Balance			800 Dr
	Closing stock c/d		200	600 Dr
	Profit and loss: transfer		600	——
July 1	Opening stock b/d	200		200 Dr

PROFIT AND LOSS ACCOUNT FOR THE YEAR ENDED
30 JUNE 1988

	£	£	£
INCOME			XX
LESS EXPENDITURE			
Stationery	800		
Less closing stock	200	600	

BALANCE SHEET AS AT 30 JUNE 1988

	£	£
CAPITAL EMPLOYED		XX
EMPLOYMENT OF CAPITAL		
FIXED ASSETS	XX	
CURRENT ASSETS		
Closing stock of stationery	200	XX

4 COSTS ACCOUNT

Date	Details	Dr	Cr	Balance
1987		£	£	£
Dec 31	Balance			80,000 Cr
	Closing work in progress c/d		10,000	90,000 Cr
	Profit and loss: transfer	90,000		—
1988				
Jan 1	Opening work in progress b/d	10,000		10,000 Dr
Dec 31	Costs		120,000	110,000 Cr
	Closing work in progress c/d		25,000	135,000 Cr
	Profit and loss: transfer	135,000		—
1989				
Jan 1	Opening work in progress b/d	25,000		25,000 Dr

PROFIT AND LOSS ACCOUNT FOR THE YEAR ENDED
31 DECEMBER 1988

INCOME	£	£	£
Costs	120,000		
Add closing work in progress	25,000		
	145,000		
Less opening work in progress	10,000	135,000	
LESS EXPENDITURE		XX	

BALANCE SHEET AS AT 31 DECEMBER 1988

	£	£
CAPITAL EMPLOYED		XX
		==
EMPLOYMENT OF CAPITAL		
FIXED ASSETS		XX
CURRENT ASSETS		
Closing work in progress	25,000	XX
		==

5   MOTOR CARS ACCOUNT

Date	Details	Dr	Cr	Balance
1987		£	£	£
July 1	Balance			25,000 Dr
Dec	Asset disposal		10,000	15,000 Dr

ASSET DISPOSAL ACCOUNT

Date	Details	Dr	Cr	Balance
1987		£	£	£
Dec	Motor cars	10,000		10,000 Dr
	Depreciation		3,000	7,000 Dr
	Cash		8,000	1,000 Cr
1988				
June 30	Profit and loss:			
	Profit on sale	1,000		—

DEPRECIATION ACCOUNT

Date	Details	Dr	Cr	Balance
1987		£	£	£
July 1	Balance			7,000 Cr
Dec	Asset disposal	3,000		4,000 Cr
1988				
June 30	Profit and loss: transfer		2,250	6,250 Cr

PROFIT AND LOSS ACCOUNT FOR YEAR ENDED 30 JUNE 1988

	£	£	£
INCOME			
Profit on sale of car		1,000	
LESS EXPENDITURE			
Depreciation, motor cars	2,250		

BALANCE SHEET AS AT 30 JUNE 1988

	£	£	£
CAPITAL EMPLOYED			XX
			==
EMPLOYMENT OF CAPITAL			
FIXED ASSETS			
Motor cars	15,000		
Less accumulated depreciation	6,250	8,750	XX
			==

6 SMITH

BAD DEBTS ACCOUNT

Date	Details	Dr	Cr	Balance
1987		£	£	£
Dec 31	Brown	124		
	Jones	86		
	Green	26		236 Dr
	Black	200		436 Dr
	Provision c/d	550		986 Dr
	Profit and loss transfer		986	—
1988				
Jan 1	Provision b/d		550	550 Cr
	Cash bad debt recovered (Green)		26	576 Cr
Dec 31	Provision c/d	200		376 Cr
	Profit and loss transfer	376		—
1989				
Jan 1	Provision b/d		200	200 Cr

PROFIT AND LOSS ACCOUNT FOR THE YEAR ENDED 31 DECEMBER 1987

	£	£	£
INCOME			XX
LESS EXPENDITURE			
Bad debts		986	

BALANCE SHEET FOR THE YEAR ENDED 31 DECEMBER 1987

	£	£	£
CAPITAL EMPLOYED			XX
			==
EMPLOYMENT OF CAPITAL			
FIXED ASSETS		XX	
CURRENT ASSETS			
Debtors	5,500		
Less provision for doubtful debts	550	4,950	XX
			==

PROFIT AND LOSS ACCOUNT FOR THE YEAR ENDED
31 DECEMBER 1988

INCOME	£	£	£
Overestimate of provision for			
doubtful debts written off		376	

BALANCE SHEET AS AT 31 DECEMBER 1988

	£	£	£
CAPITAL EMPLOYED			XX
			==
EMPLOYMENT OF CAPITAL			
FIXED ASSETS		XX	
CURRENT ASSETS			
Debtors	4,000		
Less provision for doubtful debt	200	3,800	XX
	——	——	==

7   PROFIT AND LOSS ACCOUNT FOR THE YEAR ENDED
31 DECEMBER 1988

INCOME	£	£	£
Costs		48,422	
Add closing work in progress		4,569	52,991
		——	
LESS EXPENDITURE			
Telephone and postage	1,300		
Add provision	505	1,805	
	——		
Rates		2,950	
Light and heat	1,550		
Add provision	551	2,101	
	——		
Salaries		5,270	
Depreciation:			
Motor cars	1,060		
Fixtures and fittings	260	1,320	
	——		
Bad debts and provision		187	13,633
(£122 + £65 provision)		——	——
NET PROFIT			39,358

BALANCE SHEET AS AT 31 DECEMBER 1988

	£	£	£
CAPITAL EMPLOYED			
Capital at start	40,000		
Add net profit	39,358	79,358	
Less drawings		19,000	60,358
EMPLOYMENT OF CAPITAL			
FIXED ASSETS			
Premises		32,000	
Fixtures and fittings at cost	5,200		
Less accumulated depreciation	1,560	3,640	
Motor cars at cost	10,600		
Less accumulated depreciation	3,180	7,420	43,060
CURRENT ASSETS			
Cash at bank		14,190	
Petty cash		123	
Debtors	1,300		
Less provision	65	1,235	
Closing work in progress		4,569	
		20,117	
LESS CURRENT LIABILITIES			
Creditors	1,763		
Outstanding expenses	1,056	2,819	
Net current assets			17,298
CLIENT BALANCES			
Cash at bank, client account		115,000	
Due to clients		115,000	
			60,358

8 C. HOP: PROFIT AND LOSS ACCOUNT FOR THE YEAR ENDED 31 DECEMBER 1988

INCOME	£	£	£
Costs		50,021	
Add: Closing work in progress		4,270	
		54,291	
Less: Opening work in progress		36,582	17,709
Insurance commission			59
			17,768
LESS: EXPENDITURE			
Rent and rates	626		
Less: Paid in advance	100	526	
Salaries	5,226		
Plus: Outstanding	426	5,652	
General expenses		1,735	
Interest		56	
Bad and doubtful debts		338	
Depreciation			
Cars	500		
Fixtures and Fittings	200	700	9,007
NET PROFIT			8,761

BALANCE SHEET AS AT 31 DECEMBER 1988

CAPITAL EMPLOYED	£	£	£	£
Balance at start of year		10,059		
Add: Net profit		8,761	18,820	
Less: Drawings			2,459	16,361

EMPLOYMENT OF CAPITAL	£	£	£
FIXED ASSETS			
Freehold premises		10,300	
Fixtures and fittings at cost	4,000		
Less: Accumulated depreciation	400	3,600	
Cars at cost	2,000		
Less: Accumulated depreciation	1,000	1,000	14,900
CURRENT ASSETS			
Closing work in progress		4,270	
Debtors	7,009		
Less: Provision	260	6,749	
Petty cash		55	
Payment in advance			
Rates	100	100	
		11,174	
LESS: CURRENT LIABILITIES			
Creditors	6,735		
Office account bank overdraft	2,552		
Outstanding expenses: salaries	426	9,713	1,461

CLIENT ACCOUNT		
Bank balance	£150,000	
Less: due to clients	£150,000	
		16,361

2.16   TEST ON FINAL ACCOUNTS OF A SOLE PRACTITIONER

Allow one hour to complete this test.

The following information is extracted from the books of Smith, a practising solicitor, as at 31 December 1990. Balances on ledger cards:

Capital account £42,750
Bank loan £10,000
Drawings £22,400
Due to clients £120,960
Fixtures, furniture and office equipment at cost £15,000
  Accumulated depreciation thereon to 31 December 1989 £7,000
Motor cars at cost £18,000
  Accumulated depreciation thereon to 31 December 1989 £4,500
Cash at bank (clients account): current account £20,960, deposit account
  £100,000
Lease at cost £20,000
Less amount written off to 31 December 1989 £8,000
Creditors £4,762
General expenses £53,980
Due from clients £17,854
Cash at bank (office account) £8,346
Petty cash balance £50
Interest received £4,742
Motor cars disposal account £6,000 (credit)
Profit costs £81,879
Work in progress at 31 December 1989 £16,456
Bad debts £440
Miscellaneous income £2,893

Additional information:

Depreciation to be charged as follows:
  Motor cars £2,500
  Fixtures, fittings and office equipment £1,000.
The sum of £2,000 is to be written off the cost of the lease.
The amount standing to the credit of the motor car disposal account
  (£6,000) represents the sale proceeds of a car which was sold during
  the year. The car cost £8,000 and depreciation of £1,500 had been
  made in respect of the sale. It is Smith's policy that depreciation is not
  charged in respect of the year in which a fixed asset is sold.
Work in progress at 31 December 1990 is valued at £17,472.
General expenses outstanding at the same date amount to £659.
Additional bad debts amounting to £300 are to be written off, and an
  adjustment is to be made in respect of general expenses (£800) which
  have been met out of Smith's private resources.

Miscellaneous income includes the sum of £43, representing rent receivable in respect of 1991.

From the information above prepare a profit and loss account for the year ended 31 December 1990 together with a balance sheet as at that date, using the vertical form of presentation.

(Law Society Final Examination, updated)

2.17   SUGGESTED ANSWER TO TEST ON FINAL ACCOUNTS OF A SOLE PRACTITIONER

PROFIT AND LOSS ACCOUNT FOR THE YEAR ENDED 31 DECEMBER 1990

INCOME	£	£	£
Costs	81,879		
Add closing work in progress	17,472	99,351	
Deduct opening work in progress		16,456	82,895
Miscellaneous income	2,893		
Less received in advance	43		2,850
Interest received			4,742
			90,487
LESS EXPENDITURE			
General expenses	53,980		
Add outstanding expenses	659		
Add transfer from drawings	800	55,439	
Bad debts	440		
Additional bad debts	300	740	
Depreciation:			
Cars	2,500		
Fixtures and fittings	1,000	3,500	
Reduction in value of lease		2,000	
Loss on sale of car		500	62,179
Net profit			28,308

BALANCE SHEET AS AT 31 DECEMBER 1990

CAPITAL EMPLOYED	£	£	£
Balance at start	42,750		
Add net profit	28,308	71,058	
Less drawings		21,600	49,458
(£22,400 – £800)			
Add long-term liabilities:			
Bank loan			10,000
			59,458

EMPLOYMENT OF CAPITAL			
FIXED ASSETS			
Leasehold property	20,000		
Less reduction in value	10,000	10,000	
Fixtures, fittings and equipment	15,000		
Accumulated depreciation	8,000	7,000	
Motor cars	10,000		
Less accumulated depreciation	5,500	4,500	21,500
CURRENT ASSETS			
Closing work in progress		17,472	
Debtors	17,854		
Less bad debt	300	17,554	
Cash at bank (office)		8,346	
Petty cash		50	
		43,422	
LESS CURRENT LIABILITIES			
Creditors	4,762		
General expenses outstanding	659		
Rent received in advance	43	5,464	

NET ASSETS		37,958
CLIENT ACCOUNT		
Deposit account	100,000	
Current account	20,960	120,960
Deduct due to clients		120,960
		59,458

3 Partnership Accounts

3.1 THE ACCOUNTS KEPT BY A PARTNERSHIP

3.1.1 General

The accounts kept by a partnership are largely the same as those kept by a sole practitioner. The real and nominal accounts are the same and the clients' accounts are the same, as are the accounting procedures up to the preparation of final accounts.

3.1.2 Capital accounts

In a partnership the capital is introduced by more than one person and therefore a separate capital account is kept for each partner.

The net profit is not transferred from the profit and loss account to the partners' capital account at the end of the financial year as happens with a sole practitioner.

Drawings are not transferred to the partners' capital account at the end of the year as happens with a sole practitioner.

If a partner wishes to have his share of the profit capitalised, the balance on his current account will be transferred to his capital account at the end of the financial year.

Thus a partner's capital account shows capital which he introduced into the practice and any profit which he decides to capitalise.

Example

A and B enter into partnership introducing £3,000 and £9,000 capital respectively.

CAPITAL ACCOUNT: A

Date	Details	Dr	Cr	Balance
		£	£	£
	Balance			3,000 Cr

CAPITAL ACCOUNT: B

Date	Details	Dr	Cr	Balance
		£	£	£
	Balance			9,000 Cr

3.1.3   Current accounts

A current account is opened for each partner.

A partner's current account is credited with any sums which he is entitled to receive from the practice, for example, his profit share, interest on capital and salary.

A partner's current account is debited with any sums which the partner has taken out of the practice or which he owes to the practice, for example, his drawings (transferred at the end of the financial year from the partner's drawings account), interest charged on the partner's drawings or the partner's share of a loss made by the firm.

If a partner's current account has a credit balance, the firm has a liability to the partner. If his current account has a debit balance, the partner owes money to the firm which is a current asset of the firm.

By convention the balances on the partners' current accounts are always shown on the liabilities side of the balance sheet.

Example

In the example in section 3.1.2, assume that on 30 June 1988, the end of the financial year for A and B's first year of practice, A's share of the net profit is £2,000 and B's share is £3,000. Interest on capital is allowed to both partners at the rate of 5% per annum. A has made drawings of £2,500 and B has made drawings of £2,000. Interest is charged on drawings at the rate of 5% per annum. B is paid a salary of £500 per annum. B asks that any sums due to him at the end of the year be transferred to his capital account.

CURRENT ACCOUNT: A

Date	Details	Dr	Cr	Balance
1988		£	£	£
June 30	Profit share		2,000	2,000 Cr
	Interest on capital		150	2,150 Cr
	Drawings	2,500		350 Dr
	Interest on drawings	125		475 Dr

At the end of the year A owes the firm £475.

CURRENT ACCOUNT: B

Date	Details	Dr	Cr	Balance
1988		£	£	£
June 30	Profit share		3,000	3,000 Cr
	Salary		500	3,500 Cr
	Interest on capital		450	3,950 Cr
	Drawings	2,000		1,950 Cr
	Interest on drawings	100		1,850 Cr
	Capital account: transfer	1,850		———

CAPITAL ACCOUNT: B

Date	Details	Dr	Cr	Balance
1988		£	£	£
June 30	Balance			9,000 Cr
	Current account transfer		1,850	10,850 Cr

3.1.4 Loan accounts

If a partner loans money to the firm over and above his capital contribution, a loan account will be opened in the partner's name and he will be treated as a creditor of the firm.

The loan will be shown on the balance sheet as a long-term liability.

If interest is payable on the loan, a nominal expense account will be opened to record the payment of interest; the interest payable account.

At the end of the financial year the debit balance on the interest payable account will be transferred to the profit and loss account as a business expense.

The partner may take payment of his loan interest in cash or he may have the loan interest credited to his current account.

The bookkeeping entries to record the payment of loan interest in cash will be:

(a)   Debit interest payable account.
(b)   Credit cash account.

The bookkeeping entries to record loan interest credited to the partner's current account will be:

(a)   Debit interest payable account.
(b)   Credit current account of partner making the loan.

Example

Lawrence, Andrew and Mark practise together in partnership. It is agreed that Lawrence will make a loan of £5,000 to the practice to be used towards the purchase of a word processor. Lawrence is to receive interest of £250 per annum for so long as the loan remains unpaid. Lawrence asks that the interest be dealt with in his current account.

When the loan is negotiated the entries in the accounts will be:

(a)   Debit office cash account when the loan is paid into firm's bank account.
(b)   Credit the loan account.

CASH ACCOUNT

Date	Details	Dr	Cr	Balance
	Loan: Lawrence	£ 5,000	£	£ 5,000 Dr

LOAN ACCOUNT: LAWRENCE

Date	Details	Dr	Cr	Balance
	Cash	£	£ 5,000	£ 5,000 Cr

When the first year's interest of £250 becomes due:

(a) Debit the loan interest payable account.
(b) Credit Lawrence's current account. (Had Lawrence asked for payment to be made to him, the cash account and not Lawrence's current account would have been credited.)

INTEREST PAYABLE ACCOUNT

Date	Details	Dr	Cr	Balance
		£	£	£
	Current account: Lawrence	250		250 Dr

At the end of the financial year the balance will be transferred to the profit and loss account as a business expense and the interest payable account will be closed.

CURRENT ACCOUNT: LAWRENCE

Date	Details	Dr	Cr	Balance
		£	£	£
	Interest payable: loan		250	250 Cr

3.2 DRAWINGS

A drawings account may be opened for each partner or alternatively drawings may be debited to the partners' current accounts when they are made.

Partners' drawings can be of two types:

(a) Cash drawings.
(b) Drawings in kind.

3.2.1 Cash drawings

If a drawings account is used the following entries will be made to record the partners' cash drawings.

(a) Debit drawings account.
(b) Credit cash account.

Example

On 31 March partner A draws £500, on 30 April he draws £500, on 10 May he pays his home gas bill, £150.

DRAWINGS ACCOUNT: A

Date	Details	Dr	Cr	Balance
		£	£	£
Mar 31	Cash	500		500 Dr
Apr 30	Cash	500		1,000 Dr
May 10	Cash: home gas bill	150		1,150 Dr

If the firm does not use a drawings account for the partners but debits drawings into the partners' current accounts, when the drawings are made, the above entries would have been recorded in A's current account.

3.2.2 Drawings in kind

If a partner takes partnership property as his own, the following entries will be made in the accounts when the asset is taken out of the practice.

(a) Transfer the cost price of the asset to the asset disposal account (see section 2.13).
(b) Transfer depreciation already charged on the asset from the depreciation account to the asset disposal account.
(c) Credit the asset disposal account with the value of the asset at the date of disposal to the partner.
(d) Debit the partner's current account with the value of the asset at the date of disposal to him.
(e) Transfer the profit or loss made on the disposal of the asset from the asset disposal account to the profit and loss account at the end of the financial year.

Example

On 5 January A takes over ownership of a firm's car valued at £2,500 as
it is surplus to requirements.

CURRENT ACCOUNT: A

Date	Details	Dr	Cr	Balance
		£	£	£
Jan 5	Asset disposal: car	2,500		2,500 Dr

3.2.3 End of the financial year

At the end of the financial year the partner's drawings account will be
closed and the balance on the drawings account will be transferred to
the partner's current account.

Example

Continuing the example from section 3.2.2, assume that the firm's
financial year ends on 30 June and that each partner's drawings are
debited to his drawings account during the year.

DRAWINGS ACCOUNT: A

Date	Details	Dr	Cr	Balance
		£	£	£
Mar 31	Cash	500		500 Dr
Apr 30	Cash	500		1,000 Dr
May 10	Cash: home gas bill	150		1,150 Dr
June 30	Current account: transfer		1,150	——

CURRENT ACCOUNT: A

Date	Details	Dr	Cr	Balance
		£	£	£
Jan 5	Asset disposal: car	2,500		2,500 Dr
June 30	Drawings	1,150		3,650 Dr

3.3   FINAL ACCOUNTS

3.3.1   Profit and loss account

Up to the point of calculating the firm's net profit, the profit and loss account of a partnership is the same as that of a sole practitioner. In a partnership the profit and loss account is extended to show the allocation of the net profit amongst the partners in the profit-sharing ratio provided for in the partnership agreement after such items as salaries and interest on capital, also provided for in the partnership agreement, have been taken into account. The extension of the profit and loss account is called an appropriation account.

Example

The firm has three partners A, B and C. The profit and loss account records a net profit for the year of £10,000. The partnership agreement provides that A is to receive interest on capital of £1,000 and a salary of £800, C is to receive interest on capital of £500 and a salary of £200 and B is to receive a salary of £200. Profits are shared in the ratio 2 : 2 : 1. The appropriation account for A, B and C will appear as follows:

APPROPRIATION ACCOUNT

	£	£	£
NET PROFIT			10,000
SALARIES:			
A	800		
B	200		
C	200	1,200	
INTEREST ON CAPITAL			
A	1,000		
C	500	1,500	
PROFIT SHARE:			
A 2/5ths	2,920		
B 2/5ths	2,920		
C 1/5th	1,460	7,300	10,000

Note the following with regard to the appropriation account:

(a)   Net profit is carried down from the profit and loss account and interest on drawings (if any) charged to the partners is added to the net profit.

(b)   Partners' entitlements, to salary and interest on capital for example, are deducted from net profit plus interest on drawings.

(c)   The resulting balance is shared amongst the partners in the profit-sharing ratio.

(d)   The net profit or loss for each partner is transferred to his current account.

To continue the above example, the current account for partner A would appear as follows:

CURRENT ACCOUNT: A

Date	Details	Dr	Cr	Balance
		£	£	£
	Appropriation: salary		800	800 Cr
	Appropriation: interest on capital		1,000	1,800 Cr
	Appropriation: profit share		2,920	4,720 Cr

Example where a net loss is made

D and E are in partnership as solicitors. The partnership agreement provides that D is to receive a salary of £800 per annum and 6% per annum interest on his capital, which stands at £3,000. E is to receive 6% per annum interest on his capital, which stands at £5,000. D has made drawings of £1,400 and E has made drawings of £1,500. Both partners are charged interest on their drawings at 6% per annum. Profits and losses are shared equally. The profit and loss account shows a net loss of £1,500.

APPROPRIATION ACCOUNT

	£	£
NET LOSS b/d		1,500
SALARIES		
D		800
INTEREST ON CAPITAL		
D	180	
E	300	480
		2,780
INTEREST ON DRAWINGS		
D	84	
E	90	174
DIVISION OF NET LOSS		
D: ½	1,303	
E: ½	1,303	2,606
		2,780

CURRENT ACCOUNT: D

Date	Details	Dr	Cr	Balance
		£	£	£
	Drawings	1,400		1,400 Dr
	Appropriation: salary		800	600 Dr
	Appropriation: interest on capital		180	420 Dr
	Appropriation: interest on drawings	84		504 Dr
	Appropriation: share of loss	1,303		1,807 Dr

CURRENT ACCOUNT: E

Date	Details	Dr	Cr	Balance
		£	£	£
	Drawings	1,500		1,500 Dr
	Appropriation: interest on capital		300	1,200 Dr
	Appropriation: interest on drawings	90		1,290 Dr
	Appropriation: share of loss	1,303		2,593 Dr

3.3.2 Partners' expenses

If bona fide expenses are paid to the partners these are business expenses and will be recorded by means of a debit entry in the appropriate nominal expense account. At the end of the year the balance on the nominal expense account will be transferred to the profit and loss account as a business expense.

Example

Edward, a partner in a provincial firm, travels to London on firm's business. He travels first class and pays the return train fare of £50 out of his own money. Edward submits a claim to recoup the £50.

(a)   If the cashier pays Edward his £50, the entries in the accounts will be:
   (i)   Debit travelling expenses account.
   (ii)   Credit cash account.

TRAVELLING EXPENSES ACCOUNT

Date	Details	Dr	Cr	Balance
	Cash (partner's travel)	50		50 Dr

This is a nominal expense account.

PROFIT AND LOSS ACCOUNT FOR THE YEAR ENDED . . . . .

INCOME   £
                                                                                     —

LESS EXPENDITURE
Partners' travelling expenses   50

CASH ACCOUNT

Date	Details	Dr	Cr	Balance
		£	£	£
	Travelling expenses		50	50 Cr

(b) If Edward is not to be paid in cash, the travelling expenses will be credited to his current account, in which case the entries in the accounts will be:
  (i) Debit the travelling expenses account.
  (ii) Credit the current account of Edward.

CURRENT ACCOUNT: EDWARD

Date	Details	Dr	Cr	Balance
		£	£	£
	Travelling expenses		50	50 Cr

3.3.3 Balance sheet

The balance sheet of a partnership is the same as that of a sole practitioner except:

(a) The capital accounts of the partners are shown separately. The capital accounts show capital at the start of the year. An exception to this is if the partner capitalises his current account balance, in which case the balance on the current account will be transferred to the partner's capital account before the final accounts are prepared.

(b) Net profit and drawings are *not* transferred to a partner's capital account and therefore are not shown as additions to and deductions from capital, respectively, as happens with a sole practitioner.

(c)   The current accounts of the partners are shown on the liabilities side of the balance sheet. If there is a credit balance on the current accounts, this is added to the capital account balance. If there is a debit balance on the current accounts this is deducted from the capital account balance.

(d)   It is usual to show movements on partners' current accounts on the balance sheet itself. At the end of the balance sheet is a schedule showing the movement on the current accounts.

3.3.4   Example on partners' final accounts

Crab, Shrimp and Whelk are in partnership, sharing profits and losses in the ratio 3 : 3 : 1. Each partner is entitled to interest on capital at 10% per annum and to salaries of £10,000 to Crab, £6,000 to Shrimp and £2,000 to Whelk. Interest is to be charged on drawings as follows:

Crab	£1,000
Shrimp	£800
Whelk	£1,000

Partners' drawings have been debited to their respective current accounts as soon as they have been made. An abridged trial balance, prepared from the partnership books shows the following position at 1 December 1990.

	Dr £	Cr £
Sundry assets	70,000	
Sundry liabilities		8,400
Profit for the year from the profit and loss account		49,600
Partners' current accounts		
Crab	10,000	
Shrimp	8,000	
Whelk	6,000	
Partners' capital accounts		
Crab		20,000
Shrimp		12,000
Whelk		4,000
	94,000	94,000

From the above, prepare the profit and loss appropriation account for the year ended 31 December 1990, together with a balance sheet as at that date.   (Law Society Final Examination, updated)

3.3.5   Answer to example on partners' final accounts

PROFIT AND LOSS APPROPRIATION ACCOUNT FOR THE YEAR ENDED 31 DECEMBER 1990

	£	£
NET PROFIT		49,600
INTEREST ON DRAWINGS		
Crab	1,000	
Shrimp	800	
Whelk	1,000	2,800
		52,400
INTEREST ON CAPITAL		
Crab	2,000	
Shrimp	1,200	
Whelk	400	3,600
SALARIES		
Crab	10,000	
Shrimp	6,000	
Whelk	2,000	18,000
SHARE OF PROFIT		
Crab: 3/7ths	13,200	
Shrimp: 3/7ths	13,200	
Whelk: 1/7th	4,400	30,800
		52,400

BALANCE SHEET AS AT 31 DECEMBER 1990

CAPITAL EMPLOYED	£	£	£
Capital accounts			
Crab	20,000		
Shrimp	12,000		
Whelk	4,000	36,000	
Current accounts			
Crab	14,200Cr		
Shrimp	11,600Cr		
Whelk	200Dr	25,600	61,600
EMPLOYMENT OF CAPITAL			
Assets	70,000		
Less: Liabilities	8,400		61,600

Movements on partners' current accounts

	Crab	Shrimp	Whelk
Balance	(10,000)	(8,000)	(6,000)
Salary	10,000	6,000	2,000
Interest on capital	2,000	1,200	400
Profit share	13,200	13,200	4,400
	15,200	12,400	800
Less: Interest on drawings	1,000	800	1,000
	14,200Cr	11,600Cr	(200)Dr

3.4 PARTNERSHIP CHANGES

The constitution of a partnership may change during the financial year as a result of a partner dying, retiring from the practice, a new partner joining the practice or because the partners decide to vary their profit sharing agreement.

When there is a partnership change during the year, the format of the balance sheet and the profit and loss account to the net profit stage will not change.

The format of the appropriation account will change in that there will be a split appropriation. This means that there will be one appropriation account for the period from the start of the financial year to the change and one for the period after the change to the end of the financial year. Each appropriation account will reflect the terms of the partnership agreement in force for the period to which the appropriation account relates. Unless you are told the net profit for the period before and after the change you will have to apportion the net profit for the year on a time basis.

The net profit, interest on drawings, interest on capital and salaries must be apportioned. For example, if there is a partnership change three months into the year, in the first appropriation account net profit, etc., for the year will be divided by four to reflect the fact that the appropriation account relates to only one quarter of the year.

If a sole practitioner takes in a partner part way through the year, the profits for the time when he was sole practitioner will belong wholly to him. There will be no salary, interest on capital, etc., in the first part of the appropriation account as these are relevant only where there is a partnership. It therefore follows that provision for salaries, etc., in the partnership agreement can only apply to the second appropriation period, that is, the period when the original sole practitioner has taken in a partner.

Example

A and B are in partnership. A's capital is £20,000 and B's is £10,000. They share the profits in the ratio 3 : 2. Their financial year runs from 1 November to 31 October. C joins the partnership on 1 May 1988. C is to receive a salary of £12,000 per annum and A and B interest on capital of 10% per annum. A, B and C are to share the profits in the ratio of 2 : 2 : 1.

Net profit for the year ended 31 October 1988 is £70,000.

A, B & C: PROFIT AND LOSS ACCOUNT FOR THE YEAR ENDED 31 OCTOBER 1988

	£	£	£
NET PROFIT			70,000

APPROPRIATION ACCOUNT
1 November 1987 to 30 April 1988

	£	£	£
PROFIT SHARE			
A 3/5 ths		21,000	
B 2/5 ths		14,000	35,000

1 May 1988 to 31 October 1988

	£	£	£
INTEREST ON CAPITAL			
A	1,000		
B	500	1,500	
SALARIES			
C		6,000	
PROFIT SHARE			
A 2/5 ths	11,000		
B 2/5 ths	11,000		
C 1/5 th	5,500	27,500	35,000
			70,000

3.4.1 Revaluation of partnership assets

As a consequence of a change in the partnership constitution the partners may decide to revalue some or all of the fixed assets. This ensures that the partners in the firm before the change takes place have the benefit of any increase in value and bear the burden of any reduction in value.

The revaluation of the fixed assets is recorded in a revaluation account, the corresponding double entries being made in the real account for the asset which is being revalued.

To record an increase in the value of an asset:

(a) Debit the asset account with the increase in value.

(b) Credit the revaluation account.

To record a reduction in the value of an asset:

(a)   Credit the asset account with the reduction in value.
(b)   Debit the revaluation account.

The revaluation account is closed by transferring the net increase or decrease in value to the existing partners' capital accounts in the old profit sharing ratio. If there is an increase in value the entries will be:

(a)   Debit the revaluation account.
(b)   Credit the capital accounts of the existing partners.

If the revaluation account shows a decrease in value the entries will be reversed.

If the partners receive interest on capital it is important to remember that the revaluation alters their capital account balances. Interest should therefore be calculated on the old balances for the period before the change, and on the new balances for the period after the change.

Example

A and B are in partnership, sharing profits equally. They have capital account balances of £5,000 and £8,000 respectively. C is to be admitted into the partnership on 1 April. A and B revalue premises and motor cars which have a book value of £10,000 and £8,500 respectively. On revaluation, premises are valued at £12,500 and cars at £8,000.

REVALUATION ACCOUNT

Date	Details	Dr	Cr	Balance
		£	£	£
Mar 31	Premises		2,500	2,500 Cr
	Motor cars	500		2,000 Cr
	Capital: A	1,000		
	Capital: B	1,000		——
	(transfer profit on			
	revaluation)			

PREMISES ACCOUNT

Date	Details	Dr	Cr	Balance
		£	£	£
	Balance b/d			10,000 Dr
Mar 31	Revaluation	2,500		12,500 Dr

MOTOR CARS ACCOUNT

Date	Details	Dr	Cr	Balance
		£	£	£
	Balance b/d			8,500 Dr
	Revaluation		500	8,000 Dr

CAPITAL ACCOUNT: A

Date	Details	Dr	Cr	Balance
		£	£	£
	Balance			5,000 Cr
	Revaluation		1,000	6,000 Cr

CAPITAL ACCOUNT: B

Date	Details	Dr	Cr	Balance
		£	£	£
	Balance			8,000 Cr
	Revaluation		1,000	9,000 Cr

3.5   EXERCISES ON PARTNERSHIP FINAL ACCOUNTS

1   Book and Worm practise in partnership as solicitors. Profits and losses are shared two-thirds to Book and one-third to Worm. Worm also receives a salary of £6,000 before profits are shared.

Book and Worm decide to admit Page into the partnership on 1 July 1988 and he is to receive a salary of £3,000 per annum, together with a one-fifth share of profits as from that date. The remainder of the profits are to be shared equally between Book and Worm. Page is to introduce capital of £2,500 on his admission to the partnership. From 1 July 1988 the previous profit-sharing and salary arrangements between Book and Worm are cancelled. Interest on capital is paid at the rate of 10% per annum. Book and Worm decide that the value of premises should be increased from £7,000 to £10,000 immediately before 1 July 1988.

On 30 June 1988, before the revaluation takes place, Book's capital account has a balance of £23,000 and Worms' capital account has a balance of £14,000.

The bookkeeper extracts the following balances from the firm's accounts on 31 December 1988.

	£
Drawings	
Book	22,000
Worm	16,000
Page	6,000
Library	2,700
Motor cars	9,560
Premises	10,000
Furniture	4,600
Current accounts	
Book	1,400 Cr
Worm	1,000 Cr
Administration expenses	76,521
General expenses	33,142
Cash at bank: office account	14,290 Dr
Petty cash	23
Profit costs (after deducting work in progress at 1 January 1988)	164,726 Cr
Interest receivable	3,869 Cr
Due to creditors	1,763 Cr
Cash at bank: clients' account	
Current account	12,345
Deposit account	79,642
Amount due to clients	91,987 Cr
Due from clients	20,422

Depreciation of £1,860 and £460 is to be charged against motor cars and furniture respectively.

At 31 December 1988, bills have been received for general expenses of £1,056 but no action has yet been taken in respect of them. Included in the amount due from clients is the sum of £125 which is to be written off as a bad debt.

Work in progress at 31 December 1988 is valued at £4,569. The allocation of profits between the partners is to be determined on a time basis.

From the above information, prepare a profit and loss and appropriation account for the year ended 31 December 1988, together with a balance sheet as at that date.

2   Autumn and Spring are in partnership as solicitors, sharing profits and losses so that Autumn receives two-thirds and Spring one third. Each partner is entitled to interest on capital in the firm, at the rate of 15% per annum. Spring is also entitled to a salary of £10,000 per annum, together with an allowance of £1,000 per annum in respect of the use of part of his private house as an office. The following trial balance is prepared from the firm's books for the year ended 31 December 1991.

TRIAL BALANCE AT 31 DECEMBER 1991

	Dr £	Cr £
Capital accounts		
Autumn		20,000
Spring		10,000
Current accounts		
Autumn		2,156
Spring		854
Lease at cost	5,000	
Motor cars	8,400	
Furniture, library and equipment	3,860	
Partners' drawings		
Autumn	18,763	
Spring	14,527	
Administration and general expenses	69,567	
Profit costs		89,314
Interest receivable		4,872
Due to clients		125,896
Provision for bad debts		326
Creditors		1,975

	£	£
Cash at bank: clients' account:		
Deposit account	85,420	
Current account	40,476	
Petty cash balance	85	
Cash at bank: office account	2,423	
Work in progress (1 January 1991)	8,764	
Due from clients	8,892	
Loan account: bank		7,000
Rent receivable		3,784
	266,177	266,177

Work in progress at 31 December 1991 is valued at £11,967. The provision for bad debts is considered to be understated by £56.

Depreciation of £1,680 and £370 is to be charged against motor cars, furniture, library and equipment respectively. A sum of £4,000 is to be taken into account in respect of secretarial and advisory fees, the amount not having been received until January 1992.

From the above information, prepare a profit and loss and appropriation account for the year ended 31 December 1991, together with a balance sheet as at that date. No adjustment has yet been made, in respect of the allowance to Spring for use of part of his private house as an office.

(Law Society Final Examination, updated)

3   Pen and Ink are in partnership as solicitors sharing profits and losses in the ratio 3 : 2. Each partner is entitled, under the partnership agreement, to interest on capital at the rate of 10% per annum and Ink is entitled, in addition, to a partnership salary of £12,000 per annum.

On 1 January 1991, Paper is admitted into the partnership, contributing £10,000 as his share of the capital in the firm. The new partnership agreement provides that, as from 1 January 1991, profits and losses will be shared between Pen, Ink and Paper in the ratio 2 : 2 : 1 respectively. Furthermore, partnership salaries of £20,000, £15,000 and £10,000 will be allowed to Pen, Ink and Paper respectively. No interest is to be allowed on capital, and no interest is to be charged on partners' drawings.

Partners' drawings have been debited to their respective current accounts as soon as they have occurred. An abridged trial balance, prepared from the partnership books, shows the following position as at 30 June 1991.

	£	£
NET PROFIT for the year, before charging interest on capital, and other appropriations		50,000
Partners' current accounts		
Pen	19,700	
Ink	18,400	
Paper	6,000	
Partners' capital accounts		
Pen		40,000
Ink		20,000
Paper		10,000
Sundry assets	80,500	
Sundry liabilities		4,600
	124,600	124,600
Amounts due to clients		87,322
Cash at bank: clients	87,322	
	211,922	211,922

From the above information, prepare the profit and loss appropriation account for the year ended 30 June 1991, together with a balance sheet as at that date. The allocation of profits between the partners is to be determined on a time basis. (Calculations to be made in months.) Detailed movements on partners' current accounts must be shown.

(Law Society Final Examination, updated)

4 Hale and Hearty are in partnership as solicitors. Hale receives interest on capital of 5% per annum and Hearty receives a salary of £2,000 per annum. The remaining profits are shared equally. Their financial year ends on 31 December. On 31 December 1991 the trial balance is:

	Dr	Cr
	£	£
Freehold premises	45,000	
Fixtures and fittings	5,000	
Depreciation on fixtures and fittings		1,000
Library	2,000	
Depreciation on library		500

Capital accounts:		
Hale		30,000
Hearty		25,000
Current accounts:		
Hale		1,500
Hearty		1,000
Drawings:		
Hale	4,000	
Hearty	4,500	
Costs		30,000
Insurance commission receivable		600
Salaries	20,000	
Insurance payable	1,500	
Rates	1,620	
Light and heat	1,400	
Stationery	900	
Travelling	400	
Creditors		820
Debtors	1,000	
Office bank account	3,000	
Petty cash	100	
Client bank account	65,000	
Client ledger account		65,000
	155,420	155,420

At 31 December 1991 work in progress amounts to £5,000; there is a stock of stationery valued at £300. Depreciation is charged on fixtures and fittings and library at 10%. There is an amount outstanding for electricity of £100.

Prepare final accounts for Hale and Hearty for the year ended 31 December 1991.

5 Carbue has practised as a solicitor for many years, and he decides to reduce his business commitments by admitting Retter, his senior assistant, into the firm as a partner. The partnership agreement shows, *inter alia,* the following details which are pertinent to the preparation of the annual accounts:

(a) The name of the firm is to be Carbue, Retter & Co.

(b) Retter is to be admitted into the firm as a partner, with effect from 1 October 1990.

(c) Profits and losses are to be shared between the partners, as to Carbue two-thirds and Retter one-third, after allowing a salary of £10,000 per annum for Retter.

(d) Interest is to be allowed on capital at the rate of 10 per cent per annum.

(e) Retter is to contribute the sum of £20,000 as his share of the capital of the firm.

The firm's bookkeeper produces the following list of balances, which he has extracted from the firm's books, for the year ended 31 March 1991:

	£
Lease at cost	24,000
Furniture and library at cost	12,000
Motor cars at cost	18,500
Provision for depreciation accounts at 31 March 1990:	
Furniture and library	3,200
Motor cars	7,500
Drawings:	
Carbue	34,000
Retter	8,000
Current account: Carbue	1,200 Cr
Capital accounts:	
Carbue (at 1 April 1990)	50,000
Retter (at 1 October 1990)	20,000
Clients' ledger balances:	
Office account	39,888
Clients' account	294,703
Cash at bank: Office account	7,925

Clients' account:
Deposit account	225,000
Current account	69,703
Petty cash balance	87
Sundry creditors	6,204
Profit costs	267,435
Work in progress at 31 March 1990	34,340
Interest receivable	11,768
Administrative and general expenses	198,567
Mortgage on leasehold premises	10,000

After the above balances had been produced, it was discovered that a cheque for £123 had been issued on 30 March 1991, but no entry had been made in the relevant accounts and the cheque had not been presented to the bank until 9 April 1991. The cheque was drawn in favour of a creditor, and was included in the amount of £6,204 shown above for sundry creditors.

The amount standing to the credit of Carbue's current account represents an adjustment made in respect of out of pocket expenses incurred in the year to 31 March 1991. It has subsequently been agreed that £300 of that amount (which has been charged to administrative and general expenses) should be borne by Carbue personally, but no adjustment has yet been made in respect thereof.

The following additional information is pertinent:

(a) Work in progress at 31 March 1991, is valued at £27,320.

(b) Depreciation is to be charged thus:
Motor cars	£3,600
Furniture and library	£800

(c) A provision for staff bonuses (£3,436) is to be made in respect of the year ended 31 March 1991.

(d) Profits are to be allocated between partners on a time basis. (All calculations to be made in months.)

From the foregoing information, prepare a profit and loss and appropriation account for the year ended 31 March 1991, together with a balance sheet as at that date. (Use the vertical form of presentation.)

Movements on partners' current accounts must be shown in detail.

(Solicitors' Final Examinations, updated)

3.6 SUGGESTED ANSWERS TO EXERCISES ON PARTNERSHIP FINAL ACCOUNTS

1 Book and Worm

PROFIT AND LOSS APPROPRIATION ACCOUNT FOR THE YEAR ENDED 31 DECEMBER 1988

INCOME	£	£	£
Costs less opening work in progress		164,726	
Add: Closing work in progress		4,569	169,295
Interest receivable			3,869
			173,164
LESS: EXPENDITURE			
Administration expenses		76,521	
General expenses		34,198	
Depreciation			
Motor cars	1,860		
Furniture	460	2,320	
Bad debts		125	113,164
NET PROFIT			60,000
APPROPRIATION from 1 January to 30 June 1988			
NET PROFIT (6 months)			30,000
SALARY (6 months)			
Worm		3,000	
PROFIT SHARE			
Book 2/3rds		18,000	
Worm 1/3rd		9,000	30,000
APPROPRIATION from 1 July to 31 December 1988			
NET PROFIT (6 months)			30,000

	£	£	£
SALARY (6 months)			
Page		1,500	
INTEREST on capital (6 months)			
Book	1,250		
Worm	750		
Page	125	2,125	
PROFIT SHARE			
Book: 2/5ths	10,550		
Worm: 2/5ths	10,550		
Page: 1/5th	5,275	26,375	30,000

MOVEMENTS ON PARTNERS' CURRENT ACCOUNTS

	Book	Worm	Page
	£	£	£
Balance	1,400	1,000	—
Salary	—	3,000	1,500
Interest on capital	1,250	750	125
Profit share	28,550	19,550	5,275
	31,200	24,300	6,900
Drawings	22,000	16,000	6,000
	9,200	8,300	900

BALANCE SHEET AS AT 31 DECEMBER 1988

	£	£	£
CAPITAL EMPLOYED			
Partners' capital accounts			
Book		25,000	
Worm		15,000	
Page		2,500	42,500
Partners' current accounts			
Book		9,200	
Worm		8,300	
Page		900	18,400
			60,900

	£	£	£
EMPLOYMENT OF CAPITAL			
Fixed assets			
Premises		10,000	
Library		2,700	
Furniture	4,600		
Less: Depreciation	460	4,140	
Motor cars	9,560		
Less: Depreciation	1,860	7,700	24,540
Current assets			
Closing work in progress	4,569		
Debtors (bad debt deducted £125)	20,297		
Office bank account	14,290		
Petty cash	23	39,179	
Less: Current liabilities			
Creditors	1,763		
Outstanding expenses			
General expenses	1,056	2,819	36,360
CLIENT BALANCES			
Client bank account			
Current account	12,345		
Deposit account	79,642	91,987	
Less: Due to clients		91,987	
			60,900

2   Autumn and Spring

PROFIT AND LOSS APPROPRIATION ACCOUNT FOR THE YEAR ENDED 31 DECEMBER 1991

INCOME	£	£	£
Costs		89,314	
Add: Closing work in progress		11,967	
		101,281	
Less: Opening work in progress		8,764	92,517
Interest receivable			4,872
Rent receivable			3,784
Provision for secretarial and advisory fees			4,000
			105,173
LESS: EXPENDITURE			
Administration and general expenses		69,567	
Provision for bad debts		56	
Depreciation			
Cars	1,680		
Furniture etc.	370	2,050	
Rent: Spring		1,000	72,673
NET PROFIT			32,500
SALARIES			
Spring		10,000	
INTEREST ON CAPITAL			
Autumn		3,000	
Spring		1,500	
PROFIT SHARE			
Autumn: 2/3rds		12,000	
Spring: 1/3rd		6,000	32,500

It is assumed that the allowance made to Spring for use of his home is a bona fide business rent and therefore allowable as a business expense in the profit and loss account.

If the payment to Spring were not a bona fide business expense, but an allocation of profit, it would be shown as such in the appropriation account and would not appear in the profit and loss account.

Workings for balance sheet

MOVEMENTS ON PARTNERS' CURRENT ACCOUNTS

	Autumn £	Spring £
Balance	2,156 Cr	854 Cr
Salary	–	10,000
Interest on capital	3,000	1,500
Rent allowance	–	1,000
Profit share	12,000	6,000
	17,156	19,354
Less drawings	18,763	14,527
	1,607 Dr	4,827 Cr

BAD DEBTS ACCOUNT

Date	Details	Dr	Cr	Balance
1991		£	£	£
Jan 1	Provision b/d		326	326 Cr
Dec 31	Provision c/d	382		56 Dr
	Profit and loss account:			
	transfer		56	—

BALANCE SHEET AS AT 31 DECEMBER 1991

CAPITAL EMPLOYED	£	£	£	£
Partners' capital accounts				
Autumn		20,000		
Spring		10,000		30,000
Partners' current accounts				
Autumn		1,607 Dr		
Spring		4,827 Cr		3,220
LONG-TERM LIABILITIES				
Bank loan				7,000
				40,220
EMPLOYMENT OF CAPITAL				
Fixed assets				
Leasehold premises			5,000	
Furniture, library and				
equipment at cost		3,860		
Less: Accumulated depreciation		370	3,490	
Motor cars		8,400		
Less: Accumulated depreciation		1,680	6,720	15,210
Current assets				
Closing work in progress		11,967		
Debtors	8,892			
Less: Provision	382	8,510		
Fees due		4,000		
Office bank account		2,423		
Petty cash		85	26,985	
Less: Current liabilities				
Creditors			1,975	25,010

CLIENT ACCOUNT	£	£	£	£
Bank balance				
Current account	40,476			
Deposit account	85,420	125,896		
Less: Due to clients		125,896		
				40,220

3   Pen and Ink

PROFIT AND LOSS APPROPRIATION ACCOUNT FOR PERIOD 1 JULY 1990 TO 31 DECEMBER 1990

	£	£
NET PROFIT (for 6 months)		25,000
SALARY (for 6 months)		
Ink	6,000	
INTEREST ON CAPITAL (for 6 months)		
Pen	2,000	
Ink	1,000	
PROFIT SHARE		
Pen: 3/5ths	9,600	
Ink: 2/5ths	6,400	25,000

PROFIT AND LOSS APPROPRIATION ACCOUNT FOR PERIOD 1 JANUARY 1991 TO 30 JUNE 1991

	£	£
NET PROFIT (for 6 months)		25,000
SALARIES (for 6 months)		
Pen	10,000	
Ink	7,500	
Paper	5,000	
PROFIT SHARE		
Pen: 2/5ths	1,000	
Ink: 2/5ths	1,000	
Paper: 1/5th	500	25,000

Workings

MOVEMENTS ON PARTNERS' CURRENT ACCOUNTS

	Pen	Ink	Paper
	£	£	£
Salary	10,000	13,500	5,000
Interest on capital	2,000	1,000	–
Profit share	10,600	7,400	500
	22,600	21,900	5,500
Less balance	19,700	18,400	6,000
	2,900 Cr	3,500 Cr	500 Dr

BALANCE SHEET AS AT 30 JUNE 1991

CAPITAL EMPLOYED	£	£	£
Partners' capital accounts			
Pen		40,000	
Ink		20,000	
Paper		10,000	70,000
Partners' current accounts			
Pen		2,900Cr	
Ink		3,500Cr	
Paper		500Dr	5,900
			75,900

EMPLOYMENT OF CAPITAL		
Sundry assets		80,500
Less: Sundry liabilities		4,600

CLIENT ACCOUNT		
Client bank balance	87,322	
Less: Due to clients	87,322	
		75,900

4 Hale and Hearty

PROFIT AND LOSS ACCOUNT FOR THE YEAR ENDED
31 DECEMBER 1991

INCOME	£	£	£
Costs		30,000	
Add closing work in progress		5,000	
Insurance commission receivable		600	35,600
LESS EXPENDITURE			
Salaries		20,000	
Insurance payable		1,500	
Rates		1,620	
Light and heat	1,400		
Plus outstanding expense	100	1,500	
Stationery	900		
Less closing stock	300	600	
Travel expenses		400	
Depreciation:			
Fixtures and fittings	500		
Library	200	700	26,320
NET PROFIT			9,280
APPROPRIATION ACCOUNT			
Salary:			
Hearty	2,000		
Interest on capital:			
Hale	1,500		3,500
Profit share:			
Hale ½	2,890		
Hearty ½	2,890		5,780
			9,280

BALANCE SHEET AS AT 31 DECEMBER 1991

	£	£	£
CAPITAL EMPLOYED			
Partners' capital accounts:			
Hale	30,000		
Hearty	25,000	55,000	
Partners current accounts:			
Hale	1,890		
Hearty	1,390	3,280	58,280
EMPLOYMENT OF CAPITAL			
Fixed assets:			
Premises		45,000	
Fixtures and fittings	5,000		
Less accumulated depreciation	1,500	3,500	
Library	2,000		
Less accumulated depreciation	700	1,300	49,800
Current assets:			
Closing work in progress	5,000		
Debtors	1,000		
Office bank account	3,000		
Petty cash	100		
Payment in advance	300	9,400	
Less current liaiblities:			
Creditors	820		
Outstanding expenses	100	920	8,480
CLIENT ACCOUNT			
Client bank balance		65,000	
Less amount due to clients		65,000	
			58,280

MOVEMENT ON PARTNERS' CURRENT ACCOUNTS

	Hale	Hearty
Opening balance	1,500	1,000
Salary		2,000
Interest on capital	1,500	
Profit share	2,890	2,890
	5,890	5,890
Less drawings	4,000	4,500
	1,890	1,390

5   Carbue, Retter & Co.

PROFIT AND LOSS ACCOUNT FOR THE YEAR ENDED
31 MARCH 1991

INCOME	£	£	£
Costs	267,435		
Add closing work in progress	27,320	294,755	
Less opening work in progress		34,340	
		260,415	
Interest receivable		11,768	272,183
LESS EXPENDITURE:			
Administrative and general expenses	198,567		
Add due for staff bonus	3,436		
	202,003		
Less transfer to Carbue	300	201,703	
Depreciation:			
Cars	3,600		
Furniture and library	800	4,400	206,103
NET PROFIT			66,080

APPROPRIATION ACCOUNT

		£
1 April 1990 to 30 September 1990		
Profit to Carbue		33,040
1 October 1990 to 31 March 1991		
Salary:		
Retter	5,000	
Interest on capital:		
Carbue	2,500	
Retter	1,000	8,500
Profit share:		
Carbue 2/3rds	16,360	
Retter 1/3rd	8,180	24,540
		66,080

BALANCE SHEET AS AT 31 MARCH 1991

CAPITAL EMPLOYED	£	£	£
Capital accounts:			
Carbue	50,000		
Retter	20,000	70,000	
Current accounts:			
Carbue	18,800		
Retter	6,180	24,980	
Long-term liabilities:			
Mortgage		10,000	104,980
EMPLOYMENT OF CAPITAL			
Fixed assets:			
Leasehold property		24,000	
Cars at cost	18,500		
Less accumulated depreciation	11,100	7,400	
Furniture and library at cost	12,000		
Less accumulated depreciation	4,000	8,000	39,400
(Carried forward)			(39,400)

	£	£	£
(Brought forward)			(39,400)
Current assets:			
Closing work in progress	27,320		
Debtors	39,888		
Office bank account: 7,925 less 123	7,802		
Petty cash	87	75,097	
Less current liabilities:			
Creditors: 6,204 less 123 plus 3,436		9,517	65,580
			104,980
CLIENT ACCOUNT			
Deposit account	225,000		
Current account	69,703	294,703	
Deduct due to clients		294,703	

MOVEMENT ON PARTNERS' CURRENT ACCOUNTS

	Carbue £	Retter £
Balance	1,200	
Salary		5,000
Interest on capital	2,500	1,000
Profit share	49,400	8,180
	53,100	14,180
Less drawings (£34,000 + £300)	34,300	8,000
	18,800	6,180

3.7   TEST ON PARTNERSHIP FINAL ACCOUNTS

Allow 2 hours to complete this test.

1   The bookkeeper of the firm Red and Roses, who are practising solicitors, extracts the following information from the books of account in respect of the year ended 31 December 1991.

	£
Due to clients	140,455
Profit costs	165,741
Interest receivable	6,395
General and administrative expenses	103,622
Rent receivable	2,000
Provision for bad debts	358
Partners' capital accounts	
Red	20,000
Roses	15,000
Partners' current accounts	
Red	2,274 Dr
Roses	1,785 Dr
Leasehold premises at cost	25,000
Library, furniture and equipment at cost	9,678
Accumulated depreciation written off library, furniture and equipment to 31 December 1990	3,228
Due from clients	18,765
Work in progress: 1 January 1991	12,111
Cash at bank: Client account	140,455
Office account	5,310
Petty cash balance	40
Partners' drawings:	
Red	22,679
Roses	17,890
Sundry creditors	6,432

The following information is relevant:

(a)   Profits and losses are shared between Red and Roses so that Red receives three-fifths and Roses two-fifths.

(b)   Roses is to receive a partnership salary of £8,000 per annum.

(c)   Interest is to be allowed on partners' capital, as follows:

Red   £2,000
Roses   £1,500

(d)   Work in progress at 31 December 1991 is valued at £14,135.

(e)   At 31 December 1991, prepaid general expenses amount to £240, whilst there are administration expenses outstanding and not yet accounted for amounting to £879.

(f)   An adjustment is to be made, in respect of business travelling expenses of £750 in the case of each partner, which each partner has paid from his own resources.

(g)   The provision for bad debts is to be increased to £467.

(h)   Depreciation of £950 is to be charged against library, furniture and equipment.

From the above information prepare a profit and loss appropriation account for the year ended 31 December 1991, together with a balance sheet at that date.

(Law Society Final Examination, updated)

2   Lake, Windermere & Co. are solicitors; the partnership consists of Brown and Green who share profits and losses so that Brown receives two-thirds and Green one-third. Each partner is entitled to interest on capital in the firm and, in addition, Green is entitled to a salary of £8,000 per annum.

On 1 January 1990 Brown decides to retire from the partnership and on the same day Pink is admitted into the partnership with Green, contributing £10,000 as his share of the capital in the firm. From 1 January 1990 the partnership ratio for sharing profits and losses is to be Green three-fifths and Pink two-fifths, the former salary arrangement for Green being cancelled from that date. Brown agrees to leave his share of the capital in the firm for the time being and he is to be allowed interest thereon at the rate of 15% per annum, such interest to be treated as a normal business expense. The following trial balance is prepared from the firm's books for the year ended 30 June 1990.

TRIAL BALANCE AT 30 JUNE 1990

	Dr £	Cr £
Profit costs		92,463
Interest receivable		5,394
Administration expenses	51,432	
General expenses	22,654	
Cash at bank: office account	7,876	
Petty cash balance	18	
Work in progress 1 July 1989	9,346	
Capital accounts (1 July 1989):		
Brown		25,000
Green		15,000
Capital account (1 January 1990):		
Pink		10,000
Current accounts (1 July 1989):		
Brown		1,976
Green	567	
Drawings:		
Brown	9,000	
Green	9,000	
Pink	4,000	
Motor cars	8,500	
Library	1,000	
Furniture and office equipment	2,450	
Due from clients	10,789	
Cash at bank: client account		
Current account	11,200	
Deposit account	92,000	
Due to clients		103,200
Due to creditors		3,240
Provision for bad debts (1 July 1989)		559
Loss on sale of motor cars	1,000	
Lease at cost	16,000	
	256,832	256,832

Depreciation of £490 is to be charged against furniture and office equipment and £2,125 against motor cars.

Brown, Green and Pink are entitled to interest on capital, of £1,250, £1,500 and £500 respectively, such amounts to be allocated over the relevant periods, whilst the interest on the loan made by Brown (from 1 January 1990) is agreed at £1,875.

Work in progress at 30 June 1990 is valued at £16,775. At 30 June 1990 bills have been received for administration expenses amounting to £1,344, but no action has yet been taken in respect thereof. At the same date it is considered that the provision for bad debts is overstated by the sum of £159 and the current provision should be reduced accordingly. The allocation of profits between the partners is to be determined on a time basis (calculations to be made in months).

From the above information prepare a profit and loss appropriation account for the year ended 30 June 1990, together with a balance sheet as at that date.

(Law Society Final Examination, updated)

3.8 SUGGESTED ANSWERS TO TEST ON PARTNERSHIP FINAL ACCOUNTS

1 Red and Roses

PROFIT AND LOSS APPROPRIATION ACCOUNT FOR THE YEAR
ENDED 31 DECEMBER 1991

INCOME	£	£
Costs	165,741	
Add: Closing work in progress	14,135	
	179,876	
Less: Opening work in progress	12,111	167,765
Interest receivable		6,395
Rent receivable		2,000
		176,160
LESS EXPENDITURE		
General and administrative expenses	104,261	
Bad debts	109	
Depreciation: library, furniture and equipment	950	
Travelling expenses	1,500	106,820
NET PROFIT		69,340

	£	£
SALARY		
Roses	8,000	
INTEREST ON CAPITAL		
Red	2,000	
Roses	1,500	
SHARE OF PROFIT		
Red: 3/5ths	34,704	
Roses: 2/5ths	23,136	69,340

Workings

GENERAL AND ADMINISTRATIVE EXPENSES ACCOUNT

Date	Details	Dr	Cr	Balance
1991		£	£	£
Dec 31	Balance			103,622 Dr
	Provision: outstanding			
	expenses	879		104,501 Dr
	Payments in advance		240	104,261 Dr
	Profit and loss account:			
	transfer		104,261	———

BAD DEBTS ACCOUNT

Date	Details	Dr	Cr	Balance
1991		£	£	£
Jan 1	Provision b/d		358	358 Cr
Dec 31	Provision c/d	467		109 Dr
	Profit and loss account:			
	transfer		109	———

MOVEMENTS ON PARTNERS' CURRENT ACCOUNTS

	Red £	Roses £
Travel expenses	750	750
Interest on capital	2,000	1,500
Salary	–	8,000
Profit share	34,704	23,136
	37,454	33,386
Less balance	2,274	1,785
	35,180	31,601
Less Drawings	22,679	17,890
	12,501 Cr	13,711 Cr

BALANCE SHEET AS AT 31 DECEMBER 1991

CAPITAL EMPLOYED	£	£	£	£
Partners' capital accounts				
Red			20,000	
Roses			15,000	35,000
Partners' current accounts				
Red			12,501	
Roses			13,711Cr	26,212
				61,212

EMPLOYMENT OF CAPITAL	£	£	£	£
FIXED ASSETS				
Leasehold premises at cost			25,000	
Library, furniture and equipment at cost		9,678		
Less: Accumulated depreciation		4,178	5,500	30,500
CURRENT ASSETS				
Closing work in progress		14,135		
Debtors	18,765			
Less: Provision	467	18,298		
Cash at bank: office account		5,310		
Petty cash		40		
Payment in advance: general expenses		240	38,023	
Less: Current liabilities				
Creditors		6,432		
Outstanding expenses: general expenses		879	7,311	30,712
CLIENT ACCOUNTS				
Client bank account	140,455			
Less: Due to clients	140,455			
				61,212

2   Lake, Windermere & Co

PROFIT AND LOSS APPROPRIATION ACCOUNT FOR THE YEAR ENDED 30 JUNE 1990

INCOME	£	£	£
Costs		92,463	
Add: Closing work in progress		16,775	
		109,238	
Less: Opening work in progress		9,346	99,892
Interest receivable			5,394
Bad debts provision written back			159
			105,445
LESS: EXPENDITURE			
Administration expenses		52,776	
General expenses		22,654	
Loss on sale of car		1,000	
Loan interest: Brown		1,875	
Depreciation			
Cars	2,125		
Furniture	490	2,615	80,920
			24,525

APPROPRIATION from 1 July 1989 to 31 December 1989 (6 months)

NET PROFIT		12,263
SALARY		
Green	4,000	
INTEREST ON CAPITAL		
Brown	1,250	
Green	750	
PROFIT SHARE		
Brown: 2/3rds	4,175	
Green: 1/3rd	2,088	12,263

APPROPRIATION from 1 January 1990 to 30 June 1990

		£	£
NET PROFIT			12,262
INTEREST ON CAPITAL			
Green		750	
Pink		500	
PROFIT SHARE			
Green:	3/5ths	6,607	
Pink:	2/5ths	4,405	12,262

MOVEMENTS ON PARTNERS' CURRENT ACCOUNTS

	Brown	Green	Pink
	£	£	£
Balance	1,976 Cr	567 Dr	—
Interest on capital	1,250	1,500	500
Salary	—	4,000	—
Profit share	4,175	8,695	4,405
	7,401 Cr	13,628 Cr	4,905 Cr
Less drawings	9,000	9,000	4,000
	1,599 Dr	4,628 Cr	905 Cr

BALANCE SHEET AS AT 30 JUNE 1990

CAPITAL EMPLOYED	£	£	£	£
Capital accounts				
Green			15,000	
Pink			10,000	25,000
Current accounts				
Green			4,628	
Pink			905	5,533
LONG-TERM LIABILITIES				
Brown: loan				25,000
				55,533
EMPLOYMENT OF CAPITAL				
FIXED ASSETS				
Lease			16,000	
Library			1,000	
Furniture at cost		2,450		
Less: Accumulated depreciation		490	1,960	
Motor cars at cost		8,500		
Less: Accumulated depreciation		2,125	6,375	25,335
CURRENT ASSETS				
Closing work in progress		16,775		
Bank: office account		7,876		
Petty cash		18		
Due from Brown (current account balance)		1,599		
Debtors	10,789			
Less: Provision	400	10,389	36,657	
LESS: CURRENT LIABILITIES				
Loan interest: Brown		1,875		
Creditors		3,240		
Outstanding expenses		1,344	6,459	30,198
				55,533
CLIENT ACCOUNT				
Client bank account				
Current account	11,200			
Deposit account	92,000	103,200		
Less: Due to clients		103,200		

Calculations have been made to the nearest full pound.

At the date the balance sheet is prepared, Brown is not a partner. His capital account and current account balances are therefore not shown on the balance sheet as partners' capital and current accounts. His capital account balance is to be left in the firm and is therefore a long-term liability. The debit balance on Brown's current account is a current asset to the firm.

4 Basic Solicitors' Accounts

4.1 INTRODUCTION

You should read and have a thorough understanding of the Solicitors' Accounts Rules 1991. You will not be required to write out the rules or remember their numbers but you will be required to show the examiner that you understand and can apply them.

4.2 THE SOLICITORS' ACCOUNTS RULES

4.2.1 Keeping clients' and office money separate

A solicitor must keep money belonging to his clients (clients' money) separate from his own money (office money). This necessitates his having two separate accounts at the bank, the client bank account and the office bank account. The rules define a client account as a current or deposit account at a bank or a deposit account at a building society in the name of the solicitor or his firm, in the title of which the word 'client' appears.

It follows that the solicitor must also have two cash accounts in his ledger system, the office cash account and the client cash account. For convenience these two are shown side by side, as follows:

CASH ACCOUNT

Date	Details	Office account			Client account		
		Dr £	Cr £	Balance £	Dr £	Cr £	Balance £

Each client ledger card will also show that there are two accounts at the bank:

SMITH: RE CONVEYANCING

Date	Details	Office account			Client account		
		Dr £	Cr £	Balance £	Dr £	Cr £	Balance £

Although the money for all clients will, as a general rule, be kept in one bank account, the solicitor must record separately in respect of each client the money which is being held for that client. This means that the solicitor must not use money belonging to one client for the purposes of another client, nor may the solicitor transfer the money of one client from his ledger account to the ledger account of another client except as provided for in the rules (see 4.6.3).

4.2.2   The definition of clients' money

Whenever a solicitor receives or pays money for a client, the solicitor must decide whether it is clients' or office money. The rules define clients' money as money held or received by a solicitor on account of a person for whom he or she is acting in relation to the holding or receipt of such money either as solicitor, or in connection with his or her practice as a solicitor, as agent, bailee, stakeholder or in any other capacity.

4.2.3   Payments into client account

Where a solicitor holds clients' money, the solicitor must pay it into a client account without delay. This means on the day the money is received or, if that is not possible, on the next working day.

The following should be particularly noted:

(a)   Money may not be paid into a client account if the client has asked for it not to be paid into a client account. Such a request from the client should be in writing or acknowledged in writing by the solicitor.

(b) Where a solicitor agrees to hold a cheque 'to the order' of a third party, the cheque should not be paid into a client account until it is released by the third party, as until that point it does not become the client's money.

(c) Where two firms of solicitors place stakeholder money in an account in their joint names, this is not clients' money. It is, however, still good practice for both firms to record the holding of the stakeholder money in their accounts. If the stakeholder money is in the sole control of one firm it is clients' money and must be paid into client account.

(d) Money which is received for or towards the payment of the solicitor's costs may not be paid into a client account. Thus if a fee is agreed or a bill of costs delivered to the client and afterwards money is received from the client in respect of the costs, the money must be paid into office account.

(e) A solicitor's bill of costs may include the charges of a third party instructed by the solicitor on the client's behalf, for example, counsel, an expert witness or an agent. These liabilities to third parties are excluded from the definition of 'costs' and so, unless the third-party liability has already been discharged by the solicitor when the client pays the bill, the part of the payment representing counsel's fees etc. must be paid into client account. For example, a solicitor delivers a bill showing profit costs £200, VAT £35, and counsel's fees £117.50. When the client pays the bill the solicitor has not paid counsel's fees. The solicitor must either:

(i) pay the cheque into client account and then transfer £235 for the costs and VAT to office account, or

(ii) split the cheque, by paying £235 for costs and VAT into office account and £117.50 for counsel's fees into client account.

When the solicitor subsequently pays counsel's fees it will be by way of a cheque drawn on client account.

(f) Money paid generally on account of costs and disbursements is clients' money and must be paid into client account.

(g) Money belonging to a solicitor or one of his partners cannot be treated as clients' money and must always be paid into office account. For example, if the firm acts for one of the partners in the purchase of a house in his sole name, free of mortgage, and the partner hands a cheque for the deposit to the firm's cashier, the cheque must be paid into office account. Note the following however:

(i) If the firm is acting for a partner and that partner's spouse (who is not a partner), any moneys received will be held on behalf of both as trustees and must be treated as clients' money.

(ii) If the firm is acting for a partner in the purchase of a property with the aid of a mortgage, the mortgage advance is clients' money.

(h) The following 'non-client' money may be paid into a client account:

(i) Trust moneys (see 4.2.5).

(ii) The solicitor's own money required to open or maintain the account.

(iii) Money to replace that withdrawn in contravention of the rules.

(iv) Cheques which the solicitor would be entitled to 'split' but does not.

(i) A solicitor is not obliged to pay into a client account, clients' money held or received:

(i) in cash, which is, without delay, paid in cash, in the ordinary course of business, to the client or on the client's behalf to a third party, or

(ii) in the form of a cheque or banker's draft which is endorsed over in the ordinary course of business to the client or on the client's behalf to a third party, or

(iii) which is paid into a separate bank account or building society account opened in the name of the client or a third party designated in writing by the client or acknowledged in writing by the solicitor.

Note: if a solicitor negotiates cash or endorses a cheque made out to him, then the solicitor has handled clients' money and must make entries in the account to show the receipt and payment of clients' money.

If a solicitor receives a cheque made payable to a third party which the solicitor passes on to that third party then the solicitor has not handled clients' money and should not record a receipt and payment of clients' money in the accounts. It is, however, advisable to record the fact that the cheque has been received and passed on. This can be done by a file note and/or an entry on the client's ledger account by way of memorandum.

4.2.4 Withdrawals from a client account

The following in particular should be noted with regard to the withdrawal of money from a client account:

(a) Clients' money can only be used to make payments if enough money is held in client account for the particular client on whose behalf it is desired to make the payment.

(b) If insufficient money is held in client account for the particular client the solicitor may either:

(i) pay disbursement out of office account, (the solicitor may then transfer the balance held on client account, to office account), or

(ii) draw two cheques, one on client account for the balance held and one on office account for the remainder, or

(iii) transfer the balance required to pay the disbursement from office to client account and then pay the disbursement out of client account. If the solicitor does this, the money transferred to client account becomes clients' money and is subject to the restrictions on withdrawal and the rules as to interest.

(c) Money may be withdrawn from a client account in the following circumstances:

(i) To make a payment to the client or on the client's behalf.

(ii) With the client's authority. If this is in circumstances not otherwise permitted by the rules the solicitor should always obtain the client's written authority.

(iii) To transfer moneys from a client current account to a client deposit account.

(iv) To reimburse the solicitor in part or full for money expended on the client's behalf. For the purpose of the rules a solicitor will be treated as having expended money when the solicitor draws and dispatches the cheque, unless the cheque is sent on a 'hold to order' basis in which case the solicitor will be deemed to have expended the moneys when the cheque is released.

(v) To pay the solicitor's costs, in full or part, where a bill of costs has been delivered to the client, a fee agreed or other written intimation of the costs has been given to the client and it has thereby or otherwise in writing been made clear to the client that money held for him is being or will be used towards or in satisfaction of such costs.

Note, although there is an obligation to notify the client in writing that his money is being used to pay costs it is not necessary to obtain his approval.

(vi) If money is paid into client account by mistake.

(vii) If the solicitor's own money has been paid into client account to open or maintain it and the money is no longer required for that purpose.

(d) It is permissible to draw against an uncleared cheque which has been paid into client account, but if that cheque is subsequently dishonoured an immediate transfer must be made from office account to client account of the amount by which the client account is over-drawn.

4.2.5 Controlled trusts

A solicitor may hold moneys as a 'controlled trustee'. A solicitor will be a controlled trustee if he is a sole trustee or the only other trustees are his or her partners or employees. If a solicitor is a trustee with an outside third party then the solicitor will not be a controlled trustee. The distinction is important and the following points should be noted:

(a) If the solicitor is a trustee but not a controlled trustee, any money which the solicitor holds for the trust is clients' money and must be held in a client account.

(b) If the solicitors is a controlled trustee, the money in the con-trolled trust is not clients' money.

(c)   A solicitors who is a controlled trustee is not obliged to pay money held on behalf of the controlled trust into client account, although he may do so if he wishes.

(d) If a solicitor who is a controlled trustee elects not to pay controlled trust money into a client account then it must be paid into a separate controlled trust account for that particular trust.

4.3 BASIC ENTRIES

Note that office and client columns are separate. An entry in the client column of one account must have its corresponding double entry in the client column of another account. The same obviously applies also to office account entries.

4.3.1 Receipts of office moneys

The firm must pay money owed to it into office account. The entries to record this are:

(a) Credit clients' ledger account — office column.
(b) Debit cash account — office column.

Example

On 1 February the solicitor receives £100 in respect of disbursements already paid out of office account for his client, Black.

BLACK

Date	Details	Office account			Client account		
		Dr £	Cr £	Balance £	Dr £	Cr £	Balance £
	Balance			100 Dr			
Feb 1	Cash		100	—			

4.3.2 Payments of office moneys

The firm must pay disbursements out of office account if there is insufficient money in client account for that particular client, unless the solicitor decides to transfer office moneys to client account (see 4.2.4). The entries to record a payment of office moneys are:

(a) Debit client's ledger account — office column.
(b) Credit cash account — office column.

Example

Brown's solicitors are acting on his behalf with regard to a personal injury claim. They are not holding money on Brown's behalf and pay £100 to counsel for an opinion on liability on 1 March.

BROWN: RE PERSONAL INJURY ACTION

Date	Details	Office account			Client account		
		Dr £	Cr £	Balance £	Dr £	Cr £	Balance £
Mar 1	Cash: counsel	100		100 Dr			

The client's ledger account should always show a debit balance or a nil balance on office account. A credit balance indicates a breach of the Solicitors' Accounts Rules. The only exception to this is in respect of agreed fees (see 4.5.2).

If there is money held in client account but not enough to pay the particular disbursements, so that the whole payment is made out office account, the solicitor may transfer the money held in client account to office account once the disbursement has been paid. As an alternative, two cheques could be drawn to pay the disbursement, one on client account for the amount held and the remainder on office account. In practice this is rarely done. Alternatively a transfer could be made from office to client account of the balance required (see 4.2.4).

4.3.3 Receipt of clients' money

Once it has been decided that money received is clients' money it must be paid into client account promptly. The entries are:

(a)   Credit client's ledger account − client column.
(b)   Debit cash account − client column.

Example

On 1 April the firm receives a cheque for £2,000 from the Bramchester Building Society to be used as a deposit on the purchase of Blackacre by the firm's client, White.

WHITE: RE PURCHASE OF BLACKACRE

Date	Details	Office account			Client account		
		Dr £	Cr £	Balance £	Dr £	Cr £	Balance £
Apr 1	Cash: Bram-chester Build-ing Society					2,000	2,000 Cr

If money is received from a third party on behalf of a client, as in the preceding example, the receipt is recorded in the ledger account of the client on whose behalf the money is received. An account is not opened for the third party.

Remember the solicitor must not pay the following into client account:

(a)   his own or his partner's money (except as allowed by the rules);
(b)   money received to pay costs after a bill has been delivered;
(c)   money the client asks him not to pay into client account.

4.3.4   Payment of clients' money

Before making a payment out of client account, the solicitor should check:

(a)   That he holds sufficient money in client account for the client on whose behalf he is making the payment.

(b)   That the payment is permissible within the Solicitors' Accounts Rules 1991.

The bookkeeping entries are:

(a)   Debit the client's ledger account – client column.

(b)   Credit the cash account – client column.

Example

On 7 April the firm pays the £2,000 deposit received from the Bramchester Building Society for Jones, to Fleecems the vendor's solicitors.

JONES: RE PURCHASE OF BLACKACRE

Date	Details	Office account			Client account		
		Dr £	Cr £	Balance £	Dr £	Cr £	Balance £
Apr 1	Cash: Bramchester Building Society					2,000	2,000 Cr
Apr 7	Cash: Fleecems				2,000		———

4.3.5   Indorsed cheques and cheques made payable to third parties

You may be required in the examination to show that you appreciate that when you endorse a cheque without paying it through your bank account, you have handled clients' money. This requires entries for the receipt and payment of clients' money. The details column should show that the cheque has been indorsed to avoid problems when the book-keeper prepares the client account bank reconciliation statement, as the receipt and payment will not be shown on the firm's bank statement.

Example

The firm acts for Yellow with regard to the sale of Blackacre and the purchase of Whiteacre. Completion of the sale and purchase takes place on 1 December. On completion of the sale of Blackacre, the firm receives a banker's draft for £10,000 from the purchaser's solicitors. The firm indorses the banker's draft in favour of the solicitors acting for the vendor of Whiteacre.

YELLOW: SALE OF BLACKACRE, PURCHASE OF WHITEACRE

Date	Details	Office account			Client account		
		Dr £	Cr £	Balance £	Dr £	Cr £	Balance £
Dec 1	Cash: sale of Blackacre (draft indorsed)					10,000	10,000 Cr
	Cash: purchase of Whiteacre (draft indorsed)				10,000		———

CASH ACCOUNT

Date	Details	Office account			Client account		
		Dr £	Cr £	Balance £	Dr £	Cr £	Balance £
Dec 1	Yellow: cash: sale of Black-acre (draft indorsed)				10,000		10,000 Dr
	Yellow: cash: purchase of Whiteacre (draft indorsed)					10,000	———

You may also be required in the examination to show that you appreciate that when you hand over to a third party a cheque made payable to him, you have not handled clients' money. You can do this by making no entry at all in the accounts. Alternatively, you can make what is known as a memorandum entry. If you do this, remember: no entry is made in the cash account at all, no balance column entry is made in the client's ledger account and the details column should show clearly that the entry is by way of memorandum only.

Example

You act for Charles to recover a debt owed to him by Janis. On 1 February Janis sends you a cheque for £250 made payable to Charles.

CHARLES: RE DEBT COLLECTION

Date	Details	Office account			Client account		
		Dr £	Cr £	Balance £	Dr £	Cr £	Balance £
Feb 1	Cheque received from Janis payable to Charles				250	250	

4.4 PAYMENTS OUT OF PETTY CASH

Small disbursements paid on behalf of clients, for example, commissioner's fees, may be paid in cash rather than by cheque.

The solicitor maintains a petty cash float by drawing money out of his office account at the bank.

To record dealings with petty cash, a petty cash account is used or a petty cash book if the ledger system is operated.

To record the transfer of money from the office bank account to the petty cash float the following entries are made:

(a) Credit the cash account in the office column.
(b) Debit the petty cash account.

Example

On 10 January a solicitor draws £50 out of office account for petty cash.

PETTY CASH ACCOUNT

Date	Details	Dr	Cr	Balance
		£	£	£
Jan 10	Cash	50		50 Dr

Only office money can be held in petty cash, therefore only office account columns are necessary.

CASH ACCOUNT

Date	Details	Office account			Client account		
		Dr £	Cr £	Balance £	Dr £	Cr £	Balance £
Jan 10	Petty cash		50	50 Cr			

Payments made out of petty cash are always office account payments, therefore even if there is money in client account, a petty cash payment must be recorded as coming out of office account.

To record the payment of a petty cash disbursement on a client's behalf the following entries are made in the accounts:

(a) Debit the client's ledger account in the office column.
(b) Credit the petty cash account.

Example

On 15 January the firm pays £10 out of petty cash for local advertisements in the administration of Kate's estate.

KATE DECEASED: ADMINISTRATION OF ESTATE

Date	Details	Office account			Client account		
		Dr £	Cr £	Balance £	Dr £	Cr £	Balance £
Jan 15	Petty cash: local advertisements	10		10 Dr			

PETTY CASH ACCOUNT

Date	Details	Dr	Cr	Balance
		£	£	£
Jan 10	Cash	50		50 Dr
Jan 15	Kate deceased		10	40 Dr

4.5 COSTS

4.5.1 Delivery of bills of costs

When a solicitor delivers a bill of costs to his client he must keep a prime entry record. This will, in the case of a manual accounting system, be in a bills delivered book. This may simply consist of a file of carbon copies of the bills delivered.

When a bill of costs is delivered to a client the following entries are made in the accounts:

(a) Debit client ledger account office column with profit costs and VAT (on separate lines).
(b) Credit the costs account with profit costs.
(c) Credit the Customs and Excise account with VAT.

The costs account and Customs and Excise accounts only record dealings with office money and therefore only have office columns.

Example

On 15 June 1991 the firm delivers a bill of costs to Beryl, for whom it has acted in divorce proceedings, for £100 plus £17.50 VAT.

BERYL: RE DIVORCE

Date	Details	Office account			Client account		
		Dr £	Cr £	Balance £	Dr £	Cr £	Balance £
1991 June 15	Costs VAT	100 17.50		117.50 Dr			

COSTS ACCOUNT

Date	Details	Dr	Cr	Balance
1991 June 15	Beryl	£	£ 100	£ 100 Cr

CUSTOMS AND EXCISE ACCOUNT

Date	Details	Dr	Cr	Balance
1991		£	£	£
June 15	Beryl		17.50	17.50 Cr

Entries are made to record the delivery of the bill of costs on the date of delivery regardless of the date of payment. When payment of the bill is made entries are made in the accounts to record a receipt of office moneys.

Example

Beryl pays her bill on 1 July.

Date	Details	Office account			Client account		
1991		Dr	Cr	Balance	Dr	Cr	Balance
		£	£	£	£	£	£
June 15	Costs	100					
	VAT	17.50		117.50 Dr			
July 1	Cash you		117.50	—			

4.5.2 Agreed fees

A solicitor and his client may agree a fee for work which the solicitor has done or is to do on his client's behalf. When the solicitor receives the agreed fee he must pay it into office account notwithstanding that he does not deliver a bill of costs until a later date. Entries in the accounts to record the fee should be made when the fee is agreed. It is not necessary to draw a bill when a fee is agreed.

Example

On 10 July 1991 the firm receives £70.50 from Jill in respect of a fee agreed at the beginning of the month for work done by the firm on Jill's behalf in connection with a tenancy dispute. A bill is delivered on 31 July.

JILL: RE HOUSING

Date	Details	Office account			Client account		
1991		Dr £	Cr £	Balance £	Dr £	Cr £	Balance £
	Costs (agreed fee) VAT	60 10.50		70.50 Dr			
July 10	Cash you		70.50	—			

Note:

(a)   No further entries are made on delivery of the bill.

(b)   It would be a breach of the Solicitors' Accounts Rules to pay money, expressly paid in respect of an agreed fee, into client account.

(c)   The tax point for VAT arises when the fee is agreed not when a bill is subsequently delivered.

4.6   TRANSFERS

4.6.1   Transfers from client to office account

A transfer may be made from client to office account if it is permissible, within the Solicitors' Accounts Rules 1991, to withdraw money from client account.

A solicitor may wish to transfer money from client to office account if:

(a)   He has paid disbursements out of office account on the client's behalf.

(b)   He has delivered a bill of costs to the client and wishes to obtain payment of his costs by transferring money held in client account.

(c)   He has paid a split cheque into client account (see section 4.5.4).

The bookkeeping entries to record a transfer from client to office account are:

(a)   The entries to record a payment of clients' money (see section 4.3.4).

(b)   The entries to record a receipt of office money (see section 4.3.1).

Example

On 1 December 1991 the firm delivered a bill of costs to its client Green, showing profit costs of £200 and VAT £35. The firm is holding £500 in client account for Green. On 5 December the firm transfers £235 from client to office account.

GREEN

Date	Details	Office account			Client account		
1991		Dr £	Cr £	Balance £	Dr £	Cr £	Balance £
	Balance						500 Cr
Dec 1	Costs	200					
	VAT	35		235 Dr			
(a)Dec 5	Cash: transfer			——	235		265 Cr
(b)	Cash: transfer		235				

Double entry

Double entry

CASH ACCOUNT

Date	Details	Office account			Client account		
1991		Dr £	Cr £	Balance £	Dr £	Cr £	Balance £
	Green				500		500 Dr
(a)Dec 5	Cash: transfer					235	265 Dr
(b)	Cash: transfer	235		235 Dr			

Note:

   (a)   Payment of client's money.
   (b)   Receipt of office money.

4.6.2   Transfer from office account to client account

A solicitor must make an immediate transfer from office account to client account if he or she has breached the Solicitors' Accounts Rules 1991 by overdrawing on client account, for example, by drawing against an uncleared cheque which is subsequently dishonoured.

Money may be transferred from office to client account to enable a disbursement to be paid out of client account where insufficient money is held in client account to pay it.

The bookkeeping entries to record a transfer of money from office account to client account are as follows:

(a)   Entries to record a payment of office money (see section 4.3.2).

(b)   Entries to record a receipt of clients' money (see section 4.3.3).

Example

Brown has a credit balance on client account of £50. On 20 October his solicitor inadvertently pays counsel's fee of £70 out of client account. He makes an immediate transfer from office to client account to rectify the breach.

BROWN

Date	Details	Office account			Client account		
		Dr £	Cr £	Balance £	Dr £	Cr £	Balance £
	Balance						50 Cr
Oct 20	Cash: counsel				70		20 Dr
(a)	Cash: transfer	20		20 Dr			
(b)	Cash: transfer					20	—

Double entry   Double entry

CASH ACCOUNT

Date	Details	Office account			Client account		
		Dr £	Cr £	Balance £	Dr £	Cr £	Balance £
	Brown				50		50 Dr
Oct 20	Cash: counsel: Brown					70	20 Cr
(a)	Cash: transfer: Brown		20	20 Cr			
(b)	Cash: transfer: Brown				20		—

Note:
  (a) Entries to record payment of office money.
  (b) Entries to record receipt of clients' money.

4.6.3   Transfers between client accounts

Money is not moved from one bank account to another and therefore no entries are made in the cash account.
  A transfer can be made from one client ledger account to another client ledger account if:

  (a) It is permissible within the rules to withdraw money from the account of client A.
  (b) It is permissible within the rules to pay money into the account of client B.

When a transfer is made from one client ledger account to another, a prime entry must be made. This may be in a journal if the ledger system is used or on a transfer sheet if a card system is used.
  The bookkeeping entries to record transfers between client accounts are as follows:

  (a) Debit the ledger account of the client from whose account the transfer is being made. (Make a prime entry.)
  (b) Credit the ledger account of the client to whose account the transfer is being made. (Make a prime entry.)

Example
The firm is holding £5,000 in client account for its client Blue. The firm also acts for Blue's son-in-law, Red, with regard to his house purchase. Blue is making a gift to Red of the deposit of £1,500 and asks the firm to pay Red's deposit on 7 April out of the money held for him.

BLUE

Date	Details	Office account			Client account		
		Dr £	Cr £	Balance £	Dr £	Cr £	Balance £
	Balance						5,000 Cr
Apr 7	Red: transfer				1,500		3,500 Cr

RED

Date	Details	Office account			Client account		
		Dr £	Cr £	Balance £	Dr £	Cr £	Balance £
Apr 7	Blue: transfer Cash: deposit paid				1,500	1,500	1,500 Cr ———

Note: a transfer may be made from the client account of one client to the office account of another or vice versa. For example, if one client has agreed to monies being taken from his client account to discharge another client's liability for costs. If this is done the four entries used to make a transfer from client to office account or vice versa must be shown (see 4.6.1 and 4.6.2).

Example

The firm acts for the executors of Alexander. It also acts for Olivia, Alexander's daughter and the sole beneficiary. There is a balance of £12,000 on Alexander's account. The firm has acted for Olivia in her divorce proceedings and a bill has been delivered to Olivia for £1,000 plus VAT. The executors agree to this being paid out of the estate.

EXECUTORS OF ALEXANDER DECEASED

Date	Details	Office account			Client account		
		Dr £	Cr £	Balance £	Dr £	Cr £	Balance £
	Balance Cash — Olivia				1,175		12,000 Cr 10,825 Cr

OLIVIA: RE DIVORCE

Date	Details	Office account			Client account		
		Dr £	Cr £	Balance £	Dr £	Cr £	Balance £
	Costs	1,000					
	VAT	175		1,175 Dr			
	Cash —						
	Alexander		1,175	—			

CASH ACCOUNT

Date	Details	Office account			Client account		
		Dr £	Cr £	Balance £	Dr £	Cr £	Balance £
	Alexander — transfer to Olivia					1,175	
	Olivia — transfer from Alexander	1,175					

The Solicitors' Accounts Rules 1991 restrict inter-client transfers in respect of private loans. Rule 10(2) states that no sum in respect of a private loan shall be paid out of funds held on account of the lender, either

(a)   directly, or
(b)   by means of a transfer from the ledger account of one client to that of another, without the prior written authority of the lender.

A private loan is defined as meaning a loan other than one provided by an institution which provides loans in the normal course of its activities. The solicitor should keep a register of authorities for transactions of this type.

4.6.4   Split cheques

A split cheque is one which contains part office money and part clients' money.

When a solicitor receives a split cheque he may either:

(a)   Pay the cheque into client account and then make a transfer from client to office account of the office money; or

(b)   Split the cheque by paying the clients' money into client account and the office money into office account.

The solicitor may not pay the whole cheque into office account. To do so would be a breach of the Solicitors' Accounts Rules 1991.

Example

Pink sends a cheque for £250 to his solicitor on 1 March. The cheque represents £200 owed by Pink to a creditor and £50 costs owed to the solicitor in respect of which a bill was delivered to Pink on 1 February.

(a)   If the cheque is split the entries in Pink's account will be:

PINK ACCOUNT

Date	Details	Office account			Client account		
		Dr £	Cr £	Balance £	Dr £	Cr £	Balance £
Mar 1	Balance Cash: you		50	50 Dr —		200	200 Cr

(b)   If the cheque is not split, the entries in Pink's account will be:

PINK ACCOUNT

Date	Details	Office account			Client account		
		Dr £	Cr £	Balance £	Dr £	Cr £	Balance £
Mar 1	Balance Cash: you			50 Dr		250	250 Cr

When the £50 in respect of costs is transferred to office account, entries will be made in Pink's account and the cash account to record a transfer from client to office account (see section 4.6.1).

4.7 EXERCISES ON BASIC LEDGER ENTRIES

1 The firm acts for Algernon with regard to the recovery of debts. The following events take place:

1 September Algernon sends a cheque for £20 on account of disbursements.

2 September Proceedings are issued in the county court against X and a court fee of £10 is paid.

4 September Proceedings are issued against Y and a court fee of £15 is paid.

5 September Z pays £25 in cash to settle his debt to Algernon. Algernon calls at the office the same day and the £25 cash is handed to him.

12 September A cheque for £150 is received from Y in settlement of the debt he owes Algernon and court costs.

22 September The firm receives a cheque for £100 from X. The cheque is made payable to Algernon and is handed to him.

30 September The firm sends a bill of costs to Algernon for £100 plus £17.50 VAT. Costs due to the firm are transferred from client to office account. A cheque is sent to Algernon for the balance due to him.

Prepare Algernon's account to record the above transactions.

2 The firm's client Smith asks the firm to carry out a number of transactions whilst he is abroad. Smith promises to send a cheque for £800 to cover expenditure. The following events take place with regard to Smith's account.

1 June Pay £30 to enquiry agent.
2 June Pay £60 for newspaper advertisements.
3 June Pay surveyor's bill £230.
4 June Pay counsel's fee £115.
8 June Receive Smith's cheque for £800.
9 June Send a bill of costs to Smith for £60 plus £10.50 VAT and account to Smith for the balance due to him.

Prepare Smith's account to record the above transactions.

3   Prepare clients' ledger accounts to record the following transactions.

(a)   Pay counsel's fee £47 on behalf of Nigel. Deliver a bill for £60 plus £10.50 VAT and disbursement. Receive payment.

(b)   You act for Mary. Pay search fee £10 by cash. Pay for office copy entries by cheque £15. Receive £100 from Mary on account of disbursements.

(c)   Lynn pays you £75 on account. Pay £5 out of petty cash on Lynn's behalf for inspection of deeds. Deliver a bill of costs for £100 plus VAT. Receive payment of balance from Lynn and close her account.

(d)   Receive £235 from John in respect of an agreed fee for conveyancing work.

(e)   Margaret's account shows a balance in hand of £500. Margaret asks you to transfer £300 to Daphne, another client of the firm.

(f)   Keith asks you to pay a premium of £75 to the Star Insurance Co. for whom you act. He pays £75 to you one week later, by agreement.

(g)   You act for Alan, pay counsel's fee £60 plus VAT £10.50. Deliver a bill of costs to Alan for £100 plus VAT. Receive moneys due from Alan.

(h)   You act for Carol: 1 September pay counsel's fee £40 plus VAT £7, 19 September receive £200 from Carol; 23 September pay disbursement £20 plus VAT £3.50; 30 September deliver a bill of costs £60 plus VAT £10.50. Transfer sum due from client to office account. Pay balance due to Carol.

4   Your firm is acting for John Brown who is purchasing a house for £90,000. The following events occur:

4 September	Pay search fee £15.
20 September	Receive cheque for £9,000 from client for deposit.
21 September	Contracts exchanged – pay deposit of £9,000 to vendor's solicitor.
29 September	Pay search fee £4.
9 October	Deliver a bill for £250 plus disbursements.
13 October	Receive a cheque from client for £81,269, the balance of the purchase money and costs.
14 October	Complete purchase – pay £81,000 to vendor's solicitors. Transfer costs.

Prepare the client ledger card for John Brown and the cash account to record the above transactions. The cash account need not be balanced.

5   Your firm is acting for the executors of Olive White in the administration of her estate. The following events occur:

4 October	Receive £500 from the executors' bank, a loàn to pay inheritance tax.
5 October	Pay inheritance tax £500 and probate fees of £80.
31 October	Receive £1,000 from the Longlife Insurance Company in respect of a policy which the deceased held with them.
	Pay £535 to the executors' bank to repay the loan.
5 November	Receive £2,000 from the deceased's building society account.
6 November	Receive £400 from sale of household contents.
	Pay legacy of £1,500.
10 November	Deliver a bill of costs £300.
11 November	Pay residuary beneficiary £985.
	Transfer £380 from client to office account.

Prepare the ledger account for the executors of Olive White and the cash account to record the above. The cash account need not be balanced.

4.8 SUGGESTED ANSWERS TO EXERCISES ON BASIC LEDGER ENTRIES

1

ALGERNON: DEBT RECOVERY

Date	Details	Office account Dr £	Office account Cr £	Office account Balance £	Client account Dr £	Client account Cr £	Client account Balance £
Sept 1	Cash: you					20	20 Cr
Sept 2	Cash: court fee				10		10 Cr
Sept 4	Cash: court fee	15		15 Dr			
Sept 5	Cash: Z (paid direct to you)					25	
Sept 5	Cash: you (from Z, paid direct to you)				25		
Sept 12	Cash: Y					150	160 Cr
Sept 22	Cheque from X handed direct to you. (Note that this entry is by way of a memorandum. There is no double entry in the cash book.)				100	100	
Sept 30	Costs	100					
	VAT	17.50		132.50 Dr			
	Cash: transfer: costs		132.50	—			
	Cash: transfer: costs				132.50		27.50 Cr
	Cash: you				27.50		—

2

SMITH

Date	Details	Office account			Client account		
		Dr £	Cr £	Balance £	Dr £	Cr £	Balance £
June 1	Cash: enquiry agent	30		30 Dr			
June 2	Cash: newspaper advertisements	60		90 Dr			
June 3	Cash: surveyor	230		320 Dr			
June 4	Cash: counsel	115		435 Dr			
June 8	Cash: you		435	—		365	365 Cr
June 9	Costs	60					
	VAT	10.50		70.50 Dr			
	Cash: transfer: costs		70.50	—	70.50		
	Cash: transfer: costs				294.50		294.50 Cr
	Cash: you						—

3 (a)   NIGEL

Date	Details	Office account			Client account		
1991		Dr £	Cr £	Balance £	Dr £	Cr £	Balance £
	Cash: counsel's fee	47		47 Dr			
	Costs	60					
	VAT	10.50		117.50 Dr			
	Cash: you		117.50	—			

(b)   MARY

Date	Details	Office account			Client account		
1991		Dr £	Cr £	Balance £	Dr £	Cr £	Balance £
	Petty cash: search fee	10		10 Dr			
	Cash: office copies	15		25 Dr			
	Cash: you		25	—		75	75 Cr

(c)   LYNN

Date	Details	Office account			Client account		
1991		Dr £	Cr £	Balance £	Dr £	Cr £	Balance £
	Cash: you					75	75 Cr
	Petty cash: inspection fee	5		5 Dr			
	Costs	100					
	VAT	17.50		122.50 Dr			
	Cash: you		47.50	75 Dr			
	Cash: transfer: costs				75		—
	Cash: transfer: costs		75	—			

(d) **JOHN**

Date	Details	Office account			Client account		
		Dr £	Cr £	Balance £	Dr £	Cr £	Balance £
	Costs (agreed fee)	200					
	VAT	35		235 Dr			
	Cash: you		235	—			

(e) **MARGARET**

Date	Details	Office account			Client account		
		Dr £	Cr £	Balance £	Dr £	Cr £	Balance £
	Balance						500 Dr
	Daphne: transfer (transfer journal)				300		200 Dr

DAPHNE

Date	Details	Office account			Client account		
		Dr £	Cr £	Balance £	Dr £	Cr £	Balance £
	Margaret: transfer (transfer journal)					300	300 Cr

(f)   KEITH

Date	Details	Office account			Client account		
		Dr £	Cr £	Balance £	Dr £	Cr £	Balance £
	Cash: transfer premium to Star Insurance Co	75		75 Dr			
	Cash: you		75	—			

STAR INSURANCE CO

Date	Details	Office account			Client account		
		Dr £	Cr £	Balance £	Dr £	Cr £	Balance £
	Cash: Keith: transfer premium					75	75 Cr

(g)   ALAN

Date	Details	Office account			Client account		
		Dr £	Cr £	Balance £	Dr £	Cr £	Balance £
	Cash: counsel's fee	70.50		70.50 Dr			
	Costs	100					
	VAT	17.50		188 Dr			
	Cash: you		188	—			

(h)   CAROL

Date	Details	Office account			Client account		
1991		Dr £	Cr £	Balance £	Dr £	Cr £	Balance £
Sept 1	Cash: counsel's fee	47		47 Dr			
Sept 19	Cash: you					200	200 Cr
Sept 23	Cash: disbursement				23.50		176.50 Cr
Sept 30	Costs	60					
	VAT	10.50		117.50 Dr			
	Cash: transfer: costs				117.50		59 Cr
	Cash: transfer: costs		117.50	—			
	Cash: you				59		—

4   JOHN BROWN:
                    MATTER: CONVEYANCING

Date	Details	Office account			Client account		
		Dr £	Cr £	Balance £	Dr £	Cr £	Balance £
Sept 4	Cash: search fee	15		15 Dr			
Sept 20	Cash: you					9,000	9,000 Cr
Sept 21	Cash: deposit				9,000		—
Sept 29	Cash: search fee	4		19 Dr			
Oct 9	Costs	250		269 Dr			
Oct 13	Cash: you					81,269	81,269 Cr
Oct 14	Cash: completion				81,000		269 Cr
	Cash: transfer costs		269	—		269	—

CASH ACCOUNT

Date	Details	Office account			Client account		
		Dr £	Cr £	Balance £	Dr £	Cr £	Balance £
Sept 4	Brown: search fee		15				
Sept 20	Brown				9,000		
Sept 21	Brown: deposit					9,000	
Sept 29	Brown: search fee		4				
Oct 13	Brown				81,269		
Oct 14	Brown: completion					81,000	
	Brown: transfer costs	269				269	

5   **EXECUTORS OF OLIVE WHITE DECEASED**

Date	Details	Office account			Client account		
		Dr £	Cr £	Balance £	Dr £	Cr £	Balance £
Oct 4	Cash: bank loan					500	500 Cr
Oct 5	Cash: inheritance tax				500		−
	Cash: probate fees	80		80 Dr			
Oct 31	Cash: Longlife Insurance Co					1,000	1,000 Cr
	Cash: bank loan				535		465 Cr
Nov 5	Cash: Building Society					2,000	2,465 Cr
Nov 6	Cash: sale of household contents					400	2,865 Cr
	Cash: legacy				1,500		1,365 Cr
Nov 10	Cash	300		380 Dr			
	Cash: residuary beneficiary				985		380 Cr
	Cash: transfer costs		380	−	380		−

CASH ACCOUNT

Date	Details	Office account			Client account		
		Dr £	Cr £	Balance £	Dr £	Cr £	Balance £
Oct 4	Olive White: bank loan				500		
Oct 5	Olive White: tax					500	
	Olive White: probate fee		80				
Oct 31	Olive White: Longlife Insurance Co.				1,000		
	Olive White: bank loan					535	
Nov 5	Olive White: Building Society				2,000		
	Olive White: re household contents				400		
	Olive White: legacy					1,500	
Nov 11	Olive White: legacy					985	
	Olive White: transfer costs	380				380	

4.9   VALUE ADDED TAX

4.9.1   Registering for VAT

A solicitor whose annual taxable supplies exceed the limit set by the Value Added Tax Act 1983 (currently £36,600) must register for VAT purposes. The limit is changed from time to time to take account of inflation. In practice, all solicitors register.

A solicitor's taxable supplies consist mainly of the supply of services to his client but also include supplies of goods in the course of his business, for example, the sale of office equipment.

The effect of being registered for VAT is that the solicitor must collect VAT at the standard rate (currently 17.5%) on his profit costs billed or on the sale of a business asset.

VAT becomes payable when a bill of costs is delivered to a client regardless of whether the client pays the bill. In the case of agreed fees the tax point is when the fee is agreed, regardless of whether or when a bill is subsequently delivered. Note that there is a discretion for firms with gross fees of less than £250,000 per annum. In their case VAT is payable on bills paid.

Provided a solicitor delivers a bill of costs to his client within three months of completion of the work, the date of delivery of the bill is the tax point. The tax point determines the date on which the solicitor must account to Customs and Excise for VAT charged.

A solicitor must provide a tax invoice to clients who themselves are registered for VAT. In practice, solicitors usually supply invoices to all their clients. When tax invoices are supplied, they are usually attached to the bottom of the bill of costs delivered to the client.

Example of a tax invoice

Name	Invoice No.
Address	Date

VAT No. (the solicitor's VAT registration number)

To supply of legal services	£
VAT at 17.5%	£
Total	£

A solicitor must keep copies of tax invoices and all bills delivered to clients.

4.9.2 VAT and disbursements

Some disbursements paid on behalf of a client do not attract VAT, for example, search fees, Land Registry fees and stamp duty. The solicitor must not charge his client VAT on these disbursements when delivering a bill to him.

When disbursements attract VAT, for example, counsels' fees, the VAT may be dealt with on the principal method or the agency method.

The *principal method* is used when the tax invoice is made out in the solicitor's name. The input is to the solicitor and he must therefore pay the disbursement (including VAT) out of office account.

The following entries are made in the accounts when a disbursement is paid using the principal method:

(a) Debit the client's ledger account office column with the tax exclusive value of the disbursement.

(b) Debit the Customs and Excise account with VAT paid on the disbursement.

(c) Credit the cash account office account showing the disbursement and VAT separately.

Example

Using the principal method of treatment, a solicitor pays counsel's fee of £200 plus VAT £35 on 1 June 1991 on behalf of his client Smith.

SMITH

Date	Details	Office account			Client account		
		Dr £	Cr £	Balance £	Dr £	Cr £	Balance £
1991 June 1	Cash: counsel	200		200 Dr			

CUSTOMS AND EXCISE

Date	Details	Dr	Cr	Balance
1991 June 1	Cash: Smith	£ 35	£	£ 35 Dr

CASH ACCOUNT

Date	Details	Office account			Client account		
		Dr £	Cr £	Balance £	Dr £	Cr £	Balance £
1991 June 1	Smith — Counsels (fees)		200				
June 1	Customs and Excise (Smith — VAT 0, counsels fees)		35	235 Cr			

When a bill of costs is sent to the client, the solicitor will treat the disbursement as an output from himself to his client along with profit costs charged to the client. The solicitor will charge the client VAT on the total output (i.e., profit costs and disbursement).

Continuing the example, on 30 June the firm delivers a bill of costs to Smith, charging profit costs of £300 plus VAT.

SMITH

Date	Details	Office account			Client account		
		Dr	Cr	Balance	Dr	Cr	Balance
1991		£	£	£	£	£	£
June 1	Cash: counsel	200		200 Dr			
June 30	Costs	300					
	VAT	87.50		587.50 Dr			

(VAT is £52.50 on profit cost plus £35 on supply of disbursement.)

The *agency method* is used when the tax invoice is made out to the client. When the agency method is used, the supply is made from the supplier to the client and the solicitor acts as an intermediary for making payment on the client's behalf. If money is held in client account for the client on whose behalf the disbursement is paid, payment can be made out of client account.

When a disbursement is paid on the agency method, the following entries are made in the accounts:

(a) Debit the client's ledger account with the tax-inclusive value of the disbursement.

(b) Credit the cash account.

Example

On 8 May 1991 the firm pays an estate agent's account for its client Brown. The estate agent's account is in Brown's name and is for £200 plus £35 VAT. The firm holds £1,500 in client account for Brown, following completion of his sale.

BROWN

Date	Details	Office account			Client account		
		Dr £	Cr £	Balance £	Dr £	Cr £	Balance £
May 8	Balance b/d Cash: estate agent				235		1,500 Cr 1,265 Cr

(No entry is made in the Customs and Excise account of the solicitor.)

4.9.3   Charging output tax

A solicitor will charge output tax on supply of his professional services. Thus when a bill of costs is delivered to the client VAT must be charged at 17.5% on the profit cost figure. In 4.5.1 we saw that when a solicitor delivers a bill of costs the costs are debited in the client ledger account office column and credited in the costs account. To record the VAT on the delivery of a bill:

(a)   Debit the client's ledger account – office column.
(b)   Credit the Customs and Excise account.

When a solicitor makes a taxable supply other than of his professional services, for example, on the sale of second-hand office equipment, he will make the following entries in his accounts:

(a)   Credit the appropriate asset disposal account with the tax-exclusive price charged.
(b)   Credit the Customs and Excise account with VAT charged on the supply of goods.
(c)   Debit the cash account – office column.

Example

The firm sells a second-hand typewriter for £500 plus VAT £87.50 on 30 September 1991.

ASSET DISPOSAL (OFFICE EQUIPMENT) ACCOUNT

Date	Details	Dr	Cr	Balance
		£	£	£
Sept 30	Cash (typewriter)		500	500 Cr

CUSTOMS AND EXCISE ACCOUNT

Date	Details	Dr	Cr	Balance
		£	£	£
Sept 30	Cash (typewriter) (office equipment)		87.50	87.50 Cr

CASH ACCOUNT

Date	Details	Office account Dr	Cr	Balance	Client account Dr	Cr	Balance
		Dr £	Cr £	Balance £	Dr £	Cr £	Balance £
Sept 30	Asset disposal (Office equip)ment)	500					
	Customs and Excise	87.50		587.50 Dr			

4.9.4 Paying input tax

When a solicitor pays VAT on supplies made to him, he will make the following entries in his accounts:

(a) Debit the Customs and Excise account with VAT paid.

(b) Debit the appropriate real or nominal account with the tax-exclusive price paid.

(c) Credit the cash account office column.

Example

The firm buys a word processor on 1 August 1991 and pays £1,175
which includes £175 VAT.

OFFICE EQUIPMENT ACCOUNT

Date	Details	Dr	Cr	Balance
1991 Apr 1	Cash (word processor)	£ 1,000	£	£ 1,000 Dr

CUSTOMS AND EXCISE ACCOUNT

Date	Details	Dr	Cr	Balance
1991 Apr 1	Cash: word processor	£ 175	£	£ 175 Dr

CASH ACCOUNT

Date	Details	Office account			Client account		
		Dr £	Cr £	Balance £	Dr £	Cr £	Balance £
1991 Apr 1	Office equip- ment (word processor) Customs and Excise (word processor)		1,000 175	 1,175 Cr			

4.9.5 Accounting to Customs and Excise for VAT

Solicitors who are registered for VAT must account to Customs and
Excise for the balance on the Customs and Excise account, i.e., tax
charged on supplies of services and goods (output tax) less tax paid by
the solicitor on services supplied to him (input tax).

Tax is paid to Customs and Excise quarterly. Within one month of the end of a quarterly period, the solicitor must send a completed return form and remittance to Customs and Excise.

When VAT is paid to Customs and Excise, the following entries are made in the accounts:

(a)   Debit Customs and Excise account.
(b)   Credit cash account office column.

4.10   EXERCISES ON LEDGER ACCOUNTS INCLUDING VAT

1   You are acting in litigation for your client Jenny Green. You instruct a consulting engineer to prepare a report. The engineer sends you a bill for £200 plus VAT £35 addressed to your firm. You are holding £300 in client account for Jenny Green. On 23 September you pay the engineer's bill. In November the case is concluded and on 21 November you send a bill of costs to Jenny Green of £100 plus VAT.

Show Jenny Green's ledger account and the cash account to record the above.

2   You are acting for Lucy Blue. A surveyor has been instructed to prepare a report. The surveyor sends a bill addressed to Lucy Blue for £100 plus VAT £17.50. You are holding £200 on account of costs and disbursements in client account. On 7 November you pay the surveyor's bill. On 1 December you deliver a bill of costs to Lucy for £200 plus Vat.

Show Lucy Blue's ledger account.

3   You are acting for Lyndon Tree. In the month of October the following events occur:

1 October	Pay enquiry agent's fee £75. The enquiry agent is not registered for VAT.
3 October	Pay surveyor's fee £100 plus £17.50 VAT. The bill is made out to Lyndon Tree.
4 October	Pay counsel's fee £200 plus £35 VAT. The fee note is made out to you.
8 October	Receive a payment on account of costs and disbursements of £500 from Lyndon Tree.

9 October   Deliver a bill of costs to Lyndon Tree of £60 plus
                   £10.50 VAT. Transfer moneys due to you from client
                   to office account and account to Lyndon Tree for
                   the balance.

Show Lyndon Tree's ledger account to record the above transactions.

4.11   SUGGESTED ANSWERS TO EXERCISES ON LEDGER ACCOUNTS INCLUDING VAT

1   JENNY GREEN ACCOUNT

Date	Details	Office account			Client account		
		Dr £	Cr £	Balance £	Dr £	Cr £	Balance £
	Balance					300	300 Cr
Sept 23	Cash:						
	engineer	200		200 Dr			
	(VAT £35)						
Nov 21	Costs	100					
	VAT	52.50		352.50 Dr			

CASH ACCOUNT

Date	Details	Office account			Client account		
		Dr £	Cr £	Balance £	Dr £	Cr £	Balance £
Sept 23	Jenny Green:						
	engineer's fee		200				
	Customs and						
	Excise (J.G.)		35	235 Cr			

2   LUCY BLUE ACCOUNT

Date	Details	Office account			Client account		
1991		Dr £	Cr £	Balance £	Dr £	Cr £	Balance £
	Balance					200	200 Cr
Nov 7	Cash: surveyor				117.50		82.50 Cr
Dec 1	Costs	200					
	VAT	35		235 Dr			

3   LYNDON TREE ACCOUNT

Date	Details	Office account			Client account		
1991		Dr £	Cr £	Balance £	Dr £	Cr £	Balance £
Oct 1	Cash: enquiry agent	75		75 Dr			
Oct 3	Cash: surveyor's fee	117.50		192.50 Dr			
Oct 4	Cash: counsel (VAT £35)	200		392.50 Dr			
Oct 8	Cash: you					500	500 Cr
Oct 9	Costs	60					
	VAT	45.50		498 Dr			
	Cash: transfer costs		498	—	498		2.00 Cr
	Cash: you				2.00		—

5 Conveyancing Transactions

5.1 RECEIPT OF DEPOSIT ON EXCHANGE OF CONTRACTS

A solicitor receiving a deposit on behalf of a client may hold the deposit as:

(a) Agent; or
(b) Stakeholder.

5.1.1 Receipt of deposit as agent

If a solicitor receives a deposit on exchange of contracts which he is to hold as agent, he holds it on behalf of his client vendor. To record the receipt of a deposit as agent, the solicitor will make entries in his accounts to record a receipt of clients' money on behalf of the client vendor.

Example

The firm acts for White, the vendor of Whiteacre, which is being sold for £70,000. On 23 September the firm receives a 10% deposit to hold as agents.

WHITE: SALE OF WHITEACRE

Date	Details	Office account			Client account		
		Dr £	Cr £	Balance £	Dr £	Cr £	Balance £
Sept 23	Cash: pur-chaser's solicitor, deposit					7,000	7,000 Cr

CASH ACCOUNT

Date	Details	Office account			Client account		
		Dr £	Cr £	Balance £	Dr £	Cr £	Balance £
Sept 23	Cash: pur-chaser's solicitor, deposit (White)				7,000		7,000 Dr

5.1.2 Receipt of deposit as stakeholder

When a solicitor receives a deposit as stakeholder, he does not hold the deposit for his client vendor, or for the purchaser, therefore he cannot record the receipt of a stakeholder deposit in the client vendor's ledger account.

A separate account, the stakeholder account, is opened to record dealings with deposits held by a solicitor as stakeholder. The deposit is held in the stakeholder account until completion, when it belongs to the vendor.

The stakeholder account only records dealings with clients' money.

When the firm receives a deposit as stakeholder, the following entries are made:

(a) Credit the stakeholder ledger account.
(b) Debit the cash account client column.

Note the position where money is held on joint stake (see 4.2.3).

Example

Assume that in the example in section 5.1.1 the firm receives the 10% deposit as stakeholder.

STAKEHOLDER ACCOUNT

Date	Details	Office account			Client account		
		Dr £	Cr £	Balance £	Dr £	Cr £	Balance £
Sept 23	Cash: deposit re White sale of Whiteacre					7,000	7,000 Cr

The double entry will be in the cash account as in the example in section 5.1.1.

On completion of the sale the deposit is transferred from the stakeholder account to the client vendor's account. The bookkeeping entries are those to record a transfer from one client ledger account to another.

Example

Continuing the example, assume that completion takes place on 23 October.

STAKEHOLDER ACCOUNT

Date	Details	Office account			Client account		
		Dr £	Cr £	Balance £	Dr £	Cr £	Balance £
Sept 23	Cash: deposit re White sale of Whiteacre					7,000	7,000 Cr
Oct 23	White: transfer				7,000		———

WHITE: RE SALE OF WHITEACRE

Date	Details	Office account			Client account		
		Dr £	Cr £	Balance £	Dr £	Cr £	Balance £
Oct 23	Stakeholder: transfer					7,000	7,000 Cr

5.2 MORTGAGE ADVANCES

5.2.1 Acting for mortgagee and purchaser

Rule 11(3) Solicitors' Accounts Rules 1991 provides that a solicitor acting for a borrower and lender in a conveyancing transaction shall not be required to open separate ledger accounts for the borrower and lender provided that:

(a) the funds belonging to each client are clearly identifiable and

(b) the lender is an institutional lender which provides mortgages in the normal course of its business, for example, a building society or bank.

Thus if the solicitor is acting for a purchaser, and a building society provides the mortgage, the transactions can all be recorded in the client purchaser's ledger account, without the need to open a separate ledger account for the building society.

If the solicitor is acting for a purchaser and a private lender, separate ledger accounts must be opened for each.

In (a) above, 'clearly identifiable' requires the solicitor to ensure that the purchaser's ledger account states unambiguously the nature and owner of the mortgage. Care therefore needs to be taken in completing the details entry. For example, if the Branchester Building Society makes an advance of £50,000 to Smith who is purchasing Greenacre, Smith's ledger account should state, when the advance is received:

'Cash: mortgage advance from Branchester Building Society: £50,000.'

Example (institutional lender)

The firm acts for Red who is purchasing Cosy Villa for £150,000. Red has obtained a mortgage advance of £100,000 from the High Finance Building Society for which the firm also acts. Red is providing the balance from his own funds. The firm receives the mortgage advance on 16 October 1991, with the usual instruction that the cheque is not to be negotiated until completion. Red has been informed that he will be required to pay £50,517 prior to completion. He brings a cheque to the office on 17 October. Completion takes place on 18 October and on the same date the firm sends two bills of costs to Red, one for £400 plus VAT for the conveyancing and one for £40, plus VAT for acting on behalf of the building society. The transactions will be recorded as follows.

RED: RE PURCHASE OF COSY VILLA

Date	Details	Office account			Client account		
		Dr £	Cr £	Balance £	Dr £	Cr £	Balance £
1991							
Oct 17	Cash: you					50,517	50,517 Cr
Oct 18	Cash: mortgage advance from High Finance Building Society					100,000	150,517 Cr
	Cash: vendor's solicitor				150,000		517 Cr
	Costs	400					
	VAT	70					
	Costs (High Finance Building Society re mortgage)	40					
	VAT	7		517 Dr			
	Cash: transfer costs		517	—	517		—

Example (private lender)

In the above example assume that Red is borrowing £100,000 from Black, for whom the firm also acts. On 16 October 1991 Black pays the firm £100,000 and gives written authority for that money to be used towards Red's purchase of Cosy Villa. The transactions will be recorded as follows:

RED: RE PURCHASE OF COSY VILLA

Date	Details	Office account			Client account		
		Dr £	Cr £	Balance £	Dr £	Cr £	Balance £
1991							
Oct 18	Cash: you					50,517	50,517 Cr
	Black: transfer mortgage advance					100,000	150,517 Cr
	Cash: vendor's solicitors				150,000		517 Cr
	Costs	400					
	VAT	70		470 Dr			
	Black: transfer costs	47		517 Dr			
	Cash: transfer costs		517	—	517		—

BLACK: RE MORTGAGE ADVANCE

Date	Details	Office account			Client account		
		Dr	Cr	Balance	Dr	Cr	Balance
1991		£	£	£	£	£	£
Oct 16	Cash: you					100,000	100,000
Oct 18	Costs	40					
	VAT	7		47 Dr			
	Red: transfer mortgage advance				100,000		—
	Red: transfer costs		47	—			

When this method is used the lender's costs are transferred from the purchaser's account to the lender's account by making the following entries:

(a) Debit purchaser's ledger card office account with costs and VAT.
(b) Credit lender's ledger card office account with costs and VAT.

As an alternative to transferring the gross advance from Black to Red, the solicitor could have either:

(a) Transferred the net advance, after deducting costs, in which case Black's account would have appeared as follows:

BLACK: RE MORTGAGE ADVANCE

Date	Details	Office account			Client account		
		Dr	Cr	Balance	Dr	Cr	Balance
1991		£	£	£	£	£	£
Oct 16	Cash: you					100,000	100,000 Cr
Oct 18	Costs	40					
	VAT	7		47 Dr			
	Red: transfer net advance				99,953		47 Cr
	Cash: transfer costs			—	47		—
	Cash: transfer costs		47	—			

Or:

(b) Paid the net advance to the vendor's solicitors out of Black's account. No entry will be made in Red's account in respect of the payment of the net advance.

5.2.2   Solicitor acting for mortgagee only

The accounting entries when the solicitor acts for the mortgagee only are:

(a)   The solicitor opens an account for the mortgagee.
(b)   When the mortgage advance is received, the solicitor makes entries in the mortgagee's account to record a receipt of client money.
(c)   On completion, the solicitor makes entries in the mortgagee's account to record the delivery of a bill of costs to the mortgagee.
(d)   On completion, the solicitor pays the net advance to the purchaser's solicitor and records this in the mortgagee's account as a payment of clients' money.
(e)   Following completion, the solicitor transfers his costs from client to office account.

Example

The firm acts for the High Finance Building Society which is making a mortgage advance of £100,000 to Red in connection with his purchase of Cosy Villa. Red's solicitors are Ruinems. The firm's costs for acting for the building society are £100 plus £17.50 VAT. The mortgage advance is received on 16 October and completion takes place on 18 October. Costs are transferred on 18 October.

HIGH FINANCE BUILDING SOCIETY

Date	Details	Office account			Client account		
		Dr £	Cr £	Balance £	Dr £	Cr £	Balance £
1991							
Oct 16	Cash: you					100,000	100,000 Cr
Oct 18	Costs	100					
	VAT	17.50		117.50 Dr			
	Cash: Ruinems				99,882.50		117.50 Cr
	Cash: transfer: costs				117.50		—
	Cash: transfer: costs		117.50	—			

5.2.3   Solicitor acting for purchaser/borrower only

The accounting entries when the solicitor acts for the purchaser/borrower only are:

(a)   An account is opened for the purchaser. No account is opened for the mortgagee because he is not a client.

(b)   On completion the firm records the receipt of the net advance as a receipt of clients' money, in the purchaser's ledger account.

(c)   On completion the firm records the payment of the net advance to the vendor's solicitor, as a payment of clients' money, in the purchaser's ledger account.

(d)   Entries are made in the cash account and the purchaser's ledger account to record a receipt and payment of clients' money, even if the cheque from the mortgagee is indorsed in favour of the vendor's solicitor.

Example

The firm acts for Red with regard to his purchase of Cosy Villa. Red is obtaining a mortgage advance of £100,000 from the High Finance Building Society. The solicitors acting for the building society have intimated that their costs, which are to be paid by Red, will be £100 plus £17.50 VAT. It has been agreed that these costs will be deducted from the mortgage advance. On completion on 18 October, the building society's cheque for £99,882.50 is indorsed by the firm in favour of Grabbits, the vendor's solicitor.

RED

Date	Details	Office account			Client account		
		Dr	Cr	Balance	Dr	Cr	Balance
1991		£	£	£	£	£	£
Oct 18	Cash: High Finance (cheque indorsed)					99,882.50	
	Cash: Grabbits (cheque indorsed)				99,882.50		

5.3   MORTGAGE REDEMPTION

5.3.1   Acting for the vendor and an institutional lender

If the solicitor acts for the vendor and an institutional lender, it is not necessary, when the mortgage is redeemed, to open a separate account for the lender. All the entries will be shown in the vendor's account.

Example

The firm acts for George with regard to the sale of Somehut for £40,000. Completion takes place on 28 January 1992. The Bricks and Mortar Building Society, for which the firm also acts, has a mortgage on the property and the redemption figure is £15,000. The firm's costs for acting on behalf of the building society are £40 plus VAT £7.00 and for acting for George on the sale are £200 plus VAT £35.00.

The entries to record the above will be as follows:

GEORGE: RE SALE OF SOMEHUT

Date	Details	Office account			Client account		
		Dr £	Cr £	Balance £	Dr £	Cr £	Balance £
1992 Jan 28	Cash: purchaser's solicitors					40,000	40,000 Cr
	Cash: Bricks and Mortar Building Society: redemption of mortgage				15,000		25,000 Cr
	Costs (sale)	200					
	VAT	35		235 Dr			
	Costs (redemption)	40					
	VAT	7		282 Dr			
	Cash: transfer costs					282	24,718 Cr
	Cash: transfer costs		282	—			
	Cash: you				24,718		—

5.3.2   Acting for the vendor and a private lender

If the solicitor acts for the vendor and a private lender, separate accounts will need to be opened for the vendor and the lender.

(a)   Entries on completion. When completion takes place the sale proceeds belong to the vendor and are shown as a receipt of client's money in the client vendor's account.

Example

The firm acts for George with regard to the sale of Somehut for £40,000. Completion takes place on 28 January 1992.

GEORGE: RE SALE OF SOMEHUT

Date	Details	Office account			Client account		
		Dr £	Cr £	Balance £	Dr £	Cr £	Balance £
1992 Jan 28	Cash: sale proceeds					40,000	40,000 Cr

(b) Costs. The solicitor's costs for acting on the redemption will be recorded in the lender's account, although in practice they will be paid by the vendor client.

Example

The firm's costs for acting on behalf of Albert, who has a mortgage on Somehut, of £15,000, and for whom the firm also acts, are £40 plus VAT £7.00.

ALBERT: RE MORTGAGE REDEMPTION (GEORGE)

Date	Details	Office account			Client account		
		Dr £	Cr £	Balance £	Dr £	Cr £	Balance £
1992 Jan 28	Costs	40					
	VAT	7		47 Dr			

As the redemption costs will be paid by the borrower, a transfer of the costs and VAT will be made from the borrower's account to the lender's account. The transfer will be effected by making the following entries in the accounts.

(i) Debit the vendor's ledger account office column.
(ii) Credit the lender's ledger account office column.

(c) Redemption. When the mortgage is redeemed a transfer of the redemption money is made from the vendor's account to the lender's account. The payment of the redemption money to the lender is then shown as a payment of client money from his ledger account.

Example

The firm's costs for acting for George on the sale of Somehut are £200 plus VAT £35.00. The redemption figure for the mortgage is £15,000. The mortgage is redeemed and costs transferred on 28 January. On the same

date a cheque is sent to George for the balance due to him. The entries in
the ledger accounts for George and Albert will be as follows:

GEORGE: RE SALE OF SOMEHUT

Date	Details	Office account			Client account		
		Dr £	Cr £	Balance £	Dr £	Cr £	Balance £
1992 Jan 28	Cash: sale proceeds					40,000	40,000 Cr
	Albert: transfer mortgage redemption				15,000		25,000 Cr
	Costs	200					
	VAT	35		235 Dr			
	Albert: transfer costs	47		282 Dr			
	Cash: transfer costs					282	24,718 Cr
	Cash: transfer costs		282	—			
	Cash: you				24,718		—

ALBERT: RE MORTGAGE REDEMPTION (GEORGE)

Date	Details	Office account			Client account		
		Dr £	Cr £	Balance £	Dr £	Cr £	Balance £
1992 Jan 28	Costs	40					
	VAT	7		47 Dr			
	George: transfer redemption money					15,000	15,000 Cr
	George: transfer costs		47	—			
	Cash: you (mortgage redemption)				15,000		—

5.4   COMPLETION

5.4.1   Financial statement

Prior to the completion of a sale or purchase on behalf of a conveyancing client, a financial statement will be sent to the client. This will show
the amount which the client will have to provide for completion or
the balance due to him following completion. There is no set form of
financial statement, but whichever form is used it is essential that the
statement should show all monies received from and on behalf of the
client and all payments made on his behalf.

The following is a suggested method of presentation of a financial
statement when a solicitor is acting for a client selling and buying
property simultaneously.

FINANCIAL STATEMENT

To: A. Client.
Re: Sale of Blackacre
    Purchase of Whiteacre

Sale of Blackacre		£	£	£
Receipts:	Deposit	X		
	Balance of sale price	X	X	
		—		
Less Payments:				
	Estate agent's fee	X		
	Mortgage redemption	X		
	Costs on sale	X		
	VAT thereon	X	X	
		—	—	
	Net sale proceeds			X
Less:				
Purchase of Whiteacre				
Payments:	Deposit	X		
	Balance of purchase money	X		
	Stamp duty	X		
	Land Registry fees	X		
	Search fees	X		
	Mortgage costs (incl VAT)	X		
	Purchase costs	X		
	VAT thereon	X	X	
		—		
Less:	Receipts			
	Paid by you on account	X		
	Mortgage advance	X	X	
		—	—	
	Required to complete purchase			X

	£	£	£
Amount required to complete purchase			X
Less amount due from sale			X
			—
Balance due from you prior to completion			X
			=

5.4.2   Exercises on financial statements

1.   You act for Virgil who is selling 'Olympus' for £50,000. On 1 April you receive a 10% deposit as stakeholder, Olympus is subject to a mortgage of £15,000 and you also act for the building society. The building society's costs on redemption are £40 plus VAT £7 and these are paid by Virgil. You receive an account from the estate agent for £500 plus VAT £87.50. Your costs for acting on the sale are £200 plus VAT £35. Prepare a financial statement for Virgil.

2.   You act for Samuel who is buying 'The Temple' for £80,000. He is borrowing £40,000 from the building society for whom you also act. Your local search costs £15. You receive a bridging loan of £8,000 from your client's bank for the deposit. You exchange contracts and pay the deposit. You pay bankruptcy search fee £1. Your costs for acting for the building society are £60 plus VAT and these are to be paid by Samuel. Your costs are £400 plus VAT £60, land registry fee £90 and stamp duty £800. Samuel's bank informs you that the interest on the bridging loan is £75. Prepare a financial statement for Samuel.

5.4.3   Answers to exercises on financial statements

1   FINANCIAL STATEMENT

To: Virgil
Re: Sale of 'Olympus'

		£	£	£
Receipts:	Deposit	5,000		
	Balance of sale price	45,000	50,000	
Less: Payments				
	Estate agent	587.50		
	Mortgage redemption	15,000		
	Costs on redemption	47		
	Costs on sale	200		
	VAT thereon	35	15,869.50	
Balance due to you from sale				34,130.50

2   FINANCIAL STATEMENT

To: Samuel
Re: Purchase of 'The Temple'

		£	£	£
Payments:	Deposit	8,000		
	Balance of purchase money	72,000		
	Stamp duty	800		
	Land registry fee	90		
	Search fees	16		
	Bank loan interest	75		
	Mortgage costs	70.50		
	Purchase costs	400		
	VAT thereon	70	81,521.50	
Less receipts:				
	Mortgage advance		40,000	
Balance required from you to complete				41,521.50

5.4.4   Sale completions

The solicitor's accounts must reflect all the transactions involved in completing the sale of a property on the client's behalf. The following entries will usually have to be made on the completion of a sale:

(a)   Entries to record the delivery of a bill of costs to the client for acting on his behalf with regard to the sale.

Example

The firm acts for Alfred with regard to the sale of 'Sum Hut' at a price of £30,000. On 3 May a bill of costs is delivered to Alfred in the sum of £200 plus £35 VAT. Alfred's account will appear as follows:

ALFRED

Date	Details	Office account			Client account		
		Dr £	Cr £	Balance £	Dr £	Cr £	Balance £
May 3	Costs	200					
	VAT	35		235 Dr			

(b)   Entries to record the receipt of the sale proceeds from the purchaser's solicitor (i.e., entries to record a receipt of clients' money).

Continuing the example, completion of Alfred's sale takes place on 3 May. The firm receives a bank draft for £27,000. A deposit of £3,000 was paid to the firm as stakeholders on 3 April. Alfred's account will appear as follows:

ALFRED

Date	Details	Office account			Client account		
		Dr £	Cr £	Balance £	Dr £	Cr £	Balance £
May 3	Costs	200					
	VAT	35		235 Dr			
	Cash:purchaser's solicitor					27,000	27,000 Cr

(c) Entries to record the transfer of the deposit from stakeholder account to the client's ledger account if the deposit was paid to the vendor's solicitor as stakeholder on exchange of contracts.

Continuing the example:

STAKEHOLDER ACCOUNT

Date	Details	Office account			Client account		
		Dr £	Cr £	Balance £	Dr £	Cr £	Balance £
Apr 3	Cash: deposit re Alfred					3,000	3,000 Cr
May 3	Alfred: transfer				3,000		——

ALFRED

Date	Details	Office account			Client account		
		Dr £	Cr £	Balance £	Dr £	Cr £	Balance £
May 3	Costs	200					
	VAT	35		235 Dr			
	Cash: purchaser's solicitor					27,000	27,000 Cr
	Stakeholder: transfer					3,000	30,000 Cr

(d) Entries to record the redemption of a mortgage.

Continuing the example, assume that there is a mortgage to the Timberwell Building Society on 'Sum Hut'. The mortgage of £8,000 is redeemed on 4 May. Alfred's account would appear as follows:

ALFRED

Date	Details	Office account			Client account		
		Dr £	Cr £	Balance £	Dr £	Cr £	Balance £
May 3	Costs	200					
	VAT	35		235 Dr			
	Cash: purchaser's solicitor					27,000	27,000 Cr
	Stakeholder: transfer					3,000	30,000 Cr
May 4	Cash: Timberwell Building Society				8,000		22,000 Cr

(e)   Entries to record the payment of any outstanding disbursements, e.g., estate agent's fees.

Continuing the example, assume that on 6 May the firm pays an estate agent's charges of £345. Alfred's account would appear as follows:

ALFRED

Date	Details	Office account			Client account		
		Dr £	Cr £	Balance £	Dr £	Cr £	Balance £
May 3	Costs	200					
	VAT	35		235 Dr			
	Cash: purchaser's solicitor					27,000	27,000 Cr
	Stakeholder: transfer					3,000	30,000 Cr
May 4	Cash: Timberwell Building Society: redemption				8,000		22,000 Cr
May 6	Cash: estate agent				345		21,655 Cr

(f)   Entries to record the transfer of costs from client to office account and to record the payment to the client of any balance owed to him.

Continuing the example, assume that on 6 May costs are transferred and the balance remaining in client account is paid to Alfred.

Alfred's account will appear as follows:

ALFRED

Date	Details	Office account			Client account		
		Dr £	Cr £	Balance £	Dr £	Cr £	Balance £
May 3	Costs	200					
	VAT	35		235 Dr			
	Cash: purchaser's solicitor					27,000	27,000 Cr
	Stakeholder: transfer					3,000	30,000 Cr
May 4	Cash: Timberwell Building Society: redemption				8,000		22,000 Cr
May 6	Cash: estate agent				345		21,655 Cr
	Cash: transfer: costs				235		21,420 Cr
	Cash: transfer: costs		235	—			
	Cash: you				21,420		—

5.4.5   Purchase completions

The solicitor's accounts must reflect all the transactions involved in completing the purchase of a property on the client's behalf. The following entries will usually have to be made on the completion of a purchase.

(a)   Entries to record the delivery of a bill of costs to the client for acting on his behalf with regard to the purchase.

Example

The firm acts for Alfred with regard to the purchase of 'Costa Packet' at a price of £45,000. On 3 May a bill of costs is delivered to Alfred in the sum of £300 plus VAT £52.50. The firm also acted for the mortgagee, Tall Trees Building Society, and its costs are £60 plus VAT £10.50. Alfred's account will appear as follows:

ALFRED

Date	Details	Office account			Client account		
		Dr £	Cr £	Balance £	Dr £	Cr £	Balance £
1991							
May 3	Costs	300					
	VAT	52.50		352.50 Dr			
	Costs: building society	60					
	VAT	10.50		423 Dr			

(b) Entries to record the receipt of the balance of the purchase money from the client, as shown on the financial statement.

Continuing the example, a financial statement has been delivered to Alfred, showing a balance due from him on completion of £11,473. On 3 May Alfred pays the sum of £11,473 to the firm. Alfred's account will appear as follows:

ALFRED

Date	Details	Office account			Client account		
		Dr £	Cr £	Balance £	Dr £	Cr £	Balance £
1991							
May 3	Costs	300					
	VAT	52.50		352.50 Dr			
	Costs: building society	60		423 Dr			
	VAT	10.50					
	Cash: you					11,473 Cr	11,473 Dr

(c) Entries to record the receipt of the mortgage advance from the building society. Note, if the mortgage was from a private lender for whom the firm was acting, a separate ledger account would be opened for the lender and the mortgage advance would be shown as a transfer from the lender's account.

Continuing the example, Alfred has obtained a mortgage advance of £30,000 from the Tall Trees Building Society for whom the firm also acts.

ALFRED

Date	Details	Office account			Client account		
		Dr	Cr	Balance	Dr	Cr	Balance
1991		£	£	£	£	£	£
May 3	Costs	300					
	VAT	52.50		352.50 Dr			
	Costs: building						
	society	60				11,473	11,473 Cr
	VAT	10.50		423 Dr			
	Cash: Tall Trees						
	Building Society,						
	mortgage advance					30,000	41,473 Cr

(d) Entries to record the payment of the balance of the purchase monies to the vendor's solicitors.

Continuing the example, completion takes place on 3 May. On 3 April a 10% deposit was paid to the vendor's solicitors, Redhen and Co. The balance payable to Redhen and Co. on completion is £40,500. Alfred's account would appear as follows:

ALFRED

Date	Details	Office account			Client account		
		Dr	Cr	Balance	Dr	Cr	Balance
1991		£	£	£	£	£	£
May 3	Costs	300					
	VAT	52.50		352.50			
	Costs: building						
	society	60				11,473.50	11,473.50 Cr
	VAT	10.50		423 Dr			
	Cash you					11,473	11,473 Cr
	Cash: Tall Trees						
	Building Society,						
	mortgage advance					30,000	41,473 Cr
	Cash: Redhen						
	& Co.				40,500		
							973 Cr

(e) Entries to record the payment of any disbursements after completion, e.g., stamp duty or Land Registry fees.

Continuing the example, on 4 May the firm pays stamp duty of £450 on 'Costa Packet' and on 5 May pays Land Registry fees of £100. Alfred's account will appear as follows:

ALFRED

Date	Details	Office account			Client account		
		Dr £	Cr £	Balance £	Dr £	Cr £	Balance £
1991							
May 3	Costs	300					
	VAT	52.50					
	Costs: building society	60					
	VAT	10.50		423 Dr			
	Cash you					11,473	11,473 Cr
	Cash: Tall Trees Building Society, mortgage advance					30,000	41,473.50 Cr
	Cash: Redhen & Co.				40,500		973 Cr
May 4	Cash: stamp duty				450		523 Cr
May 5	Cash: Land Registry fees				100		423 Cr

(f) Entries to record the transfer of costs from client to office account.

Continuing the example, costs are transferred to office account on 7 May. Alfred's account will appear as follows:

ALFRED

Date	Details	Office account			Client account		
		Dr £	Cr £	Balance £	Dr £	Cr £	Balance £
1991							
May 3	Costs	300		352.50 Dr			
	VAT	52.50					
	Costs: building society	60					
	VAT	10.50		423 Dr			
	Cash you					11,473	11,473 Cr
	Cash: Tall Trees Building Society, mortgage advance					30,000	41,473 Cr
	Cash: Redhen & Co.				40,500		973 Cr
May 4	Cash: stamp duty				450		523 Cr
May 5	Cash: Land Registry fees				100		423 Cr
May 7	Cash: transfer: costs				423		—
	Cash: transfer: costs		423	—			

5.4.6 Simultaneous sale and purchase

When acting for a client with regard to a simultaneous sale and purchase, entries will be made in the accounts as in 5.4.6 and 5.4.7.

Example
Question:
Pulle, Back and Stoppe, solicitors, acted for Jeane in the purchase and sale of houses and for the building society concerned. The following events took place:

1991
3 October   Paid by cash search fees of £2 in respect of purchase of 'Home' by Jeane.

10 October   Paid survey fee of £195 in respect of the purchase of 'Home'.

11 October   The Lendalot Building Society intimates that it is prepared to grant a loan of £10,000 on security of 'Home' and instructs the firm to proceed.

16 October   Received from Tight Finance Ltd cheque for £3,500 as bridging loan, on behalf of Jeane.

18 October   Exchanged contracts for the sale of Jeane's house, 'Some Hut', the deposit of 10% (£3,000) having been paid to the estate agent by the prospective purchaser. On the same day, contracts were exchanged for the purchase of 'Home' and the 10% deposit (£3,500) was paid to the vendor's solicitor to hold as stakeholder.

27 October   Received completion statement from the vendor's solicitor in respect of 'Home' showing balance due in respect of purchase money.

28 October   Sent completion statement to purchaser's solicitor in respect of 'Some Hut', showing a balance due in respect of the purchase of £27,000.

2 November   Received cheque for £10,000 from the building society. The profit costs to be charged in respect of the advance are £40 plus £7 VAT. The costs in respect of the redemption are £20 plus VAT £3.50.

3 November   Sent financial statement to Jeane showing the balance of money which will be due from him on completion of the sale and purchase, together with a bill of costs (being search fees, survey fee, stamp duty £700, Land Registry fee £86, profit

                costs £280 and VAT £49, estate agent's commission £648). The amount required to redeem the building society mortgage on 'Some Hut' on the completion date is £5,035.

6 November Cheque received from Jeane being the balance of purchase money and payment of costs.

9 November Completed purchase and sale of properties. The amount due is paid to the building society on the same day. A cheque for £2,352 is received from the estate agent, being the deposit on 'Some Hut' less commission.

9 November Loan of £3,500 paid to Tight Finance Ltd, the payment of interest on the loan being waived as Jeane is an employee of the company.

10 November Paid stamp duty and Land Registry fees on 'Some Hut'.

30 November Transferred costs and disbursements from client account to office account.

Prepare the account of Jeane, showing all entries necessary to deal with the above events, and prepare a financial statement, suitable for presentation to Jeane on 3 November 1991 (showing how the balance of money due on completion is calculated).

(Question taken from Law Society Final Examination, time allowed 1 hour. Question updated and amended.)

FINANCIAL STATEMENT

To: Jeane
Re: Sale of 'Some Hut'
    Purchase of 'Home'

Sale of 'Some Hut'	£	£	£
Receipts: Deposit (from estate agent)	3,000		
Balance of sale price	27,000	30,000	
Less: Payments			
Estate agent's fee	648		
Mortgage redemption	5,035		
Costs	280		
VAT thereon (17.5%)	49		
Redemption costs	23.50	6,035.50	
Net sale proceeds			23,964.50
Less: Purchase of 'Home'	£	£	£
Payments: Deposit	3,500		
Balance of purchase price	31,500		
Survey fee	195		
Stamp duty	700		
Search fee	2		
Land registry fee	86		
Mortgage advance costs	47	36,030	
Less: Receipts			
Mortgage advance		10,000	
Amount required to complete purchase			26,030
Amount due from sale			23,964.50
Balance due from you prior to completion			2,065.50

JEANE

Date	Details	Office account			Client account		
		Dr	Cr	Balance	Dr	Cr	Balance
1991		£	£	£	£	£	£
Oct 3	Petty cash: search fee	2		2 Dr			
Oct 10	Cash: survey fee	195		197 Dr			
Oct 16	Cash: Tight Finance					3,500	3,500 Cr
Oct 18	Cash: deposit				3,500		—
Nov 3	Costs	280					
	VAT	49					
	Costs: building society re advance	40					
	VAT	7					
	Costs: building society re redemption	20					
	VAT	3.50		596.50			
Nov 6	Cash: you					2,065.50	2,065.50 Cr
Nov 9	Cash: sale proceeds					27,000	29,065.50 Cr
	Cash: Lendalot Building Society: mortgage advance					10,000	39,065.50 Cr
	Cash: purchase money				31,500		7,565.50 Cr
	Cash: Lendalot Building Society: redemption				5,035		2,530.50 Cr
	Cash: estate agent (less commission)					2,352	4,882.50 Cr
	Cash: Tight Finance: loan repayment				3,500		1,382.50 Cr
Nov 10	Cash: stamp duty				700		682.50 Cr
	Cash: Land Registry fees				86		596.50 Cr
Nov 30	Cash: transfer: costs				596.50		—
	Cash: transfer: costs		596.50	—			

5.5 EXERCISES ON CONVEYANCING TRANSACTIONS

1   Poplin Shirte, solicitors, acted for Tye in respect of the purchase of a house 'The Throttles' and the sale of his existing house 'Respite'. 'The Throttles' is being purchased for £25,000 and 'Respite' is being sold for £16,000. The following events take place:

1991

7 March	Paid by cash search fees £3.
12 March	Instructions received from the Nohope Building Society to act in connection with the advance to Tye of £6,500 on the security of 'The Throttles'. The initial fire insurance premium of £31 is to be deducted from the advance.
23 March	Received £2,500 from Tye, being the deposit on 'The Throttles'.
26 March	Exchanged contracts for the sale of 'Respite' and received 10% deposit as stakeholder. Also exchanged contracts for purchase of 'The Throttles' and paid 10% deposit to the vendor as stakeholder.
12 April	Vendor's solicitors sent completion statement showing balance of purchase money.
15 April	**Sent financial statement to Tye (costs on sale £100 plus VAT £17.50, costs on purchase £150 plus VAT £26.25, costs on mortgage £20 plus VAT £3.50).**
20 April	Tye sent a cheque for the amount required to complete, and settle all incidental liabilities.
23 April	Paid by cash search fees £2.
24 April	Received advance cheque from building society.
25 April	Completed purchase and sale of properties.
27 April	Paid estate agent's charges £359. Paid stamp duty £250. Paid Land Registry fees £51.
30 April	Transferred costs and disbursements.

Write up the client ledger account of Tye showing all necessary entries to deal with the above events.

(Law Society Final Examination, updated)

2   Mick, Mike Michael and Co. acted for Jones in the sale of his house 'Nibblers' for £50,000 and for the Expandant Building Society who were owed £15,000 by way of mortgage on the house. The following events took place:

1991

8 May	Received cheque for £45,000 from the purchaser's solicitors, being the balance of purchase monies. The amount required to redeem the mortgage including interest is £15,325. The costs of the redemption £40 plus VAT are to be borne by Jones. The amount due to the building society is paid by cheque.
9 May	Noe de Lay and Co., estate agents, acting for Jones, send a cheque for £3,590 being the deposit less their commission of £1,200 plus VAT £210.
10 May	Sent cheque for £594 including VAT to I. Repare in respect of pre-sale repairs to the property.
12 May	Bill of costs sent to Jones for £220 plus VAT.
15 May	Costs and disbursements are transferred to office account and the balance due to Jones is paid to him.

Write up the client's ledger account for Jones, showing all necessary entries to record the above transactions. VAT is to be calculated at 17.5%.

(Law Society Final Examination, updated)

3   Panel decides to sell his house 'The Clappers' for £60,000, and purchase another house 'Runlike' for £80,000. There is a mortgage on 'The Clappers' of £10,000, and the same building society (The Predial Building Society) has agreed to advance the sum of £30,000 towards the purchase price of 'Runlike'. Both Panel and The Predial Building Society instruct the same firm of solicitors, Autumnal, Glow & Co., to act on their behalf in these matters.

The following events and transactions take place, and you are required to show the account of Panel, making all the necessary entries to deal with the events and transactions, and to prepare a suitable financial statement showing any balance of money due from Panel prior to completion. Panel's transactions for both purchase and sale, are recorded on one ledger account.

Ignore all forms of taxation, except stamp duty and VAT. The rate of VAT is to be taken as 17.5%.

In making the necessary entries, it is important that the account in which the corresponding entry would be made, is clearly identified by the appropriate entry in the details column.

1991

6 November Local land charges search fee re 'Runlike' (£12), is paid from petty cash.

8 November Paid survey fee (£280 plus VAT) in respect of 'Runlike'.

14 November Panel is unable to find the deposit on 'Runlike' from his own resources, and after negotiation, and a suitable undertaking has been given by the firm, a cheque for £8,000 is received by the firm from The Reputable Bank Ltd to be used as a bridging loan.

16 November Contracts are exchanged for the sale of 'The Clappers', the deposit of £6,000 being paid to Autumnal, Glow & Co. who are to act as stakeholders. On the same day, contracts are exchanged for the purchase of 'Runlike', the deposit of £8,000 being paid to the solicitors acting for the vendor of the house who are to act as stake-holders.

29 November Sent completion statement to purchaser's solicitors in respect of 'The Clappers' showing the balance due in respect of the purchase monies.

3 December Received completion statement in respect of 'Runlike', showing balance due (£72,000).

7 December Sent financial statement to Panel, together with bill of costs. The financial statement shows, *inter alia*, the following details:

Estate agent's commission	£1,200 plus VAT
Stamp duty	£800
Bankruptcy search fee	£2
Redemption of mortgage on 'The Clappers' (including interest to date)	£10,372
Land Registry fees	£150
Interest on bridging loan	£95

The bill of costs shows profit costs of £760 exclusive of VAT (purchase £400; sale £360). The profit costs (exclusive of VAT) for acting for The Predial Building Society (payable by Panel) are mortgage £80; redemption of mortgage £20.

10 December Received banker's draft from Panel for the sum shown on the financial statement, including costs.

12 December Paid £2 from petty cash, in respect of bankruptcy search.

13 December Banker's draft received from building society in respect of mortgage advance re 'Runlike'.

14 December Completed sale and purchase of properties.
             Repaid loan of £8,000 together with accrued interest of £95, to the Reputable Bank Ltd.
             Mortgage to Building Society redeemed.
             Paid stamp duty and Land Registry fees.

17 December Paid estate agent's commission plus VAT.
             Transferred costs and disbursements from client account to office account, thereby closing the client's ledger account.
                                     (Solicitors' Final Examination, updated)

4 Your firm acts for Andrew Arbuthnot who is purchasing 'Holywell House' for £60,000 with a private mortgage of £30,000 from Lancelot Lake for whom the firm also acts. The following events take place:

1991

 1 December Pay search fee £18.

16 December Receive cheque for £6,000 from Andrew for the deposit.

17 December Contracts exchanged. Paid £6,000 to the vendor's solicitors.

22 December Receive completion statement from vendor's solicitors showing £54,000 payable on completion.

31 December Send statement to Andrew showing amount required for completion including:
             Costs on sale: £120 plus VAT
             Costs on mortgage: £40 plus VAT
             Stamp duty: £600

Search fee: £18

Bill of costs also sent.

13 January   Receive mortgage advance and Andrew's cheque for the balance of the completion money.

14 January   Complete the purchase.

16 January   Pay stamp duty.

Transfer costs and disbursements to office account.

Prepare the ledger accounts for Andrew and Lancelot Lake and the cash account, together with the financial statement sent to Andrew on 31 December. It is not necessary to balance the cash account.

5   Mozart, having reached retirement age, decides to sell his house 'Fiddlers' for £100,000, and purchase a smaller house 'French Horn' for £50,000. There is a mortgage on 'Fiddlers' of £15,000, due to the Concerto Building Society. Both Mozart and the Concerto Building Society instruct the same firm of solicitors, Bach and Liszt, to act on their behalf in these matters.

The following events and transactions take place, and you are required to show the ledger card of Mozart, making all the necessary entries to deal with the events and transactions, and to prepare a suitable financial statement showing any balance of money due to Mozart after completion. Mozart's transactions are recorded on one ledger card.

Ignore all forms of taxation, except stamp duty and VAT. The rate of VAT is to be taken as 17.5%.

In making the necessary entries, it is important that the account in which the corresponding entry would be made, is clearly identified by the appropriate entry in the details column.

1991

6 December   Local land charges search fee re 'French Horn' (£14), and office copy entries re 'Fiddlers' (£5), are paid from petty cash.

9 December   Paid survey fee (£220 plus VAT) in respect of 'French Horn'.

13 December   Mozart requests that Bach and Liszt obtain a bridging loan of £5,000 on his behalf, and after a suitable undertaking has been given by the firm, the Chopin Loan Company Ltd sends a cheque for the relevant amount.

16 December Contracts are exchanged for the sale of 'Fiddlers', the deposit of £10,000 being paid to Bach and Liszt who are to act as stakeholders. On the same day, contracts are exchanged for the purchase of 'French Horn', the deposit of £5,000 being paid to the solicitors acting for the vendor of the house who are to act as stakeholders.

30 December Sent completion statement to purchaser's solicitors in respect of 'Fiddlers' showing balance due in respect of the purchase money.

1992

3 January Received completion statement in respect of 'French Horn', showing balance due.

7 January Sent financial statement to Mozart, together with bill of costs. The financial statement shows, *inter alia*, the following details:

Redemption of mortgage on 'Fiddlers'
(including interest to date of completion) £15,465
Land Registry fees   £150
Bankruptcy search fee   £3
Stamp duty   £500
Estate agents' commission   £1,500 plus VAT
Interest on bridging loan   £75

The bill of costs shows profit costs of £800 exclusive of VAT (purchase £300, sale £500). The profit costs for acting for the Concerto Building Society (payable by Mozart) in the redemption of the mortgage amount to £20 exclusive of VAT.

13 January Paid £3 from petty cash in respect of bankruptcy search.

15 January Completed sale and purchase of properties.
Repaid loan of £5,000 together with accrued interest of £75, to the Chopin Loan Company Ltd.
Sent cheque for the redemption money to the building society.
Paid stamp duty and Land Registry fees.

17 January	Paid estate agents' commission plus VAT.
	Bach and Liszt, acting upon further instructions from Mozart, purchase an annuity on his behalf from the Handel Annuity Company plc, the cheque (£25,000) in respect thereof being sent the same day.
20 January	Paid the balance of moneys now held on his behalf, to Mozart, and transferred costs and disbursements from client account to office account, thereby closing the client's ledger card.

(Law Society Final Examination, updated)

6 You act for Dinah Dobbs in the sale of 'Green Trees' and the purchase of 'Red Roofs'. The sale price of 'Green Trees' is £40,000 and the purchase price of 'Red Roofs' is £80,000. She is purchasing 'Red Roofs' with a mortgage of £55,000 from the Lendalot Building Society. 'Green Trees' is mortgaged to a private lender, Charles. You have also received instructions from the Lendalot Building Society and Charles. The following events occur:

1991

2 August	Pay search fee £18 out of petty cash.
3 August	Receive instructions from the Lendalot Building Society in connection with the mortgage.
16 August	A bridging loan is obtained from the Mid-West Bank for £8,000 and that sum is transferred by the bank into Dinah's account.
17 August	Exchange contracts. Receive deposit of £4,000 on 'Green Trees' as stakeholder. Pay £8,000 deposit on 'Red Roofs'.
23 August	Receive invoice from Sellalot estate agents for their commission, £400 plus VAT. The invoice is addressed to Dinah. Receive completion statement from vendor's solicitors showing amount due to complete purchase of 'Red Roofs'.
30 August	Send completion statement to purchaser's solicitors showing balance of £36,000 due on completion of sale of 'Green Trees'.
1 September	Charles informs you that the amount required to redeem the mortgage on 'Green Trees' will be £10,425. Your costs will be £40 plus VAT, payable by Dinah.
	You ascertain from the Mid-West Bank that interest on the bridging loan is £83.

4 September   Send a financial statement to Dinah showing: costs on sale
                £120 plus VAT, on the purchase £400 plus VAT and on the
                mortgage advance £60 plus VAT; stamp duty £800; Land
                Registry fee £175.
12 September   Receive mortgage advance.
14 September   Complete sale and purchase. Send cheques to Charles to
                redeem mortgage and to the Mid-West Bank to pay the
                bridging loan and interest.
15 September   Pay stamp duty, land registry fees and estate agents
                commission. Send balance due to Dinah and transfer costs
                and disbursements.

Prepare the financial statement sent to Dinah on 4 September and make
the necessary entries in Dinah's ledger account, Charles' ledger account
and the cash account to record the above transactions. It is not necessary to
balance the cash account. VAT is assumed to be 17.5%.

5.6 SUGGESTED ANSWERS TO EXERCISES ON CONVEYANCING TRANSACTIONS

1 Poplin Shirte & Co.

FINANCIAL STATEMENT

To: Tye
Re: Sale of 'Respite'
   Purchase of 'The Throttles'

	£	£	£
Sale of 'Respite'			
Receipts: Deposit	1,600		
Balance of sale price	14,400	16,000	
Less: Payments			
Estate agent's fee	359		
Costs	100		
VAT thereon at 17.5%	17.50	476.50	
Net sale proceeds			15,523.50
Less: Purchase of 'The Throttles'			
Payments: Deposit	2,500		
Balance of purchase money	22,500		
Costs	150		
VAT thereon at 17.5%	26.25		
Stamp duty	250		
Search fees	5		
Land registry fees	51		
Mortgage costs	23.50	25,505.75	
Less: Receipts			
Paid by you on account	2,500		
Mortgage advance (less fire premium)	6,469	8,969	
Required to complete purchase			16,536.75
Less: Due from sale			15,523.50
Balance required from you prior to completion			1,013.25

TYE: RE SALE OF 'RESPITE' AND PURCHASE OF 'THE THROTTLES'

Date	Details	Office account			Client account		
		Dr	Cr	Balance	Dr	Cr	Balance
1991		£	£	£	£	£	£
Mar 7	Petty cash: search fees	3		3 Dr			
Mar 23	Cash: you					2,500	2,500 Cr
Mar 26	Cash: deposit				2,500		—
Apr 16	Costs: sale	100					
	VAT	17.50		120.50 Dr			
	Costs: purchase	150					
	VAT	26.25					
	Costs: mortgage advance	20					
	VAT	3.50		320.25 Dr			
Apr 20	Cash: you					1,013.25	1,013.25 Cr
Apr 23	Petty cash: search fees	2		322.25 Dr			
Apr 25	Cash: sale proceeds					14,400	15,413.25 Cr
	Stakeholder: transfer					1,600	17,013.25 Cr
	Cash: Nohope Building society: mortgage advance					6,469	23,482.25 Cr
	Cash: purchaser's solicitors				22,500		982.25 Cr
Apr 27	Cash: estate agent				359		623.25 Cr
	Cash: stamp duty				250		373.25 Cr
	Cash: Land Registry				51		322.25 Cr
Apr 30	Cash: transfer: costs and disbursements				322.25		—
	Cash: transfer: costs and disbursements		322.25	—			

2   Mick, Mike Michael and Co.

JONES: RESALE OF 'NIBBLES'

Date	Details	Office account			Client account		
		Dr £	Cr £	Balance £	Dr £	Cr £	Balance £
1991							
May 8	Cash: sale proceeds					45,000	45,000 Cr
	Cash: Expandant Building Society: mortgage redemption				15,325		29,675 Cr
May 9	Cash: Noe de Lays (less commission £1,410)					3,590	33,265 Cr
May 10	Cash: I. Repare				594		32,671 Cr
May 12	Costs	220					
	VAT	38.50					
	Costs (Expandant Building Society, re redemption)	40					
	VAT	7		305.50 Dr			
May 15	Cash: transfer: costs				305.50		32,365.50 Cr
	Cash: transfer: costs		305.50	—			
	Cash: you				32,365.50		—

3   FINANCIAL STATEMENT
To: Panel
Re: Sale of 'Clappers'
      Purchase of 'Runlike'

Sale of 'Clappers'	£	£	£
Receipts: Deposit	6,000		
Balance of sale price	54,000	60,000	
Less: Payments:			
Estate agent's fees	1,410		
Mortgage redemption	10,372		
Redemption costs	23.50		
Sale costs	360		
VAT thereon at 17.5%	63	12,228.50	
Net sale proceeds			47,771.50
Less: Purchase of 'Runlike'			
Payments: Deposit	8,000		
Balance of purchase money	72,000		
Search fees	14		
Survey fee	329		
Stamp duty	800		
Land Registry fees	150		
Interest on bridging loan	95		
Costs on sale	400		
VAT thereon at 17.5%	70		
Mortgage costs incl VAT	94	81,952	
Less: Receipts:			
Mortgage advance		30,000	
Required to complete purchase			51,952
Less due from sale			47,771.50
Balance required from you before completion			4,180.50

PANEL: RE SALE OF 'THE CLAPPERS' AND PURCHASE OF 'RUNLIKE'

Date	Details	Office account			Client account		
		Dr £	Cr £	Balance £	Dr £	Cr £	Balance £
1991							
Nov 6	Petty cash: search fee	12		12 Dr			
Nov 8	Cash: survey fee	329		341 Dr			
Nov 14	Cash: The Reputable Bank Ltd (loan)					8,000	8,000 Cr
Nov 16	Cash: deposit				8,000		—
Dec 7	Costs (sales purchase)	760					
	VAT	133					
	Costs: mortgage advance	80					
	VAT	14					
	Costs: mortgage redemption	20					
	VAT	3.50		1,351.50 Dr			
Dec 10	Cash: you					4,180.50	4,180.50 Cr
Dec 12	Petty cash: bankruptcy search	2		1,353.50 Dr			
Dec 14	Cash: Predial Building Society: mortgage advance					30,000	34,180.50 Cr
	Cash: purchaser					54,000	88,180.50 Cr
	Stakeholder: transfer: deposit					6,000	94,180.50 Cr
	Cash: vendor				72,000		22,180.50 Cr
	Cash: The Reputable Bank Ltd (loan repayment)				8,095		14,085.50 Cr
	Cash: Predial Building Society: mortgage: redemption				10,372		3,713.50 Cr
	Cash: stamp duty				800		2,913.50 Cr
	Cash: Land Registry fee				150		2,763.50 Cr
Dec 17	Cash: estate agent				1,410		1,353.50 Cr
	Cash: transfer: costs				1,353.50		—
	Cash: transfer: costs		1,353.50	—			

FINANCIAL STATEMENT

To: Andrew Arbuthnot
Re: Purchase of Holywell House

Payments:	£	£
Deposit	6,000	
Balance of purchase money	54,000	
Cost on purchase	120	
VAT at 17.5%	21	
Costs on mortgage	40	
VAT at 17.5%	7	
Stamp duty	600	
Search fees	18	60,806
Less: Receipts		
Deposit paid by you	6,000	
Mortgage advance	30,000	36,000
Balance required from you before completion		24,806

4   CLIENT: ANDREW ARBUTHNOT
                  MATTER: PURCHASE OF HOLYWELL HOUSE

Date	Details	Office account			Client account		
		Dr £	Cr £	Balance £	Dr £	Cr £	Balance £
1991							
Dec 1	Cash: search fee	18		18 Dr			
Dec 16	Cash: you					6,000	6,000 Cr
Dec 17	Cash: deposit				6,000		
	Costs (Purchase)	120					
	VAT	21		159 Dr			
1992							
Jan 13	Cash: you					24,806	24,806 Cr
Jan 14	Lancelot Lake transfer advance					30,000	54,806 Cr
	Cash: completion				54,000		806 Cr
	Cash: stamp duty				600		206 Cr
	Lancelot Lake transfer costs	47		206 Dr			
	Cash: transfer costs		206	—	206		—

LANCELOT LAKE

Date	Details	Office account			Client account		
		Dr £	Cr £	Balance £	Dr £	Cr £	Balance £
1991							
Dec 31	Costs	40					
	VAT	7		47 Dr			
1992							
Jan 13	Cash: you					30,000	30,000 Cr
Jan 14	Arbuthnot: transfer advance				30,000		
	Arbuthnot: transfer costs		47	—			—

CASH ACCOUNT

Date	Details	Office account			Client account		
		Dr £	Cr £	Balance £	Dr £	Cr £	Balance £
1991							
Dec 1	Arbuthnot: search fee		18				
Dec 16	Arbuthnot				6,000		
Dec 17	Arbuthnot: deposit					6,000	
1992							
Jan 13	Lancelot Lake mortgage advance				30,000		
	Arbuthnot				24,806		
Jan 14	Arbuthnot: completion				54,000		
Jan 16	Arbuthnot: stamp duty				600		
	Arbuthnot: transfer: costs	206				206	

5   FINANCIAL STATEMENT

To: Mozart
Re: Sale of 'Fiddlers' and purchase of 'French Horn'

Sale of 'Fiddlers'

Receipts	£	£
Deposit	10,000	
Balance of sale price	90,000	100,000

Less: Payments		
Mortgage redemption	15,465	
Redemption costs	20	
VAT at 17.5%	3.50	
Estate agents' fee	1,762.50	
Sale costs	500	
VAT at 17.5%	87.50	17,838.50

Net sale proceeds		82,161.50

Less: Purchase of 'French Horn'

Payments:		
Deposit	5,000	
Balance of purchase money	45,000	50,000

Land Registry fees	150	
Stamp duty	500	
Survey fee	258.50	
Bridging interest	75	
Costs on purchase	300	
VAT at 17.5%	52.50	
Land charges fee	14	
Office copies	5	
Bankruptcy search	3	1,358

		51,358
Due to you	82,161.50	
	51,358	30,803.50

Less: Annuity purchase		25,000

		5,803.50

CLIENT: MOZART
MATTER: SALE OF FIDDLES AND PURCHASE OF FRENCH HORN

Date	Details	Office account			Client account		
		Dr £	Cr £	Balance £	Dr £	Cr £	Balance £
1991							
Dec 6	Petty cash: search fee	14					
	Petty cash: office copies	5		19 Dr			
Dec 9	Cash: survey fee	258.50		277.50 Dr			
Dec 13	Cash: bridging loan					5,000	5,000 Cr
Dec 16	Cash: deposit paid				5,000		—
1992							
Jan 7	Costs (Sale and purchase)	800					
	VAT	140					
	Costs: mortgage redemption	20					
	VAT	3.50		1,241 Dr			
Jan 13	Petty cash: search fee	3		1,244 Dr			
	Stakeholder: transfer					10,000	10,000 Cr
	Cash: complete sale					90,000	100,000 Cr
	Cash: complete purchase				45,000		55,000 Cr
	Cash: repayment of loan				5,075		49,925 Cr
	Cash: Concerto Building Society mortgage redemption				15,465		34,460 Cr
	Cash: stamp duty				500		33,960 Cr
	Cash: land registry				150		33,810 Cr
Jan 17	Cash: estate agent				1,762.50		32,047.50 Cr
	Cash: Handel Co. plc: annuity				25,000		7,047.50 Cr
Jan 20	Cash: transfer costs				1,244		5,803.50 Cr
	Cash: transfer costs	1,244					—
	Cash: you				5,803.50		—

6   CLIENT: DINAH DOBBS
MATTER: SALE OF GREEN TREES; PURCHASE OF RED ROOFS
                              FINANCIAL STATEMENT

Sale of Green Trees:

Receipts:	£	£
Deposit	4,000	
Balance of sale price	36,000	40,000

Less Payments:		
Estate agents' fee	470	
Mortgage redemption	10,425	
Redemption costs	47	
Sale costs	120	
VAT	21	11,083

Due from sale		28,917

Less Purchase of Red Roofs:

Payments:		
Deposit	8,000	
Balance of purchase price	72,000	
	80,000	
Search fees	18	
Bridging loan interest	83	
Purchase costs	400	
VAT	70	
Mortgage advance costs	60	
VAT	10.50	
Stamp duty	800	
Land Registry fee	175	
	81,616.50	
Less mortgage advance	55,000	

Required to complete purchase   26,616.50

Due from sale   28,917
Required to complete purchase   26,616.50

Balance due to you following completion   2,300.50

Client: Dinah Dobbs
Matter: Sale of Green Trees: Purchase of Red Roofs

Date	Details	Office account			Client account		
		Dr £	Cr £	Balance £	Dr £	Cr £	Balance £
1991							
Aug 2	Petty cash: search fees	18		18 Dr			
Aug 16	Cash: bridging loan					8,000	8,000 Cr
Aug 17	Cash: deposit paid				8,000		—
Sept 4	Costs: sale	120					
	VAT	21					
	purchase	400					
	VAT	70					
	Costs: mortgage advance	60					
	VAT	10.50		699.50 Dr			
Sept 14	Cash: sale proceeds					36,000	36,000 Cr
	Stakeholder Transfer					4,000	40,000 Cr
	Cash Lendalot Building Society mortgage advance					55,000	95,000 Cr
	Cash: purchase				72,000		23,000 Cr
	Charles: transfer mortgage redemption				10,425		12,575 Cr
	Cash: Mid-West Bank: repay loan				8,083		4,492 Cr
Sept 15	Cash: stamp duty				800		3,692 Cr
	Cash: land registry				175		3,517 Cr
	Cash: estate agent				470		3,047 Cr
	Charles: transfer: redemption costs	47		746.50 Dr			
	Cash: transfer: costs					746.50	2,300.50 Cr
	Cash: transfer costs		746.50	—			
	Cash: you				2,300.50		

Client: Charles
Matter: Mortgage Redemption

Date	Details	Office account			Client account		
		Dr £	Cr £	Balance £	Dr £	Cr £	Balance £
1991							
Sept 4	Costs	40		47 Dr			
	VAT	7					
Sept 14	Dinah: transfer: redemption money					10,425	10,425 Cr
	Cash: you (redemption)				10,425		—
Sept 15	Dinah: transfer: costs		47	—			

CASH ACCOUNT

Date	Details	Office account			Client account		
		Dr £	Cr £	Balance £	Dr £	Cr £	Balance £
1991							
Aug 16	Dinah: bridging loan				8,000		
Aug 17	Stakeholder re Dinah deposit				4,000		
	Dinah: deposit paid					8,000	
Sept 12	Dinah: mortgage advance (Lendor Building Society)				55,000		
Sept 14	Dinah: sale proceeds				36,000		
	Dinah: purchase					72,000	
	Charles: mortgage redemption					10,425	
	Dinah: loan repayment					8,083	
	Dinah: stamp duty					800	
	Dinah: land registry fees					175	
	Dinah: estate agents fees					470	
	Dinah: transfer: costs	746.50				746.50	
	Dinah: payment of balance					2,300.50	

5.7   TEST ON CONVEYANCING TRANSACTIONS

Allow 1 hour to complete this test.

During the months of November and December 1991, Smith, a practising solicitor, acted for Brown in the purchase and sale of houses. Smith was also instructed by the Lendit Building Society to act on its behalf in respect of the proposed mortgage on the house being purchased and the redemption of the mortgage on the house being sold.

   The relevant events and transactions are as follows and you are required to write up the client ledger account of Brown, showing all necessary entries, together with a financial statement showing the balance due on completion. Brown's transactions for both purchase and sale are kept in one ledger account. (The rate of VAT is to be taken as 17.5%.)

1991
   1 **November** Paid by petty cash, local land charges search re 'Purchouse' £12.
   3 **November** The building society intimates that it is prepared to grant a mortgage of £15,000 on security of 'Purchouse' and instructs the firm to proceed.
   8 **November** Paid survey fee £260 plus VAT.
   15 **November** Contracts are exchanged for the purchase of 'Purchouse', the deposit of 10 per cent (£5,500) being paid to the vendor's solicitors who are to act as stakeholders. The deposit money, not yet having been received from Brown, is paid by Smith out of available practice money. On the same morning, contracts are exchanged for the sale of 'Salehouse', the deposit of 10 per cent (£3,400) being received by Smith, for him to hold as stakeholder.
   30 **November** Sent completion statement to purchaser's solicitors in respect of 'Salehouse' showing balance due in respect of purchase money.
   3 **December** Received completion statement from vendor's solicitors, showing £49,500 due.
   3 **December** Financial statement sent to Brown, together with bill of costs showing profit costs of £700 plus VAT. (The costs are apportioned thus: purchase £380, sale £260, mortgage £40 and redemption of mortgage £20.) The following disbursements, *inter alia*, are relevant: Land Registry fees

£140, estate agent's commission £1,000 plus VAT, bankruptcy search fee £2, redemption of mortgage on 'Salehouse' £8,000, stamp duty £1,100.

8 December Paid £2 from petty cash in respect of bankruptcy search.

9 December Bank draft received from Brown, in settlement of all monies due in respect of the purchase and sale of the house. Received same day, cheque for £15,000 being mortgage advance from building society.

10 December Completed purchase and sale of properties. Sent cheque for redemption money to building society, and paid stamp duty and Land Registry fees.

13 December Paid estate agent's commission plus VAT and transferred costs and all other money due from client account to office account.

(Law Society Final Examination, updated)

5.8 SUGGESTED ANSWER TO TEST ON CONVEYANCING TRANSACTIONS

FINANCIAL STATEMENT

To: Brown
Re: Sale of 'Salehouse'
    Purchase of 'Purchouse'

Sale of 'Salehouse'	£	£	£
Receipts: Deposit	3,400		
Balance of sale price	30,600	34,000	
Less: Payments			
Estate agent's fees	1,175		
Mortgage redemption	8,000		
Mortgage redemption costs	23.50		
Sale costs	260		
VAT thereon 17.5%	45.50	9,504	
Net sale proceeds			24,496

	£	£	£
Less: Purchase of 'Purchouse'			
Payments: Deposit	5,500		
Balance of purchase money	49,500		
Stamp duty	1,100		
Land Registry fees	140		
Search fees	14		
Survey fee (260 + 45.50 VAT)	305.50		
Costs	380		
VAT thereon 17.50%	66.50		
Mortgage advance costs	47	57,053	
Less: Receipts			
Mortgage advance		15,000	
Required to complete purchase			42,053
Less: Due from sale			24,496
Balance required from you prior to completion			17,557

BROWN: RE SALE OF 'SALEHOUSE' AND PURCHASE OF 'PURCHOUSE'

Date	Details	Office account			Client account		
		Dr £	Cr £	Balance £	Dr £	Cr £	Balance £
1991							
Nov 1	Petty cash: search fee	12		12 Dr			
Nov 8	Cash: survey fee	305.50		317.50 Dr			
Nov 15	Cash: deposit	5,500		5,817.50 Dr			
Dec 3	Costs: sale	260					
	VAT	45.50					
	Costs: purchase	380					
	VAT	66.50					
	Costs: mortgage advance	40					
	VAT	7					
	Costs: mortgage redemption	20					
	VAT	3.50		6,640 Dr			
Dec 8	Petty cash: search fee	2		6,642 Dr			
Dec 9	Cash: you					17,557	17,557 Cr
Dec 10	Cash: sale proceeds					30,600	48,157 Cr
	Stakeholder: transfer: deposit					3,400	51,557 Cr
	Cash: Lendit Building Society: mortgage advance					15,000	66,557 Cr
	Cash: purchase				49,500		17,057 Cr
	Cash: Lendit Building Society: mortgage redemption				8,000		9,057 Cr
	Cash: stamp duty				1,100		7,957 Cr
	Cash: Land Registry fees				140		7,817 Cr
Dec 13	Cash: estate agent				1,175		6,642 Cr
	Cash: transfer: costs				6,642		—
	Cash: transfer: costs		6,642	—			

6 *Deposit Interest and Probate Transactions*

6.1 PAYING INTEREST TO THE CLIENT

6.1.1 The rules

(a)   Where money is held in a separate designated deposit account the solicitor must account to his or her client for the interest earned.

(b)   If the money is not held in a designated deposit account, interest is payable if the minimum amount shown below is held for a period equal to or in excess of that shown below:

  (i)   £500 held for eight weeks,
  (ii)   £1,000 held for four weeks,
  (iii)   £5,000 held for two weeks,
  (iv)   10,000 held for one week.

Sums in excess of £10,000, held for less than one week give rise to an obligation to pay interest if it is fair and reasonable that interest should be paid having regard to all the circumstances. If the solicitor accounts for such sums expeditiously, it will not usually be considered fair and reasonable that interest be paid.

(c)   The rate of interest payable, where the money is not held on designated deposit is at a rate which would have been earned had the money been kept on deposit (or its gross equivalent if the interest would have been net of tax).

(d)   The rules apply to trust money (except where the solicitor is a 'controlled trustee') and to stakeholder money as well as to client money.

(e)   A client may obtain a deposit interest certificate from the Law Society.

(f)   Where interest should be paid to a client, the solicitor may either:

(i) place the client's money on deposit in a separate designated deposit account in the client's name and pay the client the interest earned — to do this the solicitor must anticipate the need to pay interest — or

(ii) pay the client, out of the solicitor's own money, the amount which would have been earned as interest if the client's money had been placed on deposit.

6.1.2 Designated deposit

If a client's money is placed on designated deposit, the solicitor asks the bank to transfer the client's money from current client account to a deposit account in the client's name.

The bookkeeping entries to record the transfer to a deposit account are:

(a) Credit the cash account in the client column.

(b) Debit the designated deposit account cash account (only shows dealings with clients' money).

Example

The firm acts for Brown with regard to the sale of 'Costa Packet'. On completion on 7 November, the firm holds £50,000 for Brown and decides to transfer the balance to a designated deposit account, opened on Brown's behalf.

CASH ACCOUNT

Date	Details	Office account			Client account		
		Dr £	Cr £	Balance £	Dr £	Cr £	Balance £
1991 Nov 7	Cash: Brown: sale proceeds Designated deposit: cash: transfer (Brown)				50,000	50,000	50,000 Dr ————

DESIGNATED DEPOSIT CASH ACCOUNT

Date	Details	Office account			Client account		
		Dr £	Cr £	Balance £	Dr £	Cr £	Balance £
1991 Nov 7	Cash: transfer (Brown)				50,000		50,000 Dr

No entry is made in the client's account but a note should be made at the top of his ledger card.

BROWN

Designated deposit account
Opened 7 November 1991
Closed . . . .

Date	Details	Office account			Client account		
		Dr	Cr	Balance	Dr	Cr	Balance
1991		£	£	£	£	£	£
Nov 7	Cash: sale proceeds					50,000	50,000 Cr

When a client's money has been placed on deposit, the money is not available for the payment of disbursements on the client's behalf. Money must be transferred back to current account before payment can be made on the client's behalf.

When the solicitor asks the bank to close the designated deposit account, the bank will calculate the interest due and will notify the solicitor. The solicitor will make the following entries in his accounts to record the interest.

(a)   Credit the client's ledger account in the client column.
(b)   Debit the designated deposit cash account.

Continuing the example, assume that interest of £500 is allowed on the account at 1 January 1992.

BROWN

Designated deposit account
Opened 7 November 1991

Date	Details	Office account			Client account		
		Dr	Cr	Balance	Dr	Cr	Balance
1991		£	£	£	£	£	£
Nov 7	Cash: sale proceeds					50,000	50,000 Cr
1992 Jan 1	Deposit: cash: interest					500	50,500 Cr

DESIGNATED DEPOSIT CASH ACCOUNT

Date	Details	Office account			Client account		
		Dr £	Cr £	Balance £	Dr £	Cr £	Balance £
1991 Nov 7	Cash: transfer (Brown)				50,000		50,000 Dr
1992 Jan 1	Brown: interest				500		50,500 Dr

When the client's money is taken off designated deposit account, the following bookkeeping entries are made.

(a) Credit the designated deposit cash account client column with the amount placed on deposit plus interest allowed.

(b) Debit the cash account client column.

Continuing the example, assume that the designated deposit account is closed on 1 January.

DESIGNATED DEPOSIT CASH ACCOUNT

Date	Details	Office account			Client account		
		Dr £	Cr £	Balance £	Dr £	Cr £	Balance £
1991 Nov 7	Cash: transfer (Brown)				50,000		50,000 Dr
1992 Jan 1	Brown: interest				500		50,500 Dr
	Cash: transfer (Brown)					50,500	———

CASH ACCOUNT

Date	Details	Office account			Client account		
		Dr £	Cr £	Balance £	Dr £	Cr £	Balance £
1991							
Nov 7	Cash: Brown: sale proceeds				50,000		50,000 Dr
	Designated deposit: cash: transfer (Brown)					50,000	———
1992							
Jan 1	Deposit: cash: transfer (Brown)				50,500		50,500 Dr

No entry is made in the client's ledger account when money is transferred off deposit but a note should be put on the top of the ledger account to show that the designated deposit account has been closed.

Continuing the example:

BROWN

Designated deposit account
Opened 7 November 1991
Closed 1 January 1992

Date	Details	Office account			Client account		
		Dr £	Cr £	Balance £	Dr £	Cr £	Balance £
1991							
Nov 7	Cash: sale proceeds					50,000	50,000 Cr
1992							
Jan 1	Deposit: cash: interest					500	50,500 Cr

6.1.3 Payment of a sum of money in lieu of interest

If a solicitor does not place a client's money on deposit and he is required by the Solicitors' Accounts Rules 1991 to pay interest to the client, he must pay a sum out of office account equal to that which the client would have received had his money been placed on deposit.

If a solicitor pays a sum out of office account in lieu of interest, he has paid a business expense. To record payments in lieu of interest, a nominal expense account, the interest payable account, is opened.

When a solicitor pays a client a sum in lieu of interest only and does not, at the same time, account to the client for money held in client account on his behalf, the bookkeeping entries will be:

(a) Debit the interest payable account with the sum paid in lieu of interest.
(b) Credit the cash account office column.

Example

On 19 September 1991 the firm pays £20 in lieu of interest to its client Grey by sending Grey an office account cheque.

INTEREST PAYABLE ACCOUNT

Date	Details	Dr	Cr	Balance
1991		£	£	£
Sept 19	Cash: Grey	20		20 Dr

CASH ACCOUNT

Date	Details	Office account			Client account		
		Dr	Cr	Balance	Dr	Cr	Balance
1991		£	£	£	£	£	£
Sept 19	Interest payable: re Grey		20	20 Cr			

A note should be made at the top of the client's ledger account to show that a sum in lieu of interest has been paid. No entry is made in the account itself.

GREY
£20 in lieu of interest paid 19 September 1991

Date	Details	Office account	Client account

When a solicitor pays a sum in lieu of interest and at the same time accounts to the client for money held in client account on the client's behalf, he may either:

(a)   Send the client two cheques, one drawn on office account for the payment in lieu of interest and one drawn on client account; or

(b)   Send one cheque drawn on client account.

If the solicitor decides to send one cheque, drawn on client account, he will make the following three sets of entries in his accounts:

(a)   Entries to record the payment of a sum in lieu of interest out of office account.

(b)   Entries to record a receipt of client's money.

The entries in (a) and (b) above record the transfer, of money to be paid in lieu of interest, from office account to client account.

(c)   Entries to record a payment to the client, of the sum held on his behalf plus the sum paid in lieu of interest, out of client account.

Example

The firm holds £1,000 in its client account for its client Black. On 17 March 1991 the firm pays Black his £1,000 plus £40 in lieu of interest.

BLACK'S ACCOUNT

Date	Details	Office account			Client account		
		Dr £	Cr £	Balance £	Dr £	Cr £	Balance £
1991	Balance						1,000 Cr
Mar 17	Cash: interest payable					40	1,040 Cr
	Cash: you				1,040		——

CASH ACCOUNT

Double entry

Date	Details	Office account			Client account		
		Dr £	Cr £	Balance £	Dr £	Cr £	Balance £
1991	Black				1,000		1,000 Dr
Mar 17	Interest pay-able: re Black		40	40 Cr			
	Black: in lieu of interest				40		1,040 Dr
	Black					1,040	——

Double entry

INTEREST PAYABLE ACCOUNT

Date	Details	Dr	Cr	Balance
		£	£	£
Mar 17	Cash (Black)	40		40 Dr

At the end of the financial year the balance on the interest payable account is transferred to the profit and loss account as a practice expense.

6.2   EARNING INTEREST ON CLIENTS' MONEY

A solicitor is entitled to transfer a proportion of the money held in his client current account to a deposit account, including a Building Society account.

The solicitor is entitled to keep any interest earned on the client deposit account. He does not have to account to his clients for the interest earned.

When a solicitor transfers clients' money from current account to deposit account he makes the following entries in his accounts:

(a)   Credit the cash account client column.
(b)   Debit the deposit cash account client column.

Example

The firm has a balance of £100,000 on its client current account. The partners decide to place £30,000 of this on deposit on 8 September 1991.

CASH ACCOUNT

Date	Details	Office account			Client account		
		Dr £	Cr £	Balance £	Dr £	Cr £	Balance £
1991	Balance						100,000 Dr
Sept 8	Deposit cash: general deposit					30,000	70,000 Dr

DEPOSIT CASH ACCOUNT

Date	Details	Office account			Client account		
		Dr £	Cr £	Balance £	Dr £	Cr £	Balance £
1991 Sept 8	Cash: general deposit, clients' money				30,000		30,000 Dr

Interest earned on the general deposit account is practice income and the firm will open a nominal income account, the interest receivable account, to record this income.

When the bank notifies the firm that interest has been earned on the client deposit account, the following bookkeeping entries will be made:

(a) Credit the interest receivable account.
(b) Debit the cash account office column.

Example

On 8 May 1991 the bank credits £1,000 interest to office account on money held on general depossit.

INTEREST RECEIVABLE ACCOUNT

Date	Details	Dr	Cr	Balance
1991 May 8	Cash (general deposit)	£	£ 1,000	£ 1,000 Cr

CASH ACCOUNT

Date	Details	Office account			Client account		
		Dr £	Cr £	Balance £	Dr £	Cr £	Balance £
1991 May 8	Cash (general deposit): interest receivable	1,000		1,000 Dr			

At the end of the financial year the interest receivable account is closed and the balance on the account is transferred to the profit and loss account as a practice income.

6.3 EXAMPLE ON DEPOSIT INTEREST

Swanning, who intended to go on extended holiday, deposited the sum of £10,000 with the solicitor on 1 May 1991, with instructions that this sum was to be remitted to Taxhaven Ltd on 1 November 1991 to be held on Swanning's account. The solicitor decided to use a designated deposit account for the money and the sum of £10,500 was transferred to client current account on 31 October 1991.

The same firm of solicitors also acted for Martin in the collection of a debt due to him, amounting to the sum of £4,000. The debtor gave two cheques for the debt, each being £2,000. The first cheque was dated 1 July 1991 and the second was dated 1 September 1991. Both cheques were duly presented and met and the total amount due, after deduction of costs (£60 plus VAT £10.50) was paid to Martin by client account cheque on 5 September 1991. The firm has agreed to pay Martin the sum of £33 in lieu of interest.

The general deposit account for the firm earned £1,125 in interest for the six months ended 31 December 1991. Record the above transactions in the ledger accounts of the firm.

(Law Society Final Examination, updated and amended.)

6.4   SUGGESTED ANSWER TO EXAMPLE ON DEPOSIT INTEREST

SWANNING

Designated deposit account opened
1 May 1991. Closed 31 October 1991

Date	Details	Office account			Client account		
		Dr £	Cr £	Balance £	Dr £	Cr £	Balance £
1991							
May 1	Deposit: cash: you					10,000	10,000 Cr
Oct 31	Deposit: cash: interest					500	10,500 Cr
Nov 1	Cash: Taxhaven				10,500		———

MARTIN

Date	Details	Office account			Client account		
		Dr	Cr	Balance	Dr	Cr	Balance
1991		£	£	£	£	£	£
July 1	Cash: debtor					2,000	2,000 Cr
Sept 1	Cash: debtor					2,000	4,000 Cr
Sept 5	Costs	60					
	VAT	10.50		70.50 Dr			
	Cash: interest					33	4,033 Cr
	Cash: transfer: costs				70.50		3,962.50 Cr
	Cash: transfer: costs	70.50	70.50				
	Cash: you				3,962.50		—

INTEREST PAYABLE ACCOUNT

Date	Details	Dr	Cr	Balance
1991		£	£	£
Sept 5	Cash: Martin	33		33 Dr

INTEREST RECEIVABLE ACCOUNT

Date	Details	Dr	Cr	Balance
1991		£	£	£
Dec 31	Cash: interest credited by bank on client general deposit account		1,125	1,125 Cr

6.5 EXERCISES ON PROBATE TRANSACTIONS

1 Olde, Bayley & Co., solicitors, are instructed by the executors of Passway, deceased, to administer the estate on their behalf. The gross value of the estate amounts to £62,000 and consists of a house valued at £45,000 (subject to a mortgage of £12,000) and personalty valued at £17,000. There are sundry debts due by the estate amounting to £1,892. The following events take place:

1991

6 October   The deceased's bank agrees to advance the sum of £5,324 to the executors, so that they may pay the capital transfer tax in respect of the estate. The sum is credited to the client account of Olde, Bayley & Co., who then issue a cheque in favour of the Inland Revenue for the same amount. Probate fees of £50 are paid by the firm's cheque.

9 October   Grant received and registered with the bank, who transfer all monies due by them to the deceased (£1,250) to the executors' loan account with the bank.

15 October   A cheque for £16 is drawn in respect of the statutory advertisements, the cost of the local advertisement (£8) being met by a payment out of petty cash.

18 October   The deceased's account with Standoff Building Society is closed, and an amount is transferred to the executors' loan account with the bank, thus closing the account. The balance remaining in the building society (£223) is paid into client account.

21 October   Proceeds of life policy received, the whole amount (£5,000) being placed in a designated deposit account.

27 October   The household contents are sold and a cheque for £5,890 is received from the auctioneer. Commission of £620 had already been deducted.

4 November   Contracts for the sale of the house (£44,500) are exchanged, and a deposit of £4,450 is received by Olde, Bayley & Co., for them to hold as stakeholders.

18 November   Debts amounting to £1,927 are paid.

25 November   Paid funeral expenses £432.

4 December   The sale of the house is completed and a bank draft (£40,050) for the balance of the purchase money is received. The mortgage is redeemed by the payment of £12,367 which is inclusive of accrued interest.

11 December   A pecuniary legacy of £5,000 is paid to a legatee.

12 December   Bill of costs re sale of the house is prepared and agreed with the executors, profit costs being £440 plus VAT, and cash disbursements £20 (no VAT). Paid estate agents their commission £700 plus VAT.

14 December Bill of costs for the administration of the estate, profit costs £580 (plus VAT) and disbursements, rendered to executors, and after receiving their agreement, all moneys due to the firm from the estate are transferred to office account.

15 December The balance of moneys now held by Olde, Bayley & Co., on behalf of the executors, is paid over to Rich, the residuary legatee, in accordance with their instructions. Interest earned on the designated deposit account amounted to £107, whilst the interest to be allowed on other moneys held by the firm on behalf of the executors, is £208.

Show the client ledger card of the executors of Passway deceased. The rate of value added tax is to be taken as 17.5%.

2 The following balances appeared on the relevant clients' ledger accounts of Milky Way & Co., solicitors, as at 7 March 1991:

Saturn	Office account	£75	Client account	£1,294
Neptune	Office account	£15	Client account	£ nil

The firm is informed that Saturn died on the 26 February 1991, and the executors appointed in the will instruct the firm to act in the administration of the estate generally. The estate consists of a house 'Eudestar' valued at £70,000 and personalty valued at £47,500. There are sundry debts due by the estate (£1,500) together with a loan from an insurance company (secured on a life insurance policy) amounting to £5,000. The residue of the estate has been left to Neptune, a nephew who is in the process of purchasing a cottage 'The Wild Leap', a matter which is being dealt with by the firm.

During the administration, the following events take place:

1991
9 March House insurance premium (£95) on 'Eudestar', now due, and the firm debits the executors' account, the amount being transferred to the account of the insurance company, for whom the firm acts.

14 March   The deceased's bank agrees to advance £16,700 to the executors in respect of capital transfer tax and interest payable by the estate. Consequently, a cheque is drawn by the executors, payable to the Inland Revenue, and handed over to Milky Way & Co. Probate fees of £70 are paid by cheque.

19 March   The grant is received and registered with the bank, which then transfers £1,234 from the deceased's current account to the executors' loan account.

26 March   The amount invested by the deceased with the Constellation Building Society is, after registration of the grant, withdrawn and a sufficient sum to close the executors' loan account with the bank is transferred thereto, the remainder amounting to £590 being paid into client account.

27 March   With the executors' concurrence, the net amount outstanding in Saturn deceased's account at 7 March 1991, is transferred to the executors' account. The firm draws a cheque in respect of statutory advertisements (£22), and pays £12 out of petty cash in respect of the local advertisement.

29 March   Received cheque from the Pluto Insurance Co. Ltd, for the sum of £6,342, being the net sum receivable from the company after the deduction of £5,158 in respect of the loan together with accrued interest.

30 March   Debts amounting to £1,500, together with funeral expenses of £1,000, are paid out of client account.

              The executors having agreed to an interim distribution of £4,000 to Neptune, which is effected by transfer to Neptune's client account, the firm sends a cheque (£4,000) to the solicitors acting for the vendor of the cottage 'The Wild Leap', for them to hold as stakeholders, contracts being exchanged the same day.

5 April   Exchanged contracts for the sale of 'Eudestar', the deposit of £7,000 having been received by the firm for them to hold as stakeholders.

12 April   Sundry fees (£3) paid from office account re the transmission of shares to Virgo, a beneficiary in the estate of Saturn, deceased.

26 April   Received completion statement in respect of 'The Wild Leap', showing £36,000 due, being the balance of purchase money. Sent financial statement to Neptune same day, showing profit costs of £300 excluding VAT (as per bill of costs attached thereto), Land Registry fees £70, stamp duty £400 and search fees £16 of which £15 had been expended prior to 7 March 1991. Paid £1 from petty cash, in respect of bankruptcy search.

30 April   Completed purchase of 'The Wild Leap', the balance of purchase monies being received by the firm from the Bank of Aries as a loan, an undertaking having been given that the sum would be repaid to them from the proceeds of sale of 'Eudestar'. The executors had previously agreed to this arrangement.

2 May   Completed sale of 'Eudestar', receiving a bank draft (£63,000) in respect of the balance of purchase monies.

     Paid stamp duty and Land Registry fees re 'The Wild Leap'.

9 May   The firm agrees the bills of cost for the sale of the house and the administration of the estate with the executors. Profit costs with regard to the sale amount to £440 (excluding VAT), and with regard to the administration £700 (excluding VAT), together with disbursements in both cases. With the executors' agreement, a sum amounting to £36,146 is transferred from the account of the executors to the account of Neptune, and a cheque for this amount is sent to the Bank of Aries in accordance with the firm's undertaking.

16 May   All monies due to the firm from the estate are transferred to office account.

17 May   The balance of moneys held by the firm on behalf of the executors is transferred to the account of Neptune at the request of the executors, such sum being inclusive of interest allowed by the firm of £567.

     All moneys due to the firm from Neptune are transferred to office account, the balance due to Neptune being held pending further instructions.

You are required to show the ledger accounts of:

(i) Neptune;
(ii) the executors of Saturn, deceased;

The rate of VAT is to be taken as 17.5%.

In making the necessary entries, it is important that the account in which the corresponding entry would be made, is clearly identified by the appropriate entry in the details column.

(Solicitors' Final Examination, updated)

6.6 SUGGESTED ANSWERS TO EXERCISES ON PROBATE TRANSACTIONS

1   EXECUTORS OF PASSWAY DECEASED

Designated deposit account
Opened 21 October 1991
Closed 15 December 1991

Date	Details	Office account			Client account		
		Dr £	Cr £	Balance £	Dr £	Cr £	Balance £
1991							
Oct 6	Cash: bank loan					5,324	5,324 Cr
	Cash: CTT				5,324		―――
	Cash: probate fees	50		50 Dr			
Oct 15	Cash: advertise-ments	16		66 Dr			
	Petty cash: advertisements	8		74 Dr			
Oct 18	Cash: Standoff Building Society					223	223 Cr
Oct 21	Deposit cash: life policy					5,000	5,223 Cr
Oct 27	Cash: auctioneer (less commission £620)					5,890	11,113 Cr

Date	Details	Office account			Client account		
		Dr £	Cr £	Balance £	Dr £	Cr £	Balance £
1991							
Nov 18	Cash: debts				1,927		9,186 Cr
Nov 25	Cash: funeral expenses				432		8,754 Cr
Dec 4	Cash: sale proceeds					40,050	48,804 Cr
	Stakeholder: transfer					4,450	53,254 Cr
	Cash: mortgage redemption				12,367		40,887 Cr
Dec 11	Cash: legacy				5,000		35,887 Cr
Dec 12	Costs: sale	440					
	VAT	77		591 Dr			
	Petty cash: disbursements	20		611 Dr			
	Cash: estate agent				822.50		35,064.50 Cr
Dec 14	Costs: re estate	580					
	VAT	101.50		1,292.50 Dr			
	Cash: transfer: costs				1,292.50		33,772 Cr
	Cash: transfer: costs		1,292.50	—			
Dec 15	Deposit cash: interest					107	33,879 Cr
	Cash: in lieu of interest					208	34,087 Cr
	Cash: Rich				34,087		—

2   EXECUTORS OF SATURN DECEASED RE ADMINISTRATION OF ESTATE

Date	Details	Office account			Client account		
		Dr £	Cr £	Balance £	Dr £	Cr £	Balance £
1991							
Mar 9	Cash: transfer: insurance premium: client account: Eudestar	95		95 Dr			
Mar 14	Cash: probate fees	70		165 Dr			
Mar 26	Cash: Constellation Building Society					590	590 Cr
Mar 27	Saturn: transfer: net balance					1,219	1,809 Cr
	Cash: statutory advertisement				22		1,787 Cr
	Petty cash: local advertisement	12		177 Dr			
Mar 29	Cash: Pluto Insurance Co. Ltd					6,342	8,129 Cr
Mar 30	Cash: debts				1,500		6,629 Cr
	Cash: funeral expenses				1,000		5,629 Cr
	Neptune: transfer				4,000		1,629 Cr
Apr 12	Cash: fees: transmission of shares to Virgo	3		180 Dr			
May 2	Cash: purchaser's of Eudsetar					63,000	64,629 Cr
	Stakeholder: transfer					7,000	71,629 Cr

Date	Details	Office account			Client account		
		Dr £	Cr £	Balance £	Dr £	Cr £	Balance £
May 9	Costs: sale	440					
	VAT	77		697 Dr			
	Costs: admini-stration	700					
	VAT	122.50		1,519.50 Dr			
	Neptune: transfer				36,146		35,483 Cr
May 16	Cash: transfer: costs		1,519.50	—		1,519.50	33,963.50 Cr
May 17	Cash: transfer: from office account in lieu of interest					567	34,530.50 Cr
	Neptune: trnasfer residue				34,530.50		—

NEPTUNE: RE PURCHASE OF 'WILD LEAP'

Date	Details	Office account			Client account		
		Dr £	Cr £	Balance £	Dr £	Cr £	Balance £
1991							
Mar 7	Balance			15 Dr			
Mar 30	Executors of Saturn deceased: transfer					4,000	4,000 Cr
	Cash: deposit re 'The Wild Leap'				4,000		——
Apr 26	Costs	300					
	VAT	52.50					
	Petty cash: bank-ruptcy search	1		368.50 Dr			
Apr 30	Cash: Bank of Aries					36,000	36,000 Cr
	Cash: purchase of 'The Wild Leap'				36,000		——

Date	Details	Office account			Client account		
		Dr £	Cr £	Balance £	Dr £	Cr £	Balance £
1991							
May 2	Cash: stamp duty	400		768.50 Dr			
	Cash: Land Registry	70		838.50			
May 9	Executors of Saturn deceased: transfer					36,146	36,146 Cr
	Cash: Bank of Aries				36,146		—
May 17	Executors of Saturn deceased: transfer: residue					34,530.50	34,530.50 Cr
	Cash: transfer: costs		838.50	—	838.50		33,692 Cr

Although not specifically asked to do so, it would be advisable to place the sum of £33,692 on designated deposit.

6.7   TEST ON PROBATE TRANSACTIONS

Allow 1 hour to complete this test.

Tulip, Crocus & Co., solicitors, are instructed by the executors of Daffodil, deceased, to act in the administration of the estate generally. The whole of the net estate has been left to the widow of Daffodil, and consists of a house valued at £50,000 and personalty valued at £42,000. There are sundry debts due by the estate, amounting to £1,496, together with a bank loan of £5,000 which is secured on the house. During the administration the following events take place:

1991

1 March	Probate fees of £50 are paid by cheque.
4 March	Grant received and registered with the bank, who transfer all moneys due by them to the deceased, amounting to £896, to the firm's bank account.
5 March	At the request of the widow of Daffodil, the executors instruct the firm to sell the house for £50,000, together with some of the contents, and, when feasible, to send a bank draft for £5,000 to a firm in Spain, who are dealing with the purchase of a villa for the widow.
9 March	Cheque drawn on a client account for £20 in respect of statutory advertisements. The cost of the local advertisement (£12) is met out of petty cash.
10 March	Proceeds of life policy (£3,500) received, together with cheque from the Pompeii Building Society for £18,000 which closes that account.
12 March	Some of the contents of the house are sold and a cheque for £3,250 is received in respect thereof.
15 March	Paid by petty cash, fee for office copy entries re the house £4.
18 March	Exchanged contracts for the sale of the house, the deposit of £5,000 having been paid to the estate agent by the prospective purchaser.
22 March	Paid sundry debts of £1,496 together with funeral expenses of £485.
29 March	Received cheque (£11,900) in respect of the sale of units held in a unit trust by the deceased.
13 April	Bank draft in respect of the widow's villa sent to firm in Spain, the full cost of the draft (£5,012) being charged to the firm's client bank account.

16 April   The sale of the house is completed and a bank draft (£45,000) for the balance of purchase money is received. The bank loan is repaid, which together with accrued interest, amounted to £5,340. Received same day, from estate agents, the balance of the deposit on the house, less commission of £1,150 (including VAT).

19 April   Bills of costs for the sale of the house, and for administration of the estate are agreed with the executors. The bill of costs for the sale of the house, shows profit costs of £300, and disbursements £10. VAT is to be charged on the profit costs only. The bill of costs for the administration of the estate, shows profit costs of £600 (plus VAT) and disbursements.

20 April   All moneys due to the firm from the estate are transferred to office account.

21 April   The balance of moneys held by the firm, on behalf of the executors, together with interest allowed by the firm of £410, is deposited into a designated deposit account pending further instructions.

30 April   Mrs Daffodil (the residuary legatee), who is already a client of the firm, having instructed it some time previously to act for her in the purchase of a cottage, has requested that the executors pay her the sum of £2,850 on account of money due to her from the estate, this amount being the deposit on the cottage she proposes to purchase. The executors have agreed, the firm sends a cheque for that amount to the solicitors acting for the vendor, for them to hold as stakeholders, the cheque being drawn on the client account.

30 April   The firm, to date, has made disbursements amounting to £180 out of office moneys, in respect of the proposed purchase of the cottage.

24 May   A financial statement and bill of costs in respect of the purchase of the cottage, had been sent to Mrs Daffodil some time previously, showing the sum of £26,191 due, being the balance of the purchase price £25,650, sundry disbursements £380 (including VAT where relevant) and profit costs £140 plus VAT. The sum of £26,191 is transferred with the agreement of the executors, from the

executors' account to the account of Mrs Daffodil, and
completion then takes place. The account of Mrs Daffodil
is then closed.

The rate of value added tax is to be taken as 17.5%. Show the accounts of
the executors of Daffodil, deceased, and Mrs Daffodil.

(Law Society Final Examination, amended.)

6.8 SUGGESTED ANSWER TO TEST ON PROBATE TRANSACTIONS

THE EXECUTORS OF DAFFODIL DECEASED

30 April £2,850 taken off deposit
24 May £26,191 taken off deposit

Designated deposit account
Opened 21 April 1991

Date	Details	Office account			Client account		
		Dr £	Cr £	Balance £	Dr £	Cr £	Balance £
1991							
Mar 1	Cash: Probate fees	50		50 Dr			
Mar 4	Cash: bank					896	896 Cr
Mar 9	Cash: advertisements				20		876 Cr
	Petty cash: advertisements	12		62 Dr			
Mar 10	Cash: life policy					3,500	4,376 Cr
	Cash: Pompeii Building Society					18,000	22,376 Cr
Mar 12	Cash: house contents					3,250	25,626 Cr
Mar 22	Cash: debts				1,496		24,130 Cr
	Cash: funeral expenses				485		23,645 Cr
Mar 29	Cash: unit trust					11,900	35,545 Cr
Apr 13	Cash (bank draft) villa				5,012		30,533 Cr
Apr 16	Cash: sale proceeds					45,000	75,533 Cr
	Cash: bank loan repaid				5,340		70,193 Cr
	Cash: estate agent, deposit (less commission)					3,850	74,043 Cr

Date	Details	Office account			Client account		
		Dr £	Cr £	Balance £	Dr £	Cr £	Balance £
1991							
Apr 19	Costs: re sale	300					
	VAT	52.50					
	Petty cash: disbursements	10		424.50 Dr			
	Costs: re administration	600					
	VAT	105		1,129.50 Dr			
Apr 20	Cash: transfer: costs				1,129.50		72,913.50 Cr
	Cash: transfer: costs		1,129.50	—			
Apr 21	Cash: in lieu of interest					410	73,323.50 Cr
Apr 30	Mrs Daffodil: transfer				2,850		70,473.50 Cr
May 24	Mrs Daffodil: transfer				26,194.50		44,279 Cr

MRS DAFFODIL

Date	Details	Office account			Client account		
		Dr £	Cr £	Balance £	Dr £	Cr £	Balance £
1991							
Apr 30	Balance b/d			180 Dr			
	Executors of Daffodil: transfer					2,850	2,850 Cr
	Cash: vendor's solicitors				2,850		—
May 24	Executors of Daffodil: transfer					26,194.50	26,194.50 Cr
	Cash: purchase				25,650		544.50 Cr
	Cash: disbursements	200		380 Dr			
	Costs	140					
	VAT	24.50		544.50 Dr			
	Cash: transfer: costs				544.50		—
	Cash: transfer: costs		544.50	—			

7 *Miscellaneous Transactions*

7.1 COMMISSIONS

A solicitor may receive commission from a building society or insurance company for introducing business, or in the case of an insurance company, for collecting premiums.

Rule 10 of the Solicitors' Practice Rules 1990 deals with commission and provides as follows:

(a)   Where a solicitor receives a commission exceeding £10.00, he must account to his client for it unless the solicitor has disclosed to the client in writing the amount or basis of the calculation of the commission or, if neither the amount nor the basis can be ascertained, an approximation, and the client has agreed to the solicitor retaining the commission.

(b)   Where the commission actually received materially exceeds the amount or basis or approximation disclosed to the client, the solicitor must account to the client for the excess.

(c)   Rule 10 does not apply where a member of the public deposits money with a solicitor in the solicitor's capacity as agent for a building society or other financial institution and the solicitor has not advised that member of the public as a client about the disposition of the money. So solicitors who operate building society agencies will generally be able to retain the commission paid to them by the building society.

Thus as a general rule, unless the solicitor has his client's prior written authority to retain commission, it is clients' money and must be paid into a client account upon receipt. Where there is no authority to retain the commission, the entries made in the accounts when it is received, will be:

(a)   Debit cash account client column.

(b)   Credit the ledger account of the client entitled to the commission, client column.

There is nothing in the rules to prevent the solicitor from using the commission for or towards any bill of costs delivered to the client. If the commission does not exceed £10 or if the client gives written authority for the solicitor to retain it, the commission will be practice income and a nominal income account, the 'commission receivable account', will be opened.

When the commission is received the following entries will be made:

(a)   Debit cash account office column.

(b)   Credit insurance commission receivable account.

Example

The High Risk Insurance Co. pays the firm £100 for introducing its client Jones. The firm has already obtained Jones' written consent to retain the commission.

INSURANCE COMMISSION RECEIVABLE ACCOUNT

Date	Details	Dr	Cr	Balance
		£	£	£
	Cash (High Risk)		100	100 Cr

CASH ACCOUNT

Date	Details	Office account			Client account		
		Dr	Cr	Balance	Dr	Cr	Balance
		£	£	£	£	£	£
	Insurance commission receivable (High Risk)	100		100 Dr			

If a solicitor collects insurance premiums on behalf of an insurance company, he must open a client ledger account in the name of that insurance company.

To record the receipt of premiums, the solicitor will make entries in his accounts to record the receipt of clients' money.

Example

The firm collects miscellaneous premiums of £500 for the High Risk Insurance Co.

HIGH RISK INSURANCE CO.

Date	Details	Office account			Client account		
		Dr £	Cr £	Balance £	Dr £	Cr £	Balance £
1991 Jan	Cash: miscellaneous: premiums					500	500 Cr

When the firm charges the insurance company commission it makes the following entries in its accounts:

(a) Debit the insurance company's ledger account office column.

(b) Credit the insurance commission receivable account.

Continuing the example, the firm charges the High Risk Insurance Co. £50 commission.

HIGH RISK INSURANCE CO.

Date	Details	Office account			Client account		
		Dr £	Cr £	Balance £	Dr £	Cr £	Balance £
	Cash: miscellaneous: premiums					500	500 Cr
	Commission receivable	50		50 Dr			

INSURANCE COMMISSION RECEIVABLE ACCOUNT

Date	Details	Dr	Cr	Balance
		£	£	£
	High Risk Insurance Co. (commission charged)		50	50 Cr

When commission is to be deducted from premiums collected for the insurance company, a transfer of the commission is made from client to office account.

Continuing the example, on 31 January commission is transferred to office account.

HIGH RISK INSURANCE CO.

Date	Details	Office account			Client account		
		Dr £	Cr £	Balance £	Dr £	Cr £	Balance £
	Cash: miscellaneous: premiums					500	500 Cr
	Commission receivable	50		50 Dr			
	Cash: transfer: commission				50		450 Cr
	Cash: transfer: commission		50	—			

The above example is on the basis that the solicitor is taking money as an agent for a financial institution from someone who has not been advised as a client or that the solicitor has the client's written authority to retain the commission. If that were not the case and the solicitor were obliged to account to the clients for commission, the commission would be shown as a transfer from the client account of the insurance company to the client account of the clients entitled to the commission. No entries would be made in the commission receivable account because the firm has not received any income. So in the example above assume that the commission of £50 relates to two clients of the firm, Smith and Jones. Smith is entitled to £20 and Jones £30. Neither client has agreed to the solicitor retaining the commission. The entries in the accounts would then be as follows:

HIGH RISK INSURANCE CO.

Date	Details	Office account			Client account		
		Dr £	Cr £	Balance £	Dr £	Cr £	Balance £
	Smith: transfer net premium					180	
	Jones: transfer net premium					270	450 Cr

SMITH

Date	Details	Office account			Client account		
		Dr £	Cr £	Balance £	Dr £	Cr £	Balance £
	Cash: you (insurance premium High Risk Insurance Co.)					200	200 Cr
	High Risk Insurance Co.: transfer: net premium				180		20 Cr
	Cash: you (commission)				20		—

JONES

Date	Details	Office account			Client account		
		Dr £	Cr £	Balance £	Dr £	Cr £	Balance £
	Cash: you (Insurance premium: High Risk Insurance Co.)					300	300 Cr
	High Risk Insurance Co.: transfer: net premium				270		30 Cr
	Cash: you (commission)				30		—

When the net premium is paid to the insurance company, entries are made in the accounts to record a payment of client money.

Continuing the example, the net premium is paid to the High Risk Insurance Co.

HIGH RISK INSURANCE CO.

Date	Details	Office account			Client account		
		Dr £	Cr £	Balance £	Dr £	Cr £	Balance £
	Cash: miscellaneous: premiums					500	500 Cr
	Commission receivable	50		50 Dr			
	Cash: transfer: commission				50		450 Cr
	Cash: transfer: commission		50	—			
	Cash: you				450		—

7.2 AGENCY

7.2.1 Acting as agent

If a solicitor is instructed by another solicitor to act as his agent, he will open a client ledger account in the name of the instructing solicitor.

When a bill of costs is sent to the instructing solicitor entries will be made in his ledger account to record the delivery of a bill of costs.

If the agent solicitor allows the instructing solicitor commission, the agent solicitor's bill of costs will show gross costs less commission. VAT will be charged on the net costs.

Example

Brown & Co., solicitors, in Newcastle instruct the firm to represent their client Simple in matrimonial proceedings. The firm's costs for acting as Brown & Co's agents are £30. Commission of 10 per cent is allowed to Brown & Co. The bill which the firm delivers to Brown & Co. will be as follows:

	£
To professional fees	30
Less: Commission	3
	27
VAT (17.5%)	4.70
	31.70

The net costs and VAT on the net costs will be recorded in the instructing solicitor's account when the bill of costs is delivered to the instructing solicitors.

Continuing the example, the entries in the firm's accounts to record delivery of the bill of costs to Brown & Co. on 1 December 1991 will appear as follows:

BROWN & CO. RE AGENCY (MATRIMONIAL)

Date	Details	Office account			Client account		
		Dr	Cr	Balance	Dr	Cr	Balance
1991		£	£	£	£	£	£
Dec 1	Costs	27					
	VAT	4.70		31.70 Dr			

When the instructing solicitor makes payment an entry will be made to record the receipt of the office monies. Continuing the above example, assume that Brown & Co make payment of the agency fees on 31 December.

BROWN & CO. RE AGENCY (MATRIMONIAL)

Date	Details	Office account			Client account		
		Dr	Cr	Balance	Dr	Cr	Balance
1991		£	£	£	£	£	£
Dec 1	Costs	27					
	VAT	4.70		31.70 Dr			
Dec 31	Cash—						
	from you		31.70	—			

7.2.2   Instructing an agent

When a solicitor instructs another solicitor to act as his agent, the
instructing solicitor treats payment of the agent solicitor's costs as a
business expense. To record the payment of agency costs, the instructing solicitor opens a nominal expense account, the agency expenses
account.

When the instructing solicitor pays the agent solicitor's costs and
disbursements, he makes the following entries in his accounts:

(a)   Debit the agency expenses account with the agent's profit costs.
(If the agent solicitor has allowed the instructing solicitor commission,
the profit costs figure shown in the agency expenses account will be the
net figure, i.e., the costs actually paid.)

(b)   Debit the Customs and Excise account with VAT.

(c)   Debit the ledger account of the client on whose behalf the agent
was instructed with any disbursements (office account).

(d)   Credit the cash account office column with the total paid to the
agent solicitor. Note: These entries are made on the date on which
payment is made to the agent.

Example

The firm instructs Burke & Hare, London solicitors, to represent its client
Knox. Burke & Hare charge £60 plus VAT £10.50 and have paid court fees
of £10. Burke & Hare allow the firm 10 per cent commission. Burke &
Hare's bill is paid on 1 September 1991.

AGENCY EXPENSES ACCOUNT

Date	Details	Dr	Cr	Balance
1991		£	£	£
Sept 1	Cash: Burke & Hare: re Knox	54		54 Dr

The agency expenses account is a nominal expense account and therefore only has office columns.

CUSTOMS AND EXCISE ACCOUNT

Date	Details	Dr	Cr	Balance
1991		£	£	£
Sept 1	Cash: Burke & Hare: re Knox	9.45		9.45 Dr

KNOX

Date	Details	Office account			Client account		
		Dr	Cr	Balance	Dr	Cr	Balance
1991		£	£	£	£	£	£
Sept 1	Cash: agent's disbursements	10		10 Dr			

CASH ACCOUNT

Date	Details	Office account			Client account		
		Dr	Cr	Balance	Dr	Cr	Balance
1991		£	£	£	£	£	£
Sept 1	Agency fees		73.45	73.45 Cr			

When the instructing solicitor delivers a bill of costs to his client, he adds the agent solicitor's gross profit costs to his own. The instructing solicitor does not allow his client the commission allowed to him by the agent solicitor.

Continuing the example, the firm sends a bill of costs to Knox, showing its profit costs as £100 plus VAT. The bill is delivered on 30 November 1991.

	£
To professional charges	100
Agent's charges	60
	160
VAT at 17.5%	28
	188
Disbursements	10
	198

He records the total costs (including the agent's gross fees) as a delivery of a bill of costs by himself to his client. No entry is made in respect of the agent's disbursements at this stage. The entry in respect of the agent's disbursements, is as we have seen made when the agent's fees are paid.

KNOX

Date	Details	Office account			Client account		
1991		Dr £	Cr £	Balance £	Dr £	Cr £	Balance £
Sept 1	Cash: agent: disbursements	10		10 Dr			
Nov 30	Costs	160					
	VAT	28		198 Dr			

7.3 ABATEMENTS

After he has delivered his bill of costs to his client, a solicitor may decide to reduce his profit costs.

When an abatement of costs is made, a credit note is sent to the client, showing the reduction in costs and VAT.

The solicitor will make the following entries in his accounts to record an abatement:

(a) Credit the client's ledger account office column with the reduction in costs and VAT (on separate lines).

(b) Debit the costs account with the costs abatement.

(c) Debit the Customs and Excise account with the reduction in VAT.

Example

On 30 June 1991 the firm delivers a bill of costs to Charles, the executor of Fred, deceased, for £500 plus VAT. After discussing the matter with Charles, the firm agrees to reduce its bill to £400 and records the abatement in its account on 31 July 1991.

EXECUTORS OF FRED DECEASED

Date	Details	Office account			Client account		
		Dr £	Cr £	Balance £	Dr £	Cr £	Balance £
1991							
June 30	Costs	500					
	VAT	87.50		587.50 Dr			
July 31	Costs: abatement		100				
	VAT: abatement		17.50	470 Dr			

COSTS ACCOUNT

Date	Details	Dr	Cr	Balance
		£	£	£
1991				
June 30	Costs: executors of Fred deceased		500	500 Cr
July 31	Costs: abatement: executors of Fred deceased	100		400 Cr

CUSTOMS AND EXCISE ACCOUNT

Date	Details	Dr	Cr	Balance
		£	£	£
1991				
June 30	Executors of Fred deceased		87.50	87.50 Cr
July 31	Executors of Fred deceased: VAT: abatement	17.50		70 Cr

7.4 DISHONOURED CHEQUES

7.4.1 Cheque paid into office account

If a cheque paid into office account is later dishonoured, the solicitor will make the following entries in his accounts:

(a)   Debit the client ledger account office column with the value of the dishonoured cheque.

(b)   Credit the cash account office column.

Example

There is a debit balance of £117.50 on Peter's office account on 1 November 1991 in respect of costs previously charged to Peter. On 21 November Peter pays the costs by cheque. On 24 November the firm's bank notifies it that Peter's cheque has been returned by the paying banker. To record the above transactions, the following entries will be made in Peter's account.

PETER

Date	Details	Office account			Client account		
		Dr £	Cr £	Balance £	Dr £	Cr £	Balance £
1991							
Nov 1	Balance b/d			117.50 Dr			
Nov 21	Cash: you		117.50	—			
Nov 24	Cash: dis-honoured cheque	117.50		117.50 Dr			

The cash account will appear as follows:

CASH ACCOUNT

Date	Details	Office account			Client account		
		Dr £	Cr £	Balance £	Dr £	Cr £	Balance £
1991							
Nov 21	Peter	117.50		117.50 Dr			
Nov 24	Peter (dis-honoured cheque)		117.50	—			

7.4.2 Cheque paid into client account

If a cheque paid into client account is later dishonoured, the solicitor will make the following entries in his accounts:

(a) Debit the client's ledger account client column with the value of the cheque.

(b) Credit the cash account client column.

Example

On 4 February 1992 Jane paid the sum of £200 on account of costs and disbursements by cheque. On 7 February the firm's bankers notified it that Jane's cheque had been returned. The following entries will be made in the accounts to record these events.

JANE

Date	Details	Office account			Client account		
		Dr £	Cr £	Balance £	Dr £	Cr £	Balance £
1992							
Feb 4	Cash: you					200	200 Cr
Feb 7	Cash: dis-honoured cheque				200		—

CASH ACCOUNT

Date	Details	Office account			Client account		
		Dr £	Cr £	Balance £	Dr £	Cr £	Balance £
Feb 4	Jane				200		200 Dr
Feb 7	Jane (dis-honoured cheque)					200	—

7.4.3   Drawing against uncleared cheques in client account

The Solicitors' Accounts Rules 1991 do not prevent a solicitor from drawing against an uncleared cheque paid into client account but if the cheque is later dishonoured, the solicitor is in breach of the Solicitors' Accounts Rules and must make an immediate transfer from office to client account of the amount by which the client account is overdrawn.

When a solicitor has drawn on client account against a cheque which is later dishonoured, he will make the following entries in his accounts:

(a)   Entries to record the dishonour of a client account cheque (i.e., those entries in section 7.4.2).

(b)   Entries to record the transfer from office account to client account of the amount by which client account is overdrawn.

Note:

It is not necessary to transfer the full value of the cheque which has been dishonoured unless the client account is overdrawn by this amount.

Continuing the example from section 7.4.2, assume that on 4 February the firm drew a cheque on client account for £55 in respect of court fees.

JANE

Date	Details	Office account			Client account		
		Dr £	Cr £	Balance £	Dr £	Cr £	Balance £
1992							
Feb 4	Cash: you					200	200 Cr
Feb 5	Cash: court fee				55		145 Cr
Feb 7	Cash: dis-honoured cheque				200		55 Dr
	Cash: transfer	55		55 Dr			
	Cash: transfer					55	—

CASH ACCOUNT

Date	Details	Office account			Client account		
		Dr £	Cr £	Balance £	Dr £	Cr £	Balance £
1992							
Feb 4	Jane				200		200 Dr
Feb 5	Jane (court fee)					55	145 Dr
Feb 7	Jane (dis- honoured cheque)					200	55 Cr
	Jane (transfer to client account)		55	55 Cr			
	Jane (transfer from office account)				55		—

7.5 SMALL TRANSACTIONS

When a solicitor does work which involves only one accounting transaction, the charging of costs, for example, for drafting a will, the
solicitor may open a ledger account for the client and record the
delivery of a bill of costs and receipt of payment of costs in the usual
way.

Alternatively the solicitor may make entries only to record the
receipt of costs, as follows:

(a) Debit the cash account office column with costs and VAT (on
separate lines).

(b) Credit the costs account with costs.

(c) Credit the Customs and Excise account with VAT.

7.6 EXERCISES ON MISCELLANEOUS TRANSACTIONS

1 On 2 February 1992 a firm of solicitors receives a premium of £84 on
behalf of the Fale Safe Insurance Co. for whom the firm acts and which
currently owes the firm £16 commission due. On 20 February the
net amount due is paid to the Fale Safe Insurance Co., being the
gross premium received less commission of £8 and prior commission

due. Commission due to the firm is transferred from client to office account. The firm is not required to account to any client for the commission. Prepare the account of the Fale Safe Insurance Co.

2 On 12 February 1992 a firm of solicitors receives £100 from its client Green on account of his pending divorce action costs. On 13 February the sum of £15 is paid out of monies received from Green, to an Enquiry agent. On 15 February the bank notifies the firm that the cheque from Green for £100 has been returned by the paying bankers. Green intimates that he will be in funds within the next two weeks. Prepare the account of Green.

3 Brown & Brown are acting as agents in an action for the recovery of a debt, on behalf of Green & Co. On 1 June 1991 the agents pay expert witness fee of £58 and court fees £11. On 28 June 1991 the agents forward their bill of costs to Green & Co., showing costs £60 less agency commission £6 plus VAT and disbursements. The bill is accompanied by an indorsed cheque for £900, being the amount recovered. On 5 July Green & Co. bill their client Herbert for their own costs, £20, agents' fee, VAT and disbursements. On 7 July a cheque is forwarded to Herbert for the balance due to him. On 7 July Green & Co. pay Brown & Brown and transfer costs and disbursements from client to office account.

   (a) Show the entries in the accounts of Green & Co. to record the above transactions.
   (b) Show the entries in the accounts of Brown & Brown to record the above transactions.

4 You act for A who is purchasing a house:

1 May 1991	Receive a cheque for £6,000 for the deposit.
2 May 1991	Send a cheque for £6,000 to vendor's solicitors.
3 May 1991	Bank notifies you that cheque has been returned.

Prepare the account for A and the cash account to record the above. The cash account need not be balanced.

5 (a) On 20 January 1992 you deliver a bill of costs to Ann for £200 plus VAT £35. On 25 January you agree to reduce the cost to £160 plus VAT.

(b)   On 20 January 1992 you collect an insurance premium of £100 on behalf of Gamma Insurance Co. from Louise, since you are an agent for the Gamma Insurance Co. You retain a commission of £5, which is transferred to office account. You then send the net premium to the insurance company.

(c)   On 20 January 1992 Adam sends a cheque for £500: £117.50 is in payment of a bill you have delivered to him and the balance is for payment to the Wilshire County Court for an action which he lost. On 21 January you pay the money due to the county court. On 22 January Adam's cheque is dishonoured. On 28 January Adam brings in cash to replace the dishonoured cheque.

(d)   On 20 January 1992 you repay Debra the sum of £2,000 which you have been holding for two months, with £35 paid in lieu of interest.

Show the client ledger accounts and the cash account to record the above. It is not necessary to show the balances on the cash account.

6   In the month of March 1992 the following events take place:

1 March	Receive a cheque for £3,000, the deposit on the sale of a house by your client Donald, from the purchaser's solicitor. You are to hold the deposit as agent.
3 March	Receive a bill of costs from Badlot & Co., a firm of solicitors who act as your agents, for your client Neville: profit costs £200 plus VAT, and disbursements on which no VAT is payable, £25. Neville has already paid £100 on account of costs. You send a bill to Neville showing Badlot's costs and disbursements and your costs of £200 plus VAT.
4 March	You write off the sum of £115 which has been outstanding for some time, being costs and VAT owed by Maria, who is bankrupt.
7 March	Pay Badlot's bill by a cheque drawn on office account.
8 March	Lynne pays £90 premium due to Beta Insurance Co., for whom you act as agent. Commission due to you is currently £20.
9 March	Receive cheque from Neville in payment of his bill.
10 March	A designated deposit account opened for your client John is closed. The sum of £5,200 (inclusive of £200 interest) is sent by cheque to John.

11 March	The bank notifies you that Neville's cheque has been dishonoured.
13 March	The net amount due to the Beta Insurance Co. is paid to them. Commission charged is £5.00.
20 March	You act for Daphne in the collection of a debt of £36,000. The debtor sends two cheques of £18,000 each. One cheque dated 19 March is payable to Daphne. You have already agreed your costs of £100 plus VAT with Daphne. **You retain this sum and send Daphne a cheque for the balance, the debtor's cheque and receipted bill.**
29 March	Complete sale of Donald's house. Receive £27,000. Redeem mortgage of £7,221 by cheque to the High Rate Building Society. Send a bill of costs to Donald for £200 plus VAT. Pay estate agents' charges of £300 plus VAT, the bill being addressed to Donald.
30 March	Donald asks you to transfer enough money from his account to settle the indebtedness of his friend Neville. After making the necessary transfer a cheque is sent to Donald for the balance due.

Show the client ledger accounts to record the above.

7 During the month of November 1991, Teepot, Cupp & Saucer solicitors deal with the following events, and you are required to show all the relevant entries on the clients' ledger accounts, which are to be balanced. The rate of VAT is to be taken as 17.5%.

1991

1 November Cheque received (£4,000) from Peter, who is not a client of the firm, being the deposit on the sale of a house by Milko, for whom the firm acts. The firm is to hold the money as stakeholders. Exchanged contracts for the sale of Milko's house, and paid petty cash disbursements of £6 (no VAT) on his behalf, on the same day.

2 November Banker's draft received (£54,000) on completion of the sale of Lemon's house, stake money of £6,000 being transferred from stakeholder account. The mortgagee of Lemon's house, Alexander, had already instructed the firm to act on his behalf in the redemption of his charge on Lemon's house, and the redemption money (£9,675) is transferred to his

account. It has been agreed that the mortgagee's costs (£40 plus VAT) will be borne by Lemon. (Assume that Alexander is not an institutional lender.)

3 November Paid by cheque the sum of £10,000 in respect of a debt which had been incurred by Lemon to Cupp, a partner in the firm, Lemon having previously agreed to this action.

The amount due to the mortgagees of Lemon's house is paid by cheque, and the estate agent's fee (£1,200 plus VAT), is paid by the firm since the invoice was addressed to them.

A bill of costs is rendered to Lemon, showing profit costs of £800 plus VAT.

8 November Received cheque (£500) from Sucrose, on account of costs generally. The firm writes off the sum of £69 (inclusive of VAT £9) as a bad debt, the amount having been owed to the firm by Smith, since March 1990. Smith has now been adjudicated bankrupt.

10 November The designated deposit account opened by the firm re Orange, in respect of an amount of £10,000 held by them for the period of six months, is closed, and a cheque for the sum, together with interest of £450 credited by the bank, is sent to Orange.

14 November Cheque sent to Lemon in respect of balance of moneys held on his behalf, including agreed interest of £124. The amount due to the firm, is transferred to office account and Lemon's account is then closed.

21 November Bill of costs received from agent solicitors in connection with the affairs of Sucrose. The bill shows profit costs of £300 before allowing agency commission of £100 (excluding VAT) and disbursements of £80 (no VAT). The firm pays the agent's bill and now renders its own bill of costs to Sucrose, showing profit costs of £400 plus VAT and disbursements of £80 (no VAT). Both the profit costs and disbursements of the agent solicitors, are included in the foregoing amounts.

24 November Bill of costs rendered to Milko, showing profit costs (£300 plus VAT) together with disbursements already incurred.

25 November Received from Sucrose, the balance in respect of the firm's bill of costs, the account then being closed.

30 November The sale of Milko's house is completed, a banker's draft for £36,000 being received from the purchaser's solicitors. The amount due to the firm is transferred to office account, and a cheque for the balance due to Milko is sent to him.

(Solicitors' Final Examination, updated)

7.7   SUGGESTED ANSWERS TO EXERCISES ON MISCELLANEOUS TRANSACTIONS

1   Fale Safe Insurance Co. Ltd

FALE SAFE INSURANCE CO. LTD

Date	Details	Office account			Client account		
		Dr £	Cr £	Balance £	Dr £	Cr £	Balance £
1992							
Feb 2	Balance b/d	16		16 Dr			
	Cash: premiums					84	84 Cr
Feb 20	Commission receivable	8		24 Dr			
	Cash: you				60		24 Cr
	Cash: transfer: commission				24		—
	Cash: transfer: commission		24	—			

2 Green

GREEN

Date	Details	Office account			Client account		
		Dr £	Cr £	Balance £	Dr £	Cr £	Balance £
1992							
Feb 12	Cash: you					100	100 Cr
Feb 13	Cash: enquiry agent				15		85
Feb 15	Cash: re-turned cheque				100		15 Dr
	Cash: transfer	15		15 Dr			
	Cash: transfer					15	——

3 Green & Co. ledger accounts

AGENCY EXPENSES ACCOUNT

Date	Details	Dr	Cr	Balance
1991		£	£	£
July 7	Cash: Brown & Brown (Herbert)	54		54 Dr

CUSTOMS AND EXCISE ACCOUNT

Date	Details	Dr	Cr	Balance
1991		£	£	£
July 5	Herbert		12	12 Cr
July 7	Cash: Brown & Brown (Herbert)	9.45		

HERBERT

Date	Details	Office account			Client account		
		Dr £	Cr £	Balance £	Dr £	Cr £	Balance £
June 28	Cash: agents					900	900 Cr
July 5	Costs	80					
	VAT	14		94 Dr			
July 7	Cash: agency: disbursements	69		163 Dr			
	Cash: you				737		163 Cr
	Cash: transfer: costs				163		—
	Cash: transfer: costs		163	—			

CASH ACCOUNT

Date	Details	Office account			Client account		
		Dr £	Cr £	Balance £	Dr £	Cr £	Balance £
July 7	Cash: Brown & Brown		132.45	132.45 Cr			

Brown & Brown ledger cards

GREEN & CO. RE AGENCY

Date	Details	Office account			Client account		
		Dr £	Cr £	Balance £	Dr £	Cr £	Balance £
June 1	Cash: expert witness	58		58 Dr			
	Cash: court fee	11		69 Dr			
June 28	Costs	54					
	VAT	9.45		132.45 Dr			
	Cash: indorsed cheque					900	
	Cash: you: indorsed cheque				900		
July 7	Cash: from you		132.45	—			

4 <center>A. ACCOUNT</center>

Date	Details	Office account			Client account		
		Dr £	Cr £	Balance £	Dr £	Cr £	Balance £
1991							
May 1	Cash: you					6,000	6,000 Cr
May 2	Cash: deposit paid				6,000		—
May 3	Cash: dishonoured cheque				6,000		6,000 Dr
	Cash: transfer	6,000		6,000 Dr		6,000	—

CASH ACCOUNT

Date	Details	Office account			Client account		
		Dr £	Cr £	Balance £	Dr £	Cr £	Balance £
May 1	A: monies received				6,000		
May 2	A: deposit paid					6,000	
May 3	A: dis-honoured cheque					6,000	
	A: transfer		6,000		6,000		

5 (a)   ANN

Date	Details	Office account			Client account		
1992		Dr £	Cr £	Balance £	Dr £	Cr £	Balance £
Jan 20	Costs	200					
	VAT	35		235 Dr			
Jan 25	Costs abatement		40				
	VAT abatement		7	188 Dr			

(b)   GAMMA INSURANCE CO. ACCOUNT

Date	Details	Office account			Client account		
		Dr £	Cr £	Balance £	Dr £	Cr £	Balance £
Jan 20	Cash: premium (Louise)					100	100 Cr
	Commission	5		5 Dr			
	Cash: transfer		5	—	5		95 Cr
	Cash: you				95		—

(c)   ADAM ACCOUNT

Date	Details	Office account			Client account		
		Dr £	Cr £	Balance £	Dr £	Cr £	Balance £
1992 Jan 20	Balance			117.50 Dr			
	Cash: you		117.50	—		382.50	382.50 Cr
Jan 21	Cash: Wilshire County Court				382.50		—
Jan 22	Cash: dishonoured cheque	117.50		117.50 Dr	382.50		382.50 Dr
	Cash: transfer	382.50		500 Dr		382.50	—
Jan 28	Cash: you		500	—			

(d)   DEBRA ACCOUNT

Date	Details	Office account			Client account		
		Dr £	Cr £	Balance £	Dr £	Cr £	Balance £
1992 Jan 20	Balance					2,000	2,000 Cr
	Cash: interest payable					35	2,035 Cr
	Cash: you				2,035		—

CASH ACCOUNT

Date	Details	Office account			Client account		
		Dr £	Cr £	Balance £	Dr £	Cr £	Balance £
Jan 20	Gamma insurance: premium				100		
	Gamma insurance: transfer commission	5				5	
	Gamma insurance: balance of premium					95	
	Adam	117.50			382.50		
	Interest payable re Debra		35				
	Debra: in lieu of interest				35		
	Debra:					2,035	
Jan 21	Adam: Wilshire County Court					382.50	
Jan 22	Adam: dishonoured cheque		117.50			382.50	
	Adam: transfer		382.50		382.50		
Jan 28	Adam:		500				

DONALD ACCOUNT

Date	Details	Office account			Client account		
		Dr £	Cr £	Balance £	Dr £	Cr £	Balance £
1992							
Mar 1	Cash: deposit					3,000	3,000 Cr
Mar 29	Cash: completion					27,000	30,000 Cr
	Cash: High Rate Building Society				7,221		22,779 Cr
	Costs	200					
	VAT	35		235 Dr			
	Cash: estate agent				352.50		22,426.50 Cr
Mar 30	Cash: transfer to Neville				395		22,031.50 Cr
	Cash: transfer costs		235	—	235		21,796.50 Cr
	Cash: you				21,796.50		

NEVILLE ACCOUNT

Date	Details	Office account			Client account		
		Dr £	Cr £	Balance £	Dr £	Cr £	Balance £
1992							
Mar 3	Balance					100	100 Cr
	Costs	400					
	VAT	70		470 Dr			
Mar 7	Cash: agents disbursements	25		495 Dr			
Mar 9	Cash: you		395	100 Dr			
	Cash: transfer		100	—	100		—
Mar 11	Cash: dishonoured cheque	395		395 Dr			
Mar 30	Cash: Donald		395	—			

MARIA ACCOUNT

Date	Details	Office account			Client account		
		Dr £	Cr £	Balance £	Dr £	Cr £	Balance £
1992 Mar 4	Balance			115 Dr			
	Bad debts		100				
	Customs & Excise		15	–			

BETA INSURANCE CO. ACCOUNT

Date	Details	Office account			Client account		
		Dr £	Cr £	Balance £	Dr £	Cr £	Balance £
1992 Mar 8	Commission due	20		20 Dr			
	Cash: premium					90	90 Cr
Mar 13	Commission	5		25 Dr			
	Cash: transfer commission		25	–	25		65 Cr
	Cash: you				65		–

JOHN ACCOUNT

Designated deposit account
Opened: ....
Closed: 10 March 1992

Date	Details	Office account			Client account		
		Dr £	Cr £	Balance £	Dr £	Cr £	Balance £
1992	Balance					5,000	5,000 Cr
Mar 10	Deposit cash interest					200	5,200 Cr
	Cash: you				5,200		–

DAPHNE ACCOUNT

Date	Details	Office account			Client account		
		Dr £	Cr £	Balance £	Dr £	Cr £	Balance £
1992	Costs: agreed fee	100					
	VAT	17.50		117.50 Dr			
Mar 20	Cash: debtor					18,000	18,000 Cr
	Cash: transfer		117.50	—		117.50	17,882.50 Cr
	Cash: you				17,882.50		

Note:

The cheque for £18,000 payable by Daphne could have been shown on the account by way of a memorandum entry.

7 Teepot, Cupp & Saucer

MILKO

Date	Details	Office account			Client account		
		Dr £	Cr £	Balance £	Dr £	Cr £	Balance £
1991							
Nov 1	Petty cash: disbursement	6		6 Dr			
Nov 24	Costs	300					
	VAT	52.50		358.50 Dr			
Nov 30	Cash: sale proceeds					36,000	36,000 Cr
	Stakeholder: transfer: deposit					4,000	40,000 Cr
	Cash: transfer: costs from client to office account		358.50	—		358.50	39,641.50 Cr
	Cash: you				39,641.50		—

LEMON

Date	Details	Office account			Client account		
		Dr £	Cr £	Balance £	Dr £	Cr £	Balance £
1991							
Nov 2	Cash: sale proceeds					54,000	54,000 Cr
	Stakeholder: transfer: deposit					6,000	60,000 Cr
	Alexander: transfer: redemption				9,675		50,325 Cr
	Alexander: transfer: re-demption costs	47		47 Dr			
Nov 3	Cash: Cupp				10,000		40,325 Cr
	Cash: estate agent	1,200		1,247 Dr			
	Costs	800					
	VAT	350		2,397 Dr			
Nov 14	Cash: in lieu of interest					124	40,449 Cr
	Cash: transfer: Costs		2,397	——	2,397		38,052 Cr
	Cash: you				38,052		——

ALEXANDER

Date	Details	Office account			Client account		
		Dr £	Cr £	Balance £	Dr £	Cr £	Balance £
1991							
Nov 2	Costs	40					
	VAT	7		47 Dr			
	Lemon: transfer: re-demption					9,675	9,675 Cr
	Lemon: transfer: re-demption costs		47	——			
Nov 3	Cash: you				9,675		——

SUCROSE

Date	Details	Office account			Client account		
		Dr £	Cr £	Balance £	Dr £	Cr £	Balance £
1991							
Nov 8	Cash: you					500	500 Cr
Nov 21	Cash: dis-bursements	80		80 Dr			
	Costs	400					
	VAT	70		550 Dr			
Nov 25	Cash: you		50	500 Dr			
	Cash: transfer: costs		500	—	500		—

SMITH

Date	Details	Office account			Client account		
		Dr £	Cr £	Balance £	Dr £	Cr £	Balance £
1991							
	Balance			69 Dr			
Nov 8	Bad debt		60				
	Customs and Excise		9	—			

ORANGE

Designated deposit account
Opened May 1991
Closed 10 November 1991

Date	Details	Office account			Client account		
		Dr £	Cr £	Balance £	Dr £	Cr £	Balance £
1991							
	Balance						10,000 Cr
Nov 10	Deposit cash: interest					450	10,450 Cr
	Cash: you				10,450		—

STAKEHOLDER ACCOUNT

Date	Details	Office account			Client account		
		Dr	Cr	Balance	Dr	Cr	Balance
1991		£	£	£	£	£	£
	Balance					6,000	6,000 Cr
Nov 1	Cash: Milko					4,000	10,000 Cr
Nov 2	Lemon: transfers				6,000		4,000 Cr
Nov 30	Milko: transfers				4,000		———

7.8 TEST ON MISCELLANEOUS TRANSACTIONS

Allow 1 hour to complete this test.

Harry, Peter and Tom are solicitors, and they deal with the following events:

1992

2 January   Brown pays cash (£104) to the firm, who act as agents for the Nonpay Insurance Co. Ltd. Commission currently due to the firm on that agency amounts to £43. The firm is not liable to account to any client for that commission.

3 January   Paid by cheque the sum of £2,000 on behalf of Black, and received later the same day from Black, a cheque for £1,500 in partial satisfaction. The balance is to be paid from the proceeds of the sale of his house, which will be received within a few days' time.

4 January   Cheque for the agreed fee (£40 plus VAT) received from White in respect of debt collection work.

7 January   Received cheque, in respect of the sale of Black's house, amounting to £22,634, being the balance of purchase money. The sum of £2,500 is transferred from stake-holder account the same day. The firm also acts for the mortgagee's of Black, the Savall Building Society, and £7,436 is sent to that company to redeem the mortgage. Requisite bill of costs rendered to building society. The costs

of redemption of Black's mortgage (£20 plus VAT) are to be borne by Black.

10 January	Cheque received drawn in favour of White, for £1,250 (which is indorsed over to the firm). Bill of costs is sent to White in respect of debt collection, showing the agreed fee (£40 plus VAT) less abatement of fee £20 plus VAT.
10 January	Bill of costs sent to Black (£240 plus VAT).
11 January	Pink repays a personal loan of £1,000 made by Peter, a partner in the firm.
12 January	Black requests that the amount due to him should be retained by the firm for the time being, as he will not require payment for some months. The amount due to the firm is transferred to office account.
14 January	The amount due to White is paid by cheque, and the account is then closed.
14 January	The firm acts for Yellow in a court action, having already paid the counsel's fee of £100 plus VAT (the principal method was used). The firm had appointed local agents, and their bill showed profit costs of £120, less agency commission £20, plus VAT. Agency disbursements consisted of court fees £12. Bill of costs is sent to Yellow, showing profit costs of £100 (excluding agents' profit costs) plus VAT and the disbursements.
16 January	Grey pays £200 on account of his pending divorce action costs, and cash disbursements of £16 are paid in respect thereof on the same day.
17 January	The net amount due to the Nonpay Insurance Co. Ltd is paid, being the gross premium received (£104) less commission of £15 and prior commission due (£43).
18 January	Received amount due from Yellow, and paid the amount due to the local agents who acted in his court action.
22 January	Paid enquiry agent, on behalf of Grey, the sum of £40 (no VAT), the cheque being drawn on client account.
24 January	The bank notifies the firm that the cheque from Grey has been returned unpaid by the paying bankers.
29 January	The sum of £1,000, which has been held on behalf of Blue, for some three months, is repaid to Blue, together with agreed interest of £40. The payment is made by means of a cheque drawn on client account. The money has not been deposited in a designated deposit account.

Write up the client's ledger accounts, showing all relevant entries. All accounts are to be balanced. The rate of VAT is to be taken as 17.5%.

(Law Society Final Examination, updated)

7.9   SUGGESTED ANSWER TO TEST ON MISCELLANEOUS TRANSACTIONS

NONPAY INSURANCE CO. LTD

Date	Details	Office account			Client account		
		Dr £	Cr £	Balance £	Dr £	Cr £	Balance £
1992							
Jan 2	Balance	43		43 Dr			
	Cash: Brown					104	104 Cr
Jan 17	Commission	15		58 Dr			
	Cash: you				46		58 Cr
	Cash: transfer: commission				58		—
	Cash: transfer: commission		58	—			

BLACK

Designated deposit account
Opened 12 January 1992

Date	Details	Office account			Client account		
		Dr £	Cr £	Balance £	Dr £	Cr £	Balance £
1992							
Jan 3	Cash	2,000		2,000 Dr			
Jan 3	Cash: you		1,500	500 Dr			
Jan 7	Cash: purchaser's solicitors					22,634	22,634 Cr
	Stakeholder: transfer					2,500	25,134 Cr
	Cash: Savall Building Society: redemption				7,436		17,698 Cr
Jan 10	Costs	240					
	VAT	42					
	Costs (mortgage redemption)	20					
	VAT	3.50		805.50 Dr			

Date	Details	Office account			Client account		
		Dr £	Cr £	Balance £	Dr £	Cr £	Balance £
Jan 12	Cash: transfer: costs					805.50	16,892.50 Cr
	Cash: transfer: costs		805.50	—			

WHITE

Date	Details	Office account			Client account		
		Dr £	Cr £	Balance £	Dr £	Cr £	Balance £
1992 Jan 4	Costs (agreed fee)	40					
	VAT	7		47 Dr			
	Cash: you		47				
Jan 10	Cash: you					1,250	1,250 Cr
	Costs: abatement		20				
	VAT: abatement		3.50	23.50 Cr			
Jan 14	Cash: you	23.50		—	1,250		—

YELLOW

Date	Details	Office account			Client account		
		Dr £	Cr £	Balance £	Dr £	Cr £	Balance £
1992 Jan 14	Balance			100 Dr			
	Costs	220					
	VAT	56		376 Dr			
Jan 18	Cash (agent disbursement)	12		388 Dr			
	Cash: you		388	——			

GREY

Date	Details	Office account			Client account		
		Dr £	Cr £	Balance £	Dr £	Cr £	Balance £
1992							
Jan 16	Cash: you					200	200 Cr
	Petty cash: disbursements	16		16 Dr			
Jan 22	Cash: enquiry agent				40		160 Cr
Jan 24	Cash: returned cheque				200		40 Dr
	Cash: transfer	40		56 Dr			
	Cash: transfer					40	——

BLUE

Date	Details	Office account			Client account		
		Dr £	Cr £	Balance £	Dr £	Cr £	Balance £
1992							
Jan 29	Balance					1,000	1,000 Cr
	Cash: interest					40	1,040 Cr
	Cash: you				1,040		——

Note: an account is not opened for Peter as he is a partner in the firm and it would be in breach of the Solicitors' Accounts Rules 1991 to pay the money received from Pink into client account.

7.10   TEST ON LEDGER ACCOUNTS INCLUDING VAT

Allow 1 hour to complete this test.

Except where specifically referred to in the questions, taxation (including VAT) should be ignored.

Bread, Butter and Honey are solicitors, and they deal with the following events:

1991

5 April Paid £23.50 (including VAT £3.50) by cheque drawn on office account, in respect of the reproduction of documents. This disbursement is to be treated as an input of the client, Phantasia, for whom the firm are acting in a tax matter before the special commissioners.

6 April Received banker's draft for £49,500 from the purchaser's solicitors, being the balance of purchase money re the sale by Smith of his house 'Figleaf'. On the same day the sum of £19,500 is sent by cheque to the mortgagees of the property, in full payment of the amount due to them.

7 April Logger, Hedd and Co., the estate agents acting for Smith, send cheque to firm for £4,235, being the deposit on 'Figleaf' less their commission.

8 April Received the sum of £300 from Phantasia on account of costs generally.

12 April The firm acts for Jones in the collection of a debt due to him, amounting to £5,000. The debtor sends two cheques for the debt, each cheque being for the sum of £2,500 and dated 15 May 1991 and 15 June 1991, respectively.

14 April Sent cheque for £587.50 (including VAT £87.50) to A. Builder in respect of pre-sale repairs to 'Figleaf'. The invoice was addressed to the firm.

28 April Paid fee of £235 (including VAT £35) to E. X. Pert, a witness who appeared on behalf of Phantasia. The payment was made out of client account.

29 April Bill of costs sent to Smith (£300 plus VAT).

5 May Paid from client account £94 (including VAT) in respect of transcripts obtained on behalf of Phantasia.

9 May Smith requests that the amount due to him should be retained by the firm for the time being, and the sum is transferred to a designated deposit account; profit costs and disbursements are transferred to office account on the same day.

20 May Bill of costs in respect of tax matter is rendered to Phantasia, showing profit costs of £700 plus VAT.

16 June Received cheque in settlement of Phantasia's account with the firm.

17 June Bill of costs for £60 plus VAT delivered to Jones.

21 June   Both cheques from the debtor of Jones, having been presented and met, the total amount due, after deduction of costs but inclusive of interest allowed by the firm (£22), was paid over to Jones. It is the practice of the firm to record all interest payments made by the firm on the client's ledger account. The amount due to the firm is transferred from client to office account.

30 June   The bank credits the designated deposit account of Smith with interest of £375 and the firm allows interest of £250 for the period before the designated deposit account was opened for Smith.

You are required to show the ledger accounts of Phantasia, Smith and Jones, recording all the above transactions. The rate of value added tax is to be taken as 17.5%.

(Law Society Final Examination, updated)

7.11 SUGGESTED ANSWER TO TEST ON LEDGER ACCOUNTS INCLUDING VAT

PHANTASIA

Date	Details	Office account			Client account		
		Dr £	Cr £	Balance £	Dr £	Cr £	Balance £
1991							
Apr 5	Cash: production of documents	23.50		23.50 Dr			
Apr 8	Cash: you					300	300 Cr
Apr 28	Cash: E. X. Pert				235		65 Cr
May 5	Cash: transcripts				94		29 Dr
	Cash: transfer	29		52.50 Dr			
	Cash: transfer					29	—
May 20	Costs	700					
	VAT	122.50		875 Dr			
June 16	Cash: you		875	—			

SMITH

Designated deposit account
Opened 9 May 1991
Closed 30 June 1991

Date	Details	Office account			Client account		
		Dr £	Cr £	Balance £	Dr £	Cr £	Balance £
1991							
Apr 6	Cash: purchaser's solicitors					49,500	49,500 Cr
	Cash: redemption				19,500		30,000 Cr
Apr 7	Cash: estate agent (less commission)					4,235	34,235 Cr
Apr 14	Cash: A. Builder	500		500 Dr			

Date	Details	Office account			Client account		
		Dr	Cr	Balance	Dr	Cr	Balance
1991		£	£	£	£	£	£
Apr 29	Costs	300					
	VAT	140		940 Dr			
May 9	Cash: transfer: costs				940		33,295 Cr
	Cash: transfer: costs		940	—			
June 30	Deposit cash: interest					375	33,670 Cr
	Cash: interest					250	33,920 Cr

JONES

Date	Details	Office account			Client account		
		Dr	Cr	Balance	Dr	Cr	Balance
1991		£	£	£	£	£	£
May 15	Cash: debtor					2,500	2,500 Cr
June 15	Cash: debtor					2,500	5,000 Cr
June 17	Costs	60					
	VAT	10.50		70.50 Dr			
June 21	Cash: interest					22	5,022 Cr
	Cash: transfer				70.50		4,951.50 Cr
	Cash: transfer		70.50	—			
	Cash: you				4,951.50		—

8   Bank Reconciliation

8.1   PURPOSE OF THE BANK RECONCILIATION STATEMENT

A bank reconciliation statement is prepared to reconcile the balance on the cash account with the balance on the bank statement.

8.2   SOLICITORS' BANK RECONCILIATION STATEMENTS

A solicitor must prepare two bank reconciliation statements because he has two separate bank accounts:

(a)   Office account – holds the firm's money.
(b)   Client account – holds the clients money.

A solicitor can prepare an office account bank reconciliation statement at intervals to suit the needs of his practice. The Solicitors' Accounts Rules 1991 provide that a solicitor must prepare a client account bank reconciliation statement at least every five weeks and must keep a copy of the bank reconciliation statement.

8.3   ACCOUNTING FOR DIFFERENCES

The following may explain differences between the balance on the bank statement and the cash account balance:

(a)   Errors in the cash account or bank statement.
(b)   Items shown on the bank statement but not in the cash account. This usually occurs because the solicitor does not know of these items of income or expenditure until he receives his bank statement. The following are items which commonly appear on the bank statement but not in the cash account:

    (i)   Bank charges.

    (ii)   Overdraft interest.

    (iii) Dishonoured cheques.

    (iv) Direct payments from the account for example, standing orders.

    (v)   Payments made directly into the bank.

   (c)   Items in the cash account which are not shown on the bank statement:

    (i)   Unpresented cheques, i.e., cheques which the firm has drawn and which are shown in its cash account as credit entries but which have not been presented for payment by the time the bank statement is issued.

    (ii)   Late credits, i.e., receipts by the firm which are recorded as debit entries in the cash account but which are paid into the bank too late to appear on the bank statement.

8.4   COMPARING THE BANK STATEMENT AND THE CASH ACCOUNT

Compare the entries which are on the bank statement receipts column with those which are on the cash account debit side and:

   (a)   Mark off any entries on the bank statement (receipts) which have corresponding entries in the cash account (debit).

   (b)   Account for any difference in the opening balances. If the opening balance on the cash account is greater than the opening balance on the bank statement check whether there is an entry or entries on the bank statement (receipts) which does not have a corresponding entry in the cash account (debit) and which is the same amount as the difference in the opening balances. If such an item is found in the bank statement (receipts) it is usually safe to assume that it is a cheque or cheques received and entered in the cash account before the start of the period to which the bank statement relates. The cheque or cheques will have been treated as a late credit on the previous bank reconciliation statement and therefore the opening balances can be marked off as having been reconciled. The cheque or cheques which account for the difference in the opening balances can be marked off as having been taken into account in a previous bank reconciliation statement.

Compare the entries on the bank statement payments column with the entries in the cash account credit side and:

(a) Mark off any entries in the bank statement (payments) for which there is a corresponding entry in the cash account (credit).

(b) Account for any difference in the opening balances. If the opening balance in the cash account is less than the opening balance on the bank statement it is probably a result of unpresented cheques taken into account in the previous bank reconciliation statement but not shown in the bank statement (payments) until presented for payment at a later date. If entries are found in the bank statement (payments) which are not already accounted for and which amount to the difference in the opening balances, these entries and the opening balances can be marked off as reconciled.

8.5 BRINGING THE CASH ACCOUNT UP TO DATE

Before a bank reconciliation statement can be prepared, the balance on the cash account has to be adjusted. To adjust the cash account balance the following steps are taken:

(a) List entries on the bank statement (receipts) which do not have a corresponding entry in the cash account (debit). Such items are usually direct payments into the bank. Update the cash account by making debit entries.

(b) List entries in the bank statement (payments) which do not have a corresponding entry in the cash account (credit). These are usually either bank charges, overdraft interest, dishonoured cheques or standing orders. Update the cash account by making credit entries.

(c) Balance the cash account. The bank statement will be reconciled with this adjusted balance on the cash account.

8.6 PREPARING THE BANK RECONCILIATION STATEMENT

The following steps are taken to prepare a bank reconciliation statement.

(a) List any entries in the cash account (debit) which do not have a corresponding entry on the bank statement (receipts). These are late credits.

(b) List any entries in the cash account (credit) which do not have a corresponding entry on the bank statement (payments). These are unpresented cheques.

(c) Draw up the bank reconciliation statement. A bank reconciliation statement is usually set out as follows:

BANK RECONCILIATION STATEMENT AS AT (DATE)

	£
Balance as per bank statement	X
Unpresented cheques	X
	X
Late credits	X
Balance as per adjusted cash account	X

Note the following:

(a) If there is a credit balance at the bank, unpresented cheques will be deducted from that balance because they reduce the balance. Late credits will be added because they increase the credit balance.

(b) If there is a bank overdraft, unpresented cheques will be added to the overdraft because they increase it. Late credits will be deducted from the overdraft because they reduce it.

8.7   WORKED EXAMPLES ON BANK RECONCILIATION

1   Alfred, a sole practitioner, receives a bank statement for his office account for the month ending 31 December and it shows a balance in hand of £175. His office cash account shows a debit balance of £188. On checking the cash account and the bank statement, Alfred notices the following:

(a) A cheque paid to Ian for £20 has been incorrectly entered in the office cash account as £22.

(b) Bank charges of £4 have been made.

(c) James paid £15 direct to Alfred's bank account by credit transfer.

(d)   A cheque for £18 received from Charles has been dishonoured.

(e)   A cheque for £72 paid to Alan on 29 December has not been presented for payment.

(f)   Alfred paid £80 cash in respect of costs into the bank on 30 December and this is not shown on the bank statement.

Alfred takes the following steps to reconcile his bank statement and his office cash account.

(a)   He prepares an adjusted cash account.

OFFICE CASH ACCOUNT

Date	Details	Dr	Cr	Balance
		£	£	£
Dec 31	Balance	188		188 Dr
	Ian (correction of error)	2		190 Dr
	Bank charges		4	186 Dr
	James	15		201 Dr
	Charles		18	183 Dr

(b)   He lists late credits and unpresented cheques:
  (i)   Late credit: £80 costs paid into bank on 30 December.
  (ii) Unpresented cheque: for £72 in favour of Alan drawn on 30 December.

(c)   He draws his bank reconciliation statement:

BANK RECONCILIATION STATEMENT AS AT 31 DECEMBER

	£
Balance as per bank statement	175 Cr
Deduct unpresented cheques	72
	103
Add late credits	80
Balance as per adjusted cash account	183

2   Jones, a sole practitioner, endeavours to maintain a credit balance
on his office bank account at all times. However, when he receives his
office account bank statement for the month of November, it shows an
overdraft of £88. Jones cannot understand how the bank arrives at this
figure. The bank statement shows the following entries:

BLANBRO BANK
WINTOWN BRANCH
ACCOUNT: JONES. OFFICE.

Date	Details	Payment	Receipt	Balance
		£	£	£
Nov 1	Balance brought forward			1,468 Cr
Nov 8	Credits		636	2,104
Nov 15	Credits		2,348	
	248	1,368		3,084
Nov 19	Credits		172	
	244	1,850		1,406
Nov 27	Credits		1,246	2,652
Nov 30	246	1,524		
	Charges	138		
	Cheque returned	1,246		
	Paid in by a direct transfer		168	88 Dr

   Jones' office cash account is as follows:

OFFICE CASH ACCOUNT

Date	Details	Dr	Cr	Balance
		£	£	£
Nov 1	Balance			100 Dr
Nov 3	B	280		380
Nov 5	C	356		
	D	1,390		
	K		1,810	316
Nov 10	E	958		1,274
Nov 17	F	172		1,446
Nov 19	L		1,524	78 Cr
Nov 24	G	1,246		1,168 Dr
Nov 28	M		374	
	N		86	
	P		472	236 Dr
Nov 30	H	1,536		
	J	170		1,942 Dr

(Law Society Final Examination)

Jones states that the cheque issued to K on 5 November, for £1,850, was entered in the cash account as £1,810 in error.

Jones takes the following steps to prepare his bank reconciliation statement:

(a)   He reconciles the difference in the opening balances. The bank statement balance is £1,368 greater than the cash account balance. On 15 November there is an entry on the bank statement for payment of cheque number 248 £1,368. This will be an unpresented cheque already entered in the cash account and taken into account in the previous bank reconciliation statement. The opening balances and cheque number 248 can therefore be eliminated.

(b)   He compares the bank statement receipts column and the cash account debit side:

(i)   Cash account debit: 3 November £280 and 5 November £356, corresponding with the entry on the bank statement on 8 November: £636.

(ii)   Cash account debit: 5 November £1,390 and 10 November £958, corresponding with the entry on the bank statement on 5 November: £2,348.

(iii) Cash account debit: 17 November £172, corresponding with the entry on the bank statement on 19 November: £172.

(iv) Cash account debit: 24 November £1,246, corresponding with the entry on the bank statement on 27 November: £1,246.

The above entries in the cash account and bank statement can be marked off.

(c) He compares the bank statement payments column and the cash account credit side. He notes that there is a cash account entry on 19 November for £1,524 which corresponds with the entry on the bank statement on 30 November for £1,524. These two entries can therefore be marked off.

(d) He adjusts the balance on the cash account by:

(i) Correcting the error in relation to the credit entry on 5 November: K £1,810.

(ii) Listing entries in the bank statement payments column which are not in the cash account credit side. Bank charges: £138. Returned cheque: £1,246.

(iii) Listing entries in the bank statement receipts column which are not in the cash account debit side. A direct transfer of £168.

OFFICE CASH ACCOUNT

Date	Details	Dr	Cr	Balance
		£	£	£
Nov 30	Balance			1,942 Dr
	K: correction of error		40	
	Bank charges		138	
	G: dishonoured cheque		1,246	
	A: direct transfer	168		686 Dr

(e) He prepares the bank reconciliation statement by:
(i) Listing late credits: H, £1,536; J, £170.
(ii) Listing unpresented cheques: M, £374; N, £86; P, £472.

BANK RECONCILIATION STATEMENT AS AT 30 NOVEMBER

		£
Balance as per bank statement		88 Dr
Add unpresented cheques		
M	£374	
N	£86	
P	£472	932
		1,020
Deduct late credits		
H	£1,536	
J	£170	1,706
Balance as per adjusted cash account		686

8.8 EXERCISES ON BANK RECONCILIATION

1   Bill, a solicitor, receives a bank statement for his office account for the month of July and it shows an overdraft of £44 at the end of the month. Bill cannot understand how the bank arrives at this figure as he endeavours to maintain a credit balance at the bank at all times. The bank statement shows the following entries:

STIFFCHARGE BANK PLC
POUNDLAND BRANCH
ACCOUNT: BILL, OFFICE ACCOUNT

Date	Details	Payments	Receipts	Balance
		£	£	£
July 1	Balance brought forward			734 Cr
July 8	Credits		318	1,052
July 15	Credits		1,174	
	842	684		1,542
July 19	Credits		86	
	844	925		703
July 27	Credits		623	1,326
July 30	846	762		
	Charges	69		
	Cheque returned	623		
	Paid in by N		84	44 Dr

Bill's office cash account for the month of July shows:

OFFICE CASH ACCOUNT

Date	Details	Dr	Cr	Balance
		£	£	£
July 1	Balance			50 Dr
July 3	P	140		190
July 5	T	178		368
	G		905	537 Cr
	M	695		158 Dr
July 10	K	479		637
July 17	J	86		723
July 19	TP		762	39 Cr
July 24	S	623		584 Dr
July 28	R		187	397
	Q		43	354
	A		236	118
July 30	N	768		886
July 31	TWT	85		971 Dr

The cheque issued to G on 5 July was for £925 and was incorrectly entered in the cash account as £905.

Prepare a bank reconciliation statement for Bill and effect any other accounting entries which you consider necessary so that the cash account accords with normal accounting practice.

(Law Society Final Examination)

2   Tom, a solicitor, receives a bank statement for his office account for the month of June which shows a balance at the end of the month of £403 Cr. The bank statement shows the following entries:

WESTERN BANK
ANYTOWN BRANCH
ACCOUNT: TOM, OFFICE

Date	Details	Payments	Receipts	Balance
		£	£	£
June 25	Balance			284 Cr
June 26	Credit		5	289
June 28	Credit		110	399
June 29	A	35		364
	Charges	4		360
June 30	Credit transfer: H		43	403 Cr

Tom's office cash account for the month of June shows:

OFFICE CASH ACCOUNT

Date	Details	Dr	Cr	Balance
		£	£	£
June 25	Balance			284 Dr
June 26	J	50		334
June 28	B	110		444
June 29	S	36		480
	A		35	445
	H		73	372
	R		6	366
June 30	U		4	362 Dr

The cheque received from J was for £5 and is incorrectly shown in the cash account as £50.

You are required to correct the cash account and to prepare a bank reconciliation statement for Tom.

(Law Society Final Examination)

8.9   SUGGESTED ANSWERS TO EXERCISES ON BANK RECONCILIATION

1   OFFICE CASH ACCOUNT

Date	Details	Dr	Cr	Balance
		£	£	£
July 31	Balance			971 Dr
	G		20	951
	N	84		1,035
	Cheque returned		623	412
	Charges		69	343

BANK RECONCILIATION STATEMENT AS AT 31 JULY

		£
Balance as per bank statement		44 Dr
Add unpresented cheques		
R	£187	
Q	£ 43	
A	£236	466
		510
Deduct late credits		
N	£768	
TWT	£ 85	853
Balance as per adjusted cash account		343 Cr

2   OFFICE CASH ACCOUNT

Date	Details	Dr	Cr	Balance
		£	£	£
June 30	Balance			362 Dr
	Correction of error		45	317
	Credit transfer	43		360
	Bank charges		4	356 Dr

BANK RECONCILIATION STATEMENT AS AT 30 JUNE

	£
Balance as per bank statement	403 Cr
Deduct unpresented cheques	
H £73	
R £ 6	
U £ 4	83
	320
Add late credits	
S £36	36
Balance as per adjusted cash account	356 Cr

8.10   TEST ON BANK RECONCILIATION

Allow a maximum of 1 hour to complete this test.

1   The office cash account of Smith shows a debit balance of £642 as at 30 April but when the bank statement for that month is received, it shows that Smith has an overdraft of £247. Smith cannot understand how the difference between the two balances has arisen, as they have both been ascertained as at 30 April. Smith now has to meet a payment of £228 and he requests you to investigate the position. Prepare a bank reconciliation statement for Smith, and effect any other accounting entries in the office cash account you deem necessary so that the accounts accurately reflect the transactions and accord with normal accounting practice.

Smith's office cash account shows the following entries for the month of April:

OFFICE CASH ACCOUNT

Date	Details	Dr	Cr	Balance
		£	£	£
Apr 1	Balance			747 Dr
Apr 2	PQR Ltd		456	291
Apr 6	FG		679	388 Cr
Apr 7	M Ltd	463		75 Dr
Apr 8	PU & Co	197		272
Apr 10	DBN Ltd		156	116
Apr 14	STD Ltd	965		1,081
Apr 15	KOJ		431	650
Apr 16	S Ltd	87		737
Apr 20	FGR		420	317
Apr 21	TP Ltd	452		769
Apr 23	ABC	780		1,549
	JQN		95	1,454
Apr 28	GCE		323	1,131
Apr 29	KLM	345		1,476
	Smith		600	876
Apr 30	TDB	876		1,752
	Wages etc.		837	915
	JHO		273	642 Dr

The bank statement shows the following entries:

OSSIFIC PANK PLC

ACCOUNT: SMITH

Date	Details	Withdrawals	Deposits	Balance
		£	£	£
Apr 1	Balance			1,296 Cr
	Credits		295	1,591
Apr 2	223	305		1,286
Apr 6	225	456		830
Apr 7	224	539		291
	Credits		463	754
Apr 8	Giro direct transfer		323	1,077
	Credits		197	1,274
Apr 13	226	679		595
Apr 15	Credits		965	1,560
	227	156		1,404
Apr 19	Credits		87	1,491
	228	431		1,060
Apr 23	Credits		1,232	2,292
	229	420		1,872
Apr 28	Cheque returned	87		1,785
	Standing banker's order	300		1,485
Apr 29	230	295		1,190
Apr 30	233	837		353
	232	600		247 Dr

The cheque issued to JQN on 23 April for £295 was entered in the cash account as £95 in error.

(Law Society Final Examination)

2 On 30 September 1991, the office account cash book of James and Peter showed an overdraft of £500. James and Peter cannot understand how the bank arrives at the overdraft figure of £2,500 shown on the bank statement. When the cashier compares the bank statement and office account cash book, she discovers the following:

(a)   Bank charges £750.
(b)   Interest on overdraft £500.
(c)   Standing order £250.

None of these items has been recorded in the office cash book.

(d)   A cheque for £100 received by the firm has been shown incorrectly in the cash book as a payment.
(e)   A cheque for £280 in respect of client costs, paid into the office account, has been dishonoured. The first notice of dishonour given to the firm was in the bank statement.
(f)   A cheque drawn for rates for £600 was incorrectly entered in the cash book as £100.
(g)   Unpresented cheques total £160.
(h)   Late credits total £80.

From the above information, show the bank reconciliation statement and any necessary adjustments to the office cash account.

8.11   SUGGESTED ANSWERS TO TEST ON BANK RECONCILIATION

1   OFFICE CASH ACCOUNT

Date	Details	Dr	Cr	Balance
		£	£	£
Apr 30	Balance			642 Dr
	Credit transfer	323		965
	Cheque returned		87	878
	Standing order		300	578
	Correction of error		200	378 Dr

BANK RECONCILIATION STATEMENT AS AT 30 APRIL

	£
Balance as per bank statement	247 Dr
Add unpresented cheques	
GCE £323	
JHO £273	596
	843 Dr
Deduct late credits	
KLM £345	
TDB £876	1,221
Balance as per adjusted cash account	378 Cr

Note: The difference in the opening balance of £549 is accounted for as follows:

	£
(Bank statement) withdrawals	305
(Unpresented cheques from last accounting period)	539
	844
Less (bank statements) deposits	295
(Late credits from last accounting period)	549

2   OFFICE CASH ACCOUNT

Date	Details	Dr	Cr	Balance
1988		£	£	£
Sept	Balance			500 Cr
	Charges		750	1,250
	Interest		500	1,750
	Standing orders		250	2,000
	Correction of error	200		1,800
	Dishonoured cheque		280	2,080
	Correction of error			
	(rates)		500	2,580 Cr

BANK RECONCILIATION STATEMENT AS AT 30 SEPTEMBER 1988

	£
Balance as per bank statement	2,500 Dr
Add unpresented cheques	160
	2,660
Deduct late credits	80
Overdraft as per adjusted cash account	2,580 Dr

9 Revision Tests

The revision tests are intended to give practice in a full accounts examination paper. Each test is of two hours' duration and should be done under test conditions.

9.1 TEST ONE

Each question in this test is of one hour's duration and both questions are of equal weight.

1 Black, Bantam and Redhen, solicitors, act for Leghorn in the purchase of a house, 'Roosters', for £60,000 and the sale of his existing house, 'Cockrow', for £50,000. There is a mortgage on 'Cockrow' of £5,000 and the same building society has agreed to advance the sum of £15,000 towards the purchase price of 'Roosters'. The firm has been instructed by the building society to act on its behalf in these matters. The following events and transactions take place:

1991

9 April	Paid by petty cash, local land charges search fee re 'Roosters' £10.
11 April	Paid survey fee £282 (including £42) in respect of 'Roosters'.
17 April	The firm having given the necessary undertaking, a cheque for £6,000 is received from HXYZ Finance Ltd to be used as a bridging loan in the purchase of 'Roosters'.
20 April	Exchanged contracts for the sale of 'Cockrow', the deposit of £5,000 having been paid to the estate agents, by the prospective purchaser. On the same day contracts for the purchase of 'Roosters' are exchanged, the deposit of £6,000 being paid to the vendor's solicitors who are to act as stakeholders.

22 April	Received completion statement from the vendor's solicitors, showing £54,000 due, being the balance of purchase money. Sent completion statement to purchaser's solicitors, showing balance due in respect of 'Cockrow'.
29 April	Sent financial statement to Leghorn together with bill of costs. The latter shows profit costs of £660 excluding VAT (sale £250; purchase £350; mortgage £40; redemption of mortgage £20). The financial statement shows, *inter alia*, the following details:

Land Registry fees	£150
Estate agent's commission (including VAT £157.50)	£1,057.50
Stamp duty	£1,200
Interest on bridging loan	£80
Bankruptcy search fee	£1
Redemption of mortgage on 'Cockrow'	£5,063

5 May	Paid £1 from petty cash, in respect of bankruptcy search.
6 May	Received the balance of purchase money, together with costs, from Leghorn.
8 May	Received mortgage advance from building society in respect of 'Roosters'.
9 May	Completed purchase and sale of properties. Received from estate agents, the balance of the deposit on 'Cockrow' less their commission and VAT thereon. Loan of £6,000 together with accrued interest of £80 repaid to HXYZ Finance Ltd. Sent cheque for redemption monies to building society.
11 May	Paid stamp duty on transfer and Land Registry fees.
12 May	Transferred costs and disbursements from client account to office account.

Write up the ledger account of Leghorn, showing all the entries necessary to deal with the above events, and prepare a suitable financial statement for presentation to Leghorn on 29 April 1991. The rate of value added tax is to be taken as 17.5%.

(50 marks)
(Law Society Final Examination, updated)

2   Coffee and Cream practise in partnership as solicitors, and their partnership agreement shows the following relevant details:

(a)   Profits and losses to be shared so that Coffee receives 3/5ths and Cream 2/5ths.

(b)   Partnership salaries of £8,000 and £10,000 to be charged for Coffee and Cream respectively before profits are shared.

(c)   Interest is to be allowed on capital at the rate of 10 per cent per annum, and charged on drawings at 5 per cent per annum.

The firm's bookkeeper extracts the following information from the books of account, for the year ended 31 March 1991:

Partners' capital accounts	
Coffee	£30,000
Cream	£10,000
Partners' current accounts	
Coffee	£1,350 Cr
Cream	£200 Dr
Partners' drawings	
Coffee	£18,000
Cream	£12,000
General expenses	£33,249
Administration expenses	£51,372
Interest received	£4,267
Profit costs account	£132,593
Due from clients	£24,622
Due to creditors	£2,898
Furniture, library and equipment at cost	£6,394
Accumulated depreciation written off furniture, library and equipment to 31 March 1990	£3,894
Motor cars at cost	£12,456
Accumulated depreciation written off motor cars to 31 March 1990	£4,056
Leasehold premises at cost	£15,000
Amount due to clients	£112,364
Petty cash balance	£43
Work in progress at 1 April 1990	£11,230
Cash at bank: client account	£112,364
Cash at bank: office account	£4,492

Depreciation is to be charged at the following amounts:

Furniture, library and equipment	£500
Motor cars	£3,100

On 31 March 1991, administration expenses prepaid amount to £245, whilst general expenses which are outstanding and not yet accounted for amount to £1,248. At the same date, work in progress is valued at £14,894.

Interest to be allowed on partners' capital is as follows:

Coffee	£3,000
Cream	£1,000

The partners agree that the amounts to be charged in respect of interest on drawings for the year, will be £450 for Coffee and £300 for Cream.

From the above information prepare a profit and loss and appropriation account for the year ended 31 March 1991, together with a balance sheet as at that date.

50 marks
(Law Society Final Examination, updated)

9.2 SUGGESTED ANSWERS TO TEST ONE

1 Black, Bantam and Redhen

FINANCIAL STATEMENT

To: Leghorn
Re: Sale of 'Cockrow'
    Purchase of 'Roosters'

	£	£	£
Sale of Cockrow			
Receipts: Deposit	5,000		
Balance of sale price	45,000	50,000	
Less: Payments			
Mortgage redemption	5,063		
Redemption costs	23.50		
Estate agent's commission	1,057.50		
Costs	250		
VAT thereon at 17.5%	43.75	6,437.75	
Net sale proceeds			43,562.25
Less: Purchase of 'Roosters'			
Payments: Deposit	6,000		
Balance of purchase price	54,000		
Mortgage advance cost	47		
Search fees	11		
Survey fee	276		
Stamp duty	1,200		
Land registry fees	150		
Interest on bridging loan	80		
Costs	350		
VAT thereon at 17.5%	61.25	62,175.25	
Less: Receipts:			
Mortgage advance		15,000	47,175.25
Amount required to complete purchase			47,175.25
Less amount due from sale			43,562.25
Amount required to complete			3,613.00

LEGHORN ACCOUNT

Date	Details	Office account			Client account		
1991		Dr £	Cr £	Balance £	Dr £	Cr £	Balance £
Apr 9	Petty cash: search fee	10		10 Dr			
Apr 11	Cash: survey fee	276		286 Dr			
Apr 17	Cash: HXYZ (loan)					6,000	6,000 Cr
Apr 20	Cash: deposit				6,000		—
Apr 29	Costs	600					
	VAT	105		991 Dr			
	Costs (mortgage advance)	40					
	VAT	7		1,038 Dr			
	Costs (mortgage redemption	20					
	VAT	3.50		1,061.50 Dr			
May 5	Petty cash: bankruptcy search fee	1		1,062.50 Dr			
May 6	Cash: you					3,613	3,613 Cr
May 9	Cash: building society mortgage advance					15,000	18,613 Cr
	Cash: purchaser					45,000	63,613 Cr
	Cash: estate agent (deposit less commission)					3,942.50	67,555.50 Cr
	Cash: vendor				54,000		13,555.50 Cr
	Cash: HXYZ loan repayment				6,080		7,475.50 Cr
	Cash: building society: mortgage redemption				5,063		2,412.50 Cr
May 11	Cash: stamp duty				1,200		1,212.50 Cr
	Cash: Land Registry fee				150		1,062.50 Cr
May 12	Cash: transfer costs				1,062.50		—
	Cash: transfer costs		1,062.50	—			

2   Coffee & Cream

PROFIT AND LOSS AND APPROPRIATION ACCOUNT FOR THE YEAR ENDED 31 MARCH 1991

INCOME	£	£	£
Profit costs			132,593
Add: Closing work in progress			14,894
			147,487
Less: Opening work in progress			11,230
			136,257
Interest received			4,267
			140,524
LESS: EXPENDITURE			
General expenses			
£33,249 +			
£ 1,248		34,497	
Administration expenses			
£51,372 –			
£ 245		51,127	
Depreciation			
Furniture etc	500		
Cars	3,100	3,600	89,224
NET PROFIT			51,300
APPROPRIATION ACCOUNT			
NET PROFIT			51,300
INTEREST ON DRAWINGS			
Coffee	450		
Cream	300		750
			52,050

SALARIES	£	£	£
Coffee	8,000		
Cream	10,000		18,000
INTEREST ON CAPITAL			
Coffee	3,000		
Cream	1,000		4,000
PROFIT SHARE			
Coffee: 3/5ths	18,030		
Cream: 2/5ths	12,020		30,050
			52,050

MOVEMENTS ON PARTNERS' CURRENT ACCOUNTS

	Coffee	Cream
Balance	1,350 Cr	200 Dr
Salary	8,000	10,000
Interest on capital	3,000	1,000
Profit share	18,030	12,020
	30,380	22,820
Less: drawings	18,000	12,000
	12,380	10,820
Less interest on drawings	450	300
	11,930 Cr	10,520 Cr

BALANCE SHEET AS AT 31 MARCH 1991

CAPITAL EMPLOYED	£	£	£
Capital accounts			
Coffee		30,000	
Cream		10,000	40,000
Current accounts			
Coffee		11,930	
Cream		10,520	22,450
			62,450
EMPLOYMENT OF CAPITAL			
FIXED ASSETS			
Leasehold premises		15,000	
Furniture, etc., at cost	6,394		
Less: Accumulated depreciation	4,394	2,000	
Motor cars at cost	12,456		
Less: Accumulated depreciation	7,156	5,300	22,300
CURRENT ASSETS			
Closing work in progress	14,894		
Petty cash	43		
Bank: office account	4,492		
Debtors	24,622		
Payment in advance	245	44,296	
LESS: CURRENT LIABILITIES			
Creditors	2,898		
Outstanding expenses	1,248	4,146	40,150
Cash at bank client account			112,364
Less: Due to clients			112,364
			62,450

9.3   TEST TWO

1   Arm, Chair and Settle are solicitors; during the month of December 1991 they deal with the following events, and you are required to write up the clients' ledger accounts, showing all the entries relevant to those events. All the accounts are to be balanced and the rate of value added tax is to be taken as 17.5%.

1 December   The sum of £5,000, which has been held on behalf of Jack for three months, is repaid to Jack, together with interest of £175, which was credited by the bank in the designated deposit account opened by the firm.

2 December   Received cheque drawn in favour of George, for £2,345, which is forwarded to George. A bill of costs is sent to George in respect of services rendered by the firm, showing the agreed fee of £80 plus VAT, which amount had been received by the firm in the previous month. This fee is now abated by £20 plus VAT. The amount due to George is paid by cheque, and the account is then closed.

4 December   Following a request by Tom, a cheque for £1,000 is sent to one of his creditors, and later the same day, a cheque is received from Tom for £800 in partial satisfaction.

8 December   Cheque received (£3,500) from Ken (who is not a client) being the deposit on the sale of a house by Harold, the firm to hold as stakeholders. Paid cash disbursements of £3 same day in respect of the sale of Harold's house.

10 December   The bank notifies the firm that the cheque from Tom has been returned unpaid by the paying bankers.

11 December   A bill of costs is received from the solicitor acting as agent on behalf of the firm, in connection with the affairs of Casanova. The bill shows disbursements of £15 (no VAT) and profit costs of £120 less agency commission of £40 (exclusive of VAT). Casanova had already paid £150 on account of costs generally, and a bill of costs is now sent to him, showing profit costs £140 plus VAT (including agent's profit costs) and disbursements £15.

14 December   The firm decides to write off the sum of £115 (inclusive of VAT), which is owed to the firm by Jill who has been adjudicated bankrupt.

16 December Cheque received for £3,000, by the firm, indorsed over to Phillip, who is a client.

18 December Received cheque from Gladys (£500) on account of costs generally. Cheque (£50) drawn on client account same day, and sent to enquiry agent.

21 December Chair, a partner in the firm, hands over a cheque to the firm's cashier for £2,000, being the deposit on a country cottage which he is purchasing. The firm is acting on his behalf in this matter.

22 December Sent cheque to agent who acted on behalf of firm, in the matter relating to Casanova, the cheque being drawn on office account.

23 December Received cheque from Casanova, in settlement of his account.

30 December Banker's draft for £31,500 received in respect of the sale of Harold's house (contracts having been exchanged on 8 December 1991), the relevant amount being transferred from stakeholder account the same day. The firm also acts for the mortgagees of the house, Ben a private lender, and £4,934 is transferred to that client account, representing the principal sum together with accrued interest. It has been agreed that Ben's costs (£20 plus VAT), will be borne by Harold. The amount due to Ben is paid the same day.

31 December Paid by cheque, estate agent's fees (£700 plus VAT) re the sale of Harold's house. Harold agrees to the transfer of £1,000 from the proceeds of sale, to the account of Tom, who is his nephew, and Tom's cheque for £800 is then cancelled. Bill of costs rendered to Harold, showing profit costs of £400 plus VAT, and cash disbursements £3 (no VAT).

50 marks

(Law Society Final Examination, amended and updated)

2   Zebedee and Nedd are in partnership as solicitors, sharing profits and losses so that Zebedee receives three quarters and Nedd one quarter. A partnership salary of £15,000 per annum is payable to Nedd, and each partner is entitled to interest on capital at the rate of 10 per cent per annum.

Credo is admitted into the partnership on 1 October 1991, contributing £20,000 as his share of capital in the firm. From the inception of the new partnership, profits and losses are to be shared between the partners so that Zebedee receives one half, Nedd one quarter and Credo one quarter. The former arrangements for partnership salary and interest on capital are cancelled.

The following balances are extracted from the firm's books for the year ended 31 March 1992:

Drawings	£
Zebedee	27,000
Nedd	18,000
Credo	10,000
Current accounts	
Zebedee	8,622 Cr
Nedd	1,124 Dr
Capital accounts	
Zebedee	40,000
Nedd	20,000
Credo	20,000
Lease at cost	30,000
Motor cars at cost	20,000
to 31 March 1991 motor cars,	
to 31 March 1982	12,000
Library, furniture and computer at cost	26,300
Profit costs	240,678
Interest receivable	15,956
Administrative and general expenses	159,205
Due from clients	30,470
Bad debts	843
Cash at bank: office account	4,786
Petty cash balance	124
Cash at bank: client account	176,897
Due to clients	176,897
Due to creditors	4,456
Work in progress as at 1 April 1991	33,860

The partners decided to charge depreciation of £4,000 against motor cars and £4,200 against the library, furniture and computer. They also decide to write off £3,000 from the cost of the lease. The following information is relevant:

(a) Work in progress at 31 March 1992 is valued at £40,298.

(b) Zebedee and Nedd are entitled to interest on capital of £2,000 and £1,000 respectively.

(c) Administrative and general expenses amounting to £1,896 are owing at 31 March 1992, and no action has yet been taken in respect of them.

(d) Additional bad debts, amounting to £270, are written off, and a provision is to be made for estimated bad debts of £658.

(e) The allocation of profits between partners is to be determined on a time basis (calculations to be made in months).

From the above information, prepare a profit and loss and appropriation account for the year ended 31 March 1992, together with a balance sheet as at that date, using the vertical form of presentation.

Movements on partners' current accounts must be shown in detail.

50 marks
(Law Society Final Examination, updated)

9.4 SUGGESTED ANSWERS TO TEST TWO

1 Arm, Chair and Settle

JACK

Designated deposit account
Opened September 1991
Closed 1 December 1991

Date	Details	Office account			Client account		
		Dr £	Cr £	Balance £	Dr £	Cr £	Balance £
1991 Dec 1	Balance					5,000	5,000 Cr
	Deposit: cash: interest					175	5,175 Cr
	Cash: you				5,175		———

GEORGE

Date	Details	Office account			Client account		
1991		Dr £	Cr £	Balance £	Dr £	Cr £	Balance £
Nov	Cost (agreed fee)	80					
	VAT	14		94 Dr			
	Cash: you		94	—			
Dec 2	Cheque in favour of you					2,345	
	Cheque to you (memorandum only)				2,345		
	Costs: abatement		20				
	VAT: abatement		3.50	23.50 Cr			
	Cash: you	23.50		—			

TOM

Date	Details	Office account			Client account		
1991		Dr £	Cr £	Balance £	Dr £	Cr £	Balance £
Dec 4	Cash: creditor	1,000		1,000 Dr			
	Cash: you		800	200 Dr			
Dec 10	Cash: dishonoured cheque	800		1,000 Dr			
Dec 31	Cash: transfer from Harold		1,000	——			

STAKEHOLDER

Date	Details	Office account			Client account		
		Dr £	Cr £	Balance £	Dr £	Cr £	Balance £
1991							
Dec 8	Cash: deposit (Harold)					3,500	
Dec 30	Harold: transfer				3,500		——

JILL

Date	Details	Office account			Client account		
		Dr £	Cr £	Balance £	Dr £	Cr £	Balance £
1991							
	Balance			115 Dr			
Dec 14	Bad debts (written off)		100				
	Customs and Excise: VAT written off		15	——			

HAROLD

Date	Details	Office account			Client account		
		Dr £	Cr £	Balance £	Dr £	Cr £	Balance £
1991							
Dec 8	Petty cash: disbursement	3		3 Dr			
Dec 30	Cash: sale proceeds					31,500	31,500 Cr
	Stakeholder: transfer: deposit					3,500	35,000 Cr
	Ben: transfer: redemption				4,934		30,066 Cr
	Ben: transfer: costs	23.50		26.50 Dr			
Dec 31	Cash: estate agent				805		29,261 Cr
	Cash: transfer to Tom				1,000		28,261 Cr
	Costs	400					
	VAT	70		496.50			

Date	Details	Office account			Client account		
		Dr £	Cr £	Balance £	Dr £	Cr £	Balance £
	Cash: transfer: costs				496.50		27,764.50 Cr
	Cash: transfer: costs		496.50	—			

PHILLIP

Date	Details	Office account			Client account		
		Dr £	Cr £	Balance £	Dr £	Cr £	Balance £
1991 Dec 16	Cash (indorsed cheque)					3,000	3,000 Cr
	Cash: you (indorsed cheque)				3,000		—

CASANOVA

Date	Details	Office account			Client account		
		Dr £	Cr £	Balance £	Dr £	Cr £	Balance £
1991 Dec 11	Cash: you					150	150 Cr
	Costs	140					
	VAT	24.50		164.50 Dr			
Dec 22	Cash: disbursement	15		179.50			
Dec 23	Cash: you		29.50	150			
	Cash: transfer: costs				150		—
	Cash: transfer: costs		150	—			

GLADYS

Date	Details	Office account			Client account		
		Dr £	Cr £	Balance £	Dr £	Cr £	Balance £
1991 Dec 18	Cash: you					500	500 Cr
	Cash: enquiry agent				50		450 Cr

BEN

Date	Details	Office account			Client account		
		Dr £	Cr £	Balance £	Dr £	Cr £	Balance £
1991 Dec 30	Harold: transfer: redemption					4,934	4,934 Cr
	Costs	20					
	VAT	3.50		23.50 Dr			
	Harold: transfer: costs		23.50	—			
	Cash: you				4,934		—

Note:

As Chair is a partner he cannot be treated as a client and so a client ledger account should not be shown for him.

2   Zebedee, Nedd & Credo

PROFIT AND LOSS AND APPROPRIATION ACCOUNT FOR THE YEAR ENDED 31 MARCH 1992

INCOME	£	£	£
Profit costs		240,678	
Add: Work in progress 31 March 1992		40,298	
		280,976	
Less: Work in progress 1 April 1991		33,860	
			247,116
Interest receivable			15,956
			263,072
EXPENDITURE			
Administration and general expenses		161,101	
Bad debts		1,771	
Depreciation			
Motor cars	4,000		
Library, furniture and computer	4,200		
Amount written off lease	3,000	11,200	
			174,072
NET PROFIT FOR THE YEAR			89,000

DIVISIBLE thus:		Six months to 30 Sept. 1991		Six months to 31 March 1992	
Partner's salary: Nedd		7,500			7,500
Interest on capital					
Zebedee	£2,000				
Nedd	£1,000	3,000			3,000
Share of net profit					
Zebedee	¾	25,500	½	22,250	47,750
Nedd	¼	8,500	¼	11,125	19,625
Credo			¼	11,125	11,125
		44,500		44,500	89,000

MOVEMENTS ON PARTNERS' CURRENT ACCOUNTS

	Zebedee £	Nedd £	Credo £
Balance at 1 April 1991	8,622	(1,124)	
Salary		7,500	
Interest on capital	2,000	1,000	
Share of net profit	47,750	19,625	11,125
	58,372	27,001	11,125
Drawings	27,000	18,000	10,000
Balance at 31 March 1992	31,372	9,001	1,125

ZEBEDEE, NEDD & CREDO
BALANCE SHEET AS AT 31 MARCH 1992

CAPITAL EMPLOYED	£	£	£
Partners' capital accounts			
Zebedee		40,000	
Nedd		20,000	
Credo		20,000	
			80,000
Partners' current accounts			
Zebedee		31,372	
Nedd		9,001	
Credo		1,125	
			41,498
			121,498

EMPLOYMENT OF CAPITAL

FIXED ASSETS	£	£	£
Lease at cost	30,000		
Less: Amount written off	3,000		
		27,000	
Motor cars at cost	20,000		
Less: Accumulated depreciation	16,000		
		4,000	
Library, furniture and computer			
at cost	26,300		
Less: Depreciation	4,200		
		22,100	
			53,100

CURRENT ASSETS				
Work in progress		40,298		
Debtors	£30,200			
Less: Provision	£ 658			
		29,542		
Cash at bank		4,786		
Petty cash		124		
			74,750	

CURRENT LIABILITIES			
Creditors	4,456		
Accrued expenses	1,896		
		6,352	
			68,398

CLIENT ACCOUNT		
Balance at bank		176,897
Less: Due to clients		176,897
		121,498

9.5   TEST THREE

1   Ruff, Clobber & Co., solicitors, are instructed by the executors of Stringvest deceased to administer the estate on their behalf. The gross value of the estate amounts to £42,000 and consists of a house valued

at £28,000 (subject to a mortgage of £7,000) and personalty valued at £14,000. There are sundry debts due by the estate amounting to £625. The following events take place.

1991

4 November The deceased's bank agrees to advance the sum of £3,415 to the executors so that they may pay the capital transfer tax in respect of the estate. The sum is credited to the client account of Ruff, Clobber & Co., who then issue a cheque in favour of the Inland Revenue for the same amount. Probate fees of £50 are paid by the firm's cheque.

9 November Grant received and registered with the bank who transfer all monies due by them to the deceased (£353) to the executors' loan account with the bank.

15 November A cheque for £12 is drawn in respect of the statutory advertisements, the cost of the local advertisement (£5) being met by a payment out of petty cash.

18 November The deceased's account with the Grandiose Building Society is closed, and an amount is transferred to the executors' loan account with the bank, thus closing the account. The balance remaining in the building society account (£48) is paid into client account.

21 November Proceeds of life policy received, the whole amount (£8,000) being placed in a designated deposit account.

27 November The household contents are sold and a cheque for £2,190 is received from the auctioneer. Commission of £241 including VAT, had already been deducted.

4 December Contracts are exchanged for the sale of the house for £28,500, and a deposit of £2,850 is received by the firm to hold as stakeholders.

21 December Debts amounting to £782 are paid.

31 December Paid funeral expenses £319.

1992

4 January The sale of the house is completed and a bank draft (£25,650) for the balance of the purchase money is received. The mortgage is redeemed by the payment of £7,226 which is inclusive of accrued interest.

10 January   A pecuniary legacy amounting to £5,000 is paid to the legatee.

12 January   Bill of costs re sale is prepared and agreed with the executors, profit costs being £250 and VAT thereon £43.75, estate agent's charges paid by cheque £655 (including VAT) and cash disbursements of £15. The amount due is transferred to office account.

14 January   Bill of costs for the administration of the estate, profit costs £400 (exclusive of VAT) plus VAT thereon £70 and disbursements, rendered to the executors and after receiving their agreement, the amount due is transferred to office account.

20 January   The balance of monies now held by Ruff, Clobber & Co. is paid to Tophat, the residuary legatee, on behalf of the executors. Interest earned on the designated deposit account amounted to £135, whilst the interest to be allowed on other monies held by the firm on behalf of of the executors is £53.

Show the client's ledger account of the executors of Stringvest deceased.   *50 marks*

(**Law Society Final Examination, updated**)

2   Smith practises as a solicitor, and he decides to admit Jones into the practice as a partner on 1 January 1992. Their partnership agreement shows the following relevant details:

(a)   Jones is to be allowed a salary of £6,000 per annum, together with a one fifth share of the profits or losses remaining, after the salary and interest on partners' capital has been charged.

(b)   Interest is to be allowed on partners' capital at the rate of 10 per cent per annum.

The firm's bookkeeper has already produced a draft set of accounts for the year ended 31 March 1992, and these can be summarised as follows:

	£
Net profit for the year, before charging any amounts in respect of interest on capital or partnership salary	20,112
Furniture, library and equipment at cost	5,920
Accumulated depreciation written off furniture, library and equipment to 31 March 1992	2,320
Motor cars at cost	11,540
Accumulated depreciation written off motor cars to 31 March 1992	5,300
Freehold premises at cost	45,000
Mortgage on freehold premises (credit balance)	25,000
Clients' ledger balances	
Office account	18,675
Client account	196,342
Amounts due to creditors	2,876
Work in progress at 31 March 1992	11,874
Cash at bank: Office account	3,822
Client account:	
Deposit account	150,000
Current account	46,342
Petty cash balance	27
Partners' capital accounts	
Smith (balance at 1 April 1991)	57,000
Jones (balance at 1 January 1992)	5,000
Partners' drawings	
Smith	18,500
Jones	2,250

After the bookkeeper has presented the partners with the draft set of accounts, it is decided that an amount of £162, owed to the firm by a client, should be written off as irrecoverable and that a further amount of £150 should be provided for doubtful debts.

As is customary in such cases, the allocation of profits between the partners is to be determined on a time basis.

The partners of the firm request that you prepare a profit and loss appropriation account for the year ended 31 March 1992, together with a balance sheet as at that date.

50 marks
(Law Society Final Examination, updated)

9.6   SUGGESTED ANSWERS TO TEST THREE

1   Ruff, Clobber & Co.

EXECUTORS OF STRINGVEST, DECEASED

Designated deposit
Account opened 21 November 1991
Closed 20 January 1992

Date	Details	Office account			Client account		
		Dr £	Cr £	Balance £	Dr £	Cr £	Balance £
1991							
Nov 4	Cash: bank loan					3,415	3,415 Cr
	Cash: CTT				3,415		—
	Cash: probate fee	50		50 Dr			
Nov 15	Cash: statutory advertisements	12		62			
	Petty cash: local advertisements	5		67			
Nov 18	Cash: Grandiose Building Society					48	48 Cr
Nov 21	Deposit: cash: life policy					8,000	8,048 Cr
Nov 27	Cash: contents (less auctioneer's commission)					2,190	10,238 Cr
Dec 21	Cash: debts				782		9,456 Cr
Dec 31	Cash: funeral expenses				319		9,137 Cr
1992							
Jan 4	Cash: sale					25,650	34,787 Cr
	Stakeholder: transfer					2,850	37,637 Cr
	Cash: mortgage redemption				7,226		30,411 Cr
Jan 10	Cash: legacy				5,000		25,411 Cr
Jan 12	Costs: sale	250					
	VAT	43.75		360.75			
	Cash: estate agent				655		24,756 Cr
	Cash: disbursements	15		375.75			
	Cash: transfer: costs				308.75		24,447.25 Cr
	Cash: transfer: costs		308.75	67			

Date	Details	Office account			Client account		
		Dr £	Cr £	Balance £	Dr £	Cr £	Balance £
Jan 14	Costs: administration	400					
	VAT	70					
	Cash: transfer: costs		527	537 Dr	537		
				—			23,910.25 Cr
Jan 20	Deposit cash: interest					135	24,045.25 Cr
	Cash: interest					53	24,098.25 Cr
	Cash: Tophat				24,098.25		—

2   Smith & Jones

PROFIT AND LOSS AND APPROPRIATION ACCOUNT TO 31 MARCH 1992

	£	£
Net profit		20,112
Less: Bad debts	162	
Provision	150	312
Adjusted net profit		19,800

APPROPRIATION ACCOUNT FOR 9 MONTHS TO 31 DECEMBER 1991

Net profit to 31 December 1991 to Smith (9 months)	14,850

APPROPRIATION ACCOUNT FOR 3 MONTHS TO 31 MARCH 1992

	£	£
Profit		4,950
SALARY		
Jones		1,500
INTEREST ON CAPITAL		
Smith	1,425	
Jones	125	1,550
SHARE OF PROFIT		
Smith	1,520	
Jones	380	
		1,900
		4,950

MOVEMENTS ON PARTNERS' CURRENT ACCOUNTS

	Smith	Jones
Interest on capital	1,425	125
Salary	–	1,500
Profit share	16,370	380
	17,795	2,005
Less Drawings	18,500	2,250
	705 Dr	245 Dr

BALANCE SHEET AS AT 31 MARCH 1992

CAPITAL EMPLOYED	£	£	£
Capital accounts			
Smith		57,000	
Jones		5,000	62,000
Current accounts			
Smith		705	
Jones		245	950
			61,050
Long-term liabilities			
Mortgage			25,000
			86,050

EMPLOYMENT OF CAPITAL

	£	£	£
FIXED ASSETS			
Premises		45,000	
Furniture, library and equipment at cost	5,920		
Less: Accumulated depreciation	2,320	3,600	
Motor cars at cost	11,540		
Less: Accumulated depreciation	5,300	6,240	54,840
CURRENT ASSETS			
Work in progress		11,874	
Cash at bank: office account		3,822	
Petty cash		27	
Debtors	18,675		
Less: Bad debts not already written off, and provision	312	18,363	
		34,086	
LESS: CURRENT LIABILITIES			
Creditors		2,876	31,210
CLIENT BALANCES			
Client bank balance			
Current account	46,342		
Deposit account	150,000		196,342
Less: Due to clients			196,342
			86,050

9.7   TEST FOUR

1   Brass, Gold and Silver, are solicitors, and they deal with the following events during the month of May, 1991:

1991

1 May	The firm decides to write off the sum of £345 (inclusive of VAT), which has been outstanding for some time, and is in respect of services rendered on behalf of Lead who has been adjudicated bankrupt.
3 May	A bill of costs is received from Antimony, Zinc & Co. a firm of solicitors acting as agents on behalf of the firm in connection with the affairs of Nickel. The bill shows profit costs of £600 (exclusive of VAT), and disbursements of £80 (no VAT). The sum of £400 has already been paid by Nickel on account of costs generally, and the firm now renders its own bill of costs to Nickel, showing disbursements of £80 (no VAT) and profit costs of £800 plus VAT. Both the disbursements and profit costs of the agent solicitors, are included in the foregoing amounts.
7 May	Cheque received from Germanium, being the deposit on the sale of a house by Gallium, for whom the firm act. The firm are to hold the sum (£5,000) as stakeholders.
8 May	The firm pays by cheque, the bill rendered by Antimony, Zinc & Co. in respect of the affairs of Nickel, the cheque being drawn on office account.
10 May	Exchanged contracts for the sale of Gallium's house, and paid petty cash disbursements of £12 (no VAT) on his behalf, the same day.
15 May	A designated deposit account which had been opened by the firm at the request of Cobalt, is closed, and the sum of £22,453 (inclusive of interest credited by the bank the same day, of (£953) is remitted by cheque to Cobalt.
17 May	Received cheque from Nickel, in respect of the balance due to the firm. The account is then closed.
20 May	Niobium pays cash (£124) to the firm, who act as agents for the Boron Insurance Co. Ltd. Commission currently due to the firm on that agency, amounts to £29. The firm is not under an obligation to pay commission to clients.

23 May   The bank notifies the firm, that the cheque received from Nickel has been returned unpaid by the paying bankers.

24 May   The firm acts for Copper in the collection of a debt due to him, amounting to £4,000. The debtor sends two cheques in respect of the debt, each cheque being for the sum of £2,000. One of the cheques is dated 22 May 1991 and is made payable to Brass, Gold and Silver; the other cheque is dated 22 June 1991 and is payable to Copper. A fee of £40 plus VAT has already been agreed with Copper, and this amount is deducted from the amount received by the firm from the debtor, a cheque for the balance, together with the debtor's other cheque, being sent to Copper.

28 May   Banker's draft (£45,000) received from Erbiums, Solicitors, on completion of the sale of Gallium's house. Thoriums are the mortgagees and the redemption moneys (£14,678) are remitted by cheque. Paid estate agents' fees (£1,000 plus VAT) same day, the invoice being addressed to Gallium.

29 May   Gallium agrees with the bill of costs rendered by the firm, showing profit costs of £500 (excluding VAT).

         Gallium requests that sufficient money be transferred from his account, to settle in full, his friend Nickel's indebtedness to the firm.

         After effecting the necessary transfers, a cheque for the net sum is sent to Gallium and both accounts are then closed.

31 May   The net amount due to the Boron Insurance Co. Limited is paid, being the gross premium received (£124) less commission of £17 and prior commission due (£29). The account is then closed.

You are required to show all the relevant entries on the clients' ledger accounts, and it is important that the account in which the corresponding entry would be made, is clearly identified by the appropriate entry in the details column. All accounts are to be balanced.

Ignore all forms of taxation, except VAT, which is to be taken as 17.5%.
50 marks

2   The office accountant of Smith, a practising solicitor, has prepared a trial balance from the office books, and it shows the following position:

Trial balance at 31 March 1992

	Debit £	Credit £
Capital account		70,822
Drawings	32,362	
Motor cars at cost	28,950	
Furniture and library at cost	4,880	
Computer and ancillary equipment	8,140	
Provision for depreciation accounts at 1 April 1991:		
Motor cars		12,450
Furniture and library		1,879
Computer and ancillary equipment		1,864
Administrative and general expenses	126,632	
Sundry creditors		9,204
Profit costs		173,567
Work in hand at 31 March 1991	15,448	
Due from clients	18,704	
Due to clients		141,789
Petty cash balance	87	
Interest receivable		12,675
Cash at bank – Clients' account		
Current account	42,289	
Deposit account	99,500	
Bank overdraft – Office account		2,742
Freehold land and buildings	50,000	
	426,992	426,992

After the above trial balance had been prepared, the office accountant and practice secretary decided that the following adjustments were necessary, so that the accounts would accord with normal accounting requirements:

(a) Included in the account for computer and ancillary equipment, is a cheque for £620 which represents the difference between the cost of some new equipment (£2,000) and the part exchange value of some old equipment (£1,380) which was purchased for £1,600 in the previous year. Depreciation of £400 had been charged in respect of the latter equipment and is included in the relevant depreciation account. It is the practice of the firm, not to charge depreciation on fixed assets which are sold, or disposed of, in any accounting year. No accounting entries have yet been made in respect of the purchase or sale of the equipment, other than the posting of the aforementioned cheque.

(b) An amount of £1,250 in respect of car repairs, had inadvertently been entered in the account for motor cars.

(c) Depreciation is to be charged (straight line basis) at the following rates:

Motor cars	20 per cent per annum
Furniture and library	15 per cent per annum
Computer and ancillary equipment	25 per cent per annum

(d) A member of the staff had been allowed to use the office computer on the condition that he would be charged a nominal sum in respect thereof. This sum was agreed at £100 and was paid on 21 April 1992. The adjustment is to be effected through the account for administrative and general expenses.

(e) Work in hand at 31 March 1992, was valued at £15,786.

(f) Allowance is to be made in respect of a rebate of £300, which is to be applied in reduction of a bill (still unpaid) which had been previously agreed with the client, in February 1992. VAT on the bill is to be ignored.

(g) In addition to the above adjustments, there are bills outstanding at 31 March 1992, in respect of administrative and general expenses, which have not yet been accounted for, and these amount to £876.

From the foregoing information, you are asked to prepare a profit and loss account for the year ended 31 March 1992, together with a balance sheet as at that date.

Taxation is to be ignored, for the purposes of the preparation of these accounts.

50 marks
(Solicitors Final Examination, updated)

9.8 SUGGESTED ANSWERS TO TEST FOUR

1 Brass, Gold and Silver

(a)   LEAD. SUNDRY MATTERS

Date	Details	Office account			Client account		
		Dr £	Cr £	Balance £	Dr £	Cr £	Balance £
1991	Balance			345 Dr			
May 1	Bad debts		300				
	Customs and Excise (VAT)		45	——			

(b)   NICKEL: SUNDRY MATTERS

Date	Details	Office account			Client account		
		Dr £	Cr £	Balance £	Dr £	Cr £	Balance £
1991							
May 1	Balance						400 Cr
May 3	Costs	800					
	VAT	140		940 Dr			
May 8	Cash: Antimony Zinc & Co.	80		1,020 Dr			
May 17	Cash: you		620				
	Cash: transfer: costs from client account		400	——	400		——
May 23	Cash: returned cheque	620		620 Dr			
May 29	Cash: transfer: from Gallium		620				

(c)   STAKEHOLDER

Date	Details	Office account			Client account		
		Dr £	Cr £	Balance £	Dr £	Cr £	Balance £
1991							
May 7	Cash Germanium (for Gallium)					5,000	5,000 Cr
May 28	Gallium: transfer				5,000		——

(d)

GALLIUM: SALE OF HOUSE

Date	Details	Office account Dr £	Cr £	Balance £	Client account Dr £	Cr £	Balance £
1991 May 10	Petty cash disbursements	12		12 Dr			
May 28	Cash balance of purchase moneys					45,000	45,000 Cr
	Stakeholder transfer deposit					5,000	50,000 Cr
	Cash: Thoriums: redemption				14,678		35,322 Cr
	Cash: estate agent				1,150		34,172 Cr
May 29	Costs	500					
	VAT	87.50		599.50 Dr			
	Cash: transfer to Nickel				600		33,572 Cr
	Cash: transfer		599.50	—	599.50		33,172.50 Cr
	Costs & disbursements						
	Cash: You				33,172.50		

(e)

COBALT

Designated deposit account opened . . .
Closed 15 May 1991

Date	Details	Office account Dr £	Cr £	Balance £	Client account Dr £	Cr £	Balance £
1991 May 15	Balance						21,500 Cr
	Deposit Cash: interest					953	22,453
	Cash: You				22,453		—

(f)   BORON INSURANCE COMPANY: INSURANCE AGENCY

Date	Details	Office account			Client account		
		Dr £	Cr £	Balance £	Dr £	Cr £	Balance £
1991							
May 20	Balance			29 Dr			
	Cash: Niobium					124	124 Cr
May 31	Commission receivable	17		46 Dr			
	Cash: transfer commission		46	—	46		78
	Cash: You				78		—

(g)   COPPER: DEBT COLLECTION

Date	Details	Office account			Client account		
		Dr £	Cr £	Balance £	Dr £	Cr £	Balance £
1991							
May 24	Cash: Debtor					2,000	2,000 Cr
	Costs	40					
	VAT	7		47 Dr			
	Cash to you				1,953		47 Cr
	Cash: transfer: Costs		47		47		—

Note: A memorandum entry could be made to show that the other cheque for £2,000 has been handed to the client.

2 Smith

PROFIT AND LOSS ACCOUNT FOR THE YEAR ENDED 31 MARCH 1992

Income	£	£	£
Profit costs (173,527 – 300 rebate)			173,267
Add: Closing work in progress			15,786
			189,053
Less: Opening work in progress			15,448
			173,605
Interest receivable			12,675
Profit on sale of computer equipment			180
			186,460
Less Expenditure:			
Administrative and general expenses		128,658	
(126,632 + 1,250 + 876 – 100)			
Depreciation:			
Cars		5,540	
Furniture and library		732	
Computer equipment		1,980	136,910
Net profit			49,550

BALANCE SHEET AS AT 31 MARCH 1992

Capital:	
Capital account at start	70,822
Add net profit	49,550
	120,372
Less drawings	32,362
	88,010

EMPLOYMENT OF CAPITAL	£	£	£
Fixed assets:			
Freehold premise			50,000
Cars at cost		27,700	
Less: Accumulated depreciation		17,990	9,710
Computer equipment		7,920	
Less: Accumulated depreciation			
(1,876 + 1,980 – 400)		3,444	4,476
Furniture and library at cost		4,880	
Less: Accumulated depreciation		2,611	2,269
			66,455
Current assets:			
Closing work in progress		15,786	
Debtors (18,704 + 100 – 300)		18,504	
Petty cash		87	
		34,377	
Less: Current liabilities:			
Creditors	9,204		
Outstanding expenses	876		
Office account overdraft	2,742	12,822	
Net assets			21,555
Client balances			
Client bank:			
Current account	42,289		
Deposit account	99,500	141,789	
Less due to clients		141,789	
			88,010

9.9   TEST FIVE

1   Rousseau died on 8 March 1991, and the executors of his estate appoint the firm of Dickens, Voltaire & Co., Solicitors, to act in the administration of the estate generally. The estate consists of personalty valued at £43,000 and the house 'Realty' valued at £80,000, which is subject to a mortgage of £20,000. Sundry debts due by the estate amount to £2,954. The residue of the estate, save for a legacy of £10,000 left to Carlyle, was bequeathed to Shakespeare. Both of the legatees are clients of the firm, and the balances on their clients' ledger accounts as at 1 April 1991 are: Carlyle Office Account £100, Shakespeare Office Account £60.

During the administration of the estate, the following events take place:

24 April	The deceased's bank agrees to advance £9,087 to the executors in respect of capital transfer tax and interest payable by the estate. A loan account is opened by the bank for the executors and a cheque for £9,087 is sent to Dickens, Voltaire & Co., who bank it and then issue a cheque in favour of the Inland Revenue for the same amount. Probate fees of £80 are paid by cheque.
30 April	The grant is received and registered with the bank, who transfer the sum of £6,296 to the executors' loan account from the deceased's deposit account.
1 May	Cheque drawn for £20 plus VAT in respect of statutory advertisements, the cost of the local advertisement (£20 plus VAT) is paid from petty cash.
6 May	Proceeds of life assurance policy amounting to £7,500 received by the firm, and £2,853 is paid to the bank for the credit of the executors' loan account (which is then closed).
9 May	Exchanged contracts for the sale of 'Realty' for £80,000, the deposit of £8,000 having been paid to Hugo, the estate agent, by the prospective purchaser.
12 May	Cheque for £4,978 received from the auctioneer in respect of the sale of household contents. Commission of £345 (including VAT) had already been deducted.
19 May	Debts amounting to £2,954, together with funeral expenses of £850, are paid out of client account.

23 May   Paid £47 (including VAT £7) by cheque to Dumas on behalf of Carlyle. This disbursement is to be treated as an input of the client.

6 June   The sale of the house is completed and a bank draft (£72,000) for the balance of the purchase money is received and banked. The mortgage is redeemed by the payment by cheque, of £20,435 which is inclusive of accrued interest. Dickens, Voltaire & Co., act for the mortgagees, Plato Finance Ltd. The balance of the deposit (£6,160) is received from the estate agent, commission of £1,840 (including VAT) having already been deducted.

13 June   The executors and Carlyle agree that the pecuniary legacy of £10,000 should be transferred to Carlyle's client account, and after this has been done, a cheque for the net amount due to Carlyle, is sent to him.

16 June   The firm agrees the bills of costs for the sale of the house and the administration of the estate with the executors. Profit costs with regard to the sale amount to £360 (excluding VAT), and with regard to the administration £800 (excluding VAT), together with disbursements.

19 June   The balance of monies held by the firm on behalf of the executors including interest allowed by the firm of £369, is transferred to the account of Shakespeare at the request of the executors, sufficient moneys being retained in client account to meet the sums due to the firm.

20 June   All monies due to the firm by the executors, and by Carlyle and Shakespeare, are transferred to office account, the balance due to Shakespeare being placed in a designated deposit account pending further instructions.

You are required to show the ledger accounts of: (i) the executors of Rousseau, deceased; (ii) Carlyle; (iii) Shakespeare; recording all the above transactions. Show also the cash account (*not* the designated deposit cash account), recording the entries for the month of June 1991.

The rate of VAT is to be taken as 17.5%.

In making the necessary entries, it is important that the account in which the corresponding entry would be made, is clearly identified by the appropriate entry in the details column. There is no need to complete the balance columns in the cash account.   *55 marks*

(Law Society Final Examination, updated)

2   Shrimp has been in practice as a solicitor for many years, and he decides to admit Whelk, his senior assistant, into the firm as a partner. Those parts of the partnership agreement which are relevant to the preparation of the annual accounts, are as follows:

(a)   The name of the firm is to be Shrimp and Whelk.
(b)   Whelk is to be admitted into the firm as a partner, with effect from 1 January 1991.
(c)   Profits and losses are to be shared between the partners, as to Shrimp three-fifths and Whelk two-fifths, after allowing a salary of £12,000 per annum for Whelk, and providing for interest on capital.
(d)   Interest is to be allowed on capital at the rate of 10 per cent per annum.
(e)   The following business asset owned by Shrimp, is to be revalued as at 31 December 1990, the new valuation to be entered into the books being:

Freehold premises   £80,000

(f)   Whelk is to contribute the sum of £30,000 as his share of the capital of the firm.

The firm's accountant produces the following list of balances, which he has extracted from the firm's books, for the year ended 30 June 1991:

	£
Capital accounts	
Shrimp (at 1 July 1990)	40,000
Whelk (at 1 January 1991)	30,000
Cash at bank: Clients' account	
Deposit account	300,000
Current account	47,586
Office account	8,965
Petty cash balance	45
Clients' ledger balances	
Office account	33,242
Clients' account	347,486
Drawings	
Shrimp	42,000
Whelk	9,500

Profit costs	284,596
Work in Progress at 30 June 1990	22,993
Interest receivable	14,986
Sundry creditors	8,942
Administrative and general expenses	204,649
Freehold premises	60,000
Furniture and library at cost	8,400
Motor cars at cost	18,750
Provision for depreciation accounts at 1 July 1990	
Furniture and library	2,520
Motor cars	7,500
Bank loan	20,000

During the year, Shrimp has been appointed legal adviser to a trade association and his remuneration due in respect of the appointment, at 30 June 1991, amounts to £4,000. It has been agreed between the partners that one half of the remuneration should be treated as partnership income and should be taken into account in determining the profits and losses for the year ended 30 June 1991, notwithstanding the fact that the amount was not received until July 1991. The other half of the remuneration is to be treated as the personal income of Shrimp.

Subsequent to the extraction of the above balances, it has been discovered that a cheque received (£80) from a client, has been returned by the paying bankers marked 'refer to drawer'. The cheque had been banked and recorded in the office books, on 27 June 1991. It has been decided that the amount should be written off as a bad debt, as at 30 June 1991.

The following additional information is pertinent:

(a) Depreciation is to be charged at the following rates (straight-line basis):

Furniture and library	10 per cent per annum
Motor cars	20 per cent per annum

(b) The new valuation for the fixed asset as at 1 January 1991, has not yet been recorded in the partnership books.

(c) There are bills outstanding at 30 June 1991 in respect of administrative and general expenses, which have not yet been accounted for, and these amount to £3,863.

(d)   The firm had paid a personal bill (£100) on behalf of Shrimp, and the amount has inadvertently been included in administrative and general expenses. No adjustment has yet been made in respect of this amount.

(e)   Work in progress at 30 June 1991 is valued at £12,193.

(f)   Profits are to be allocated between partners on a time basis. (All calculations to be made in months.)

From the foregoing information, prepare a profit and loss and appropriation account for the year ended 30 June 1991, together with a balance sheet as at that date. (Use the vertical form of presentation.)

Movements on partners' current accounts must be shown in detail.

Taxation (including VAT) is to be ignored, for the purpose of the preparation of these accounts.

45 marks
(Law Society Final Examination, updated)

9.10   SUGGESTED ANSWERS TO TEST FIVE

1   ROUSSEAU

CLIENT: EXECUTORS OF ROUSSEAU, DECEASED
MATTER: ADMINISTRATION OF ESTATE

Date	Details	Office account			Client account		
		Dr £	Cr £	Balance £	Dr £	Cr £	Balance £
1991							
Apr 11	Cash: bank loan					9,087	9,087 Cr
	Cash: Inland Revenue				9,087		–
	Cash: probate fees	80		80 Dr			
May 1	Cash: advertise-ment	23		103 Dr			
	Petty cash: advertisement	23		126 Dr			
May 6	Cash: life insurance proceeds					7,500	7,500 Cr
	Cash: repay bank loan				2,853		4,647 Cr
May 12	Cash: sale of contents less commission (£345)					4,978	9,625 Cr
May 19	Cash: debts				2,954		6,671 Cr
	Cash: funeral expenses				850		5,821 Cr
Jun 6	Cash: sale pro-ceeds of house					72,000	77,821 Cr
	Cash: Plato Finance: mortgage redemption				20,435		57,386 Cr
	Cash: deposit from estate agent (less fee £1,840)					6,160	63,546 Cr
Jun 13	Carlyle: transfer				10,000		53,546
Jun 16	Costs: sale	360					
	VAT	63		549 Dr			
	Costs: administration	800					
	VAT	140		1,489 Dr			
Jun 19	Interest payable		369	1,120 Dr			
	Shakespeare transfer				52,426		1,120
Jun 20	Cash: transfer		1,120	–	1,120		–

CLIENT: CARLYLE

Date	Details	Office account			Client account		
		Dr £	Cr £	Balance £	Dr £	Cr £	Balance £
1991							
Apr 1	Balance			100 Dr			
May 23	Cash: Dumas	47		147 Dr			
Jun 13	Executors of Rousseau: transfer					10,000	10,000 Cr
	Cash: you				9,853		147 Cr
Jun 20	Cash: transfer		147	—	147		—

CLIENT: SHAKESPEARE

Designated deposit account
opened 20 June 1991
(£52,395)

Date	Details	Office account			Client account		
		Dr £	Cr £	Balance £	Dr £	Cr £	Balance £
1991							
Apr 1	Balance			60 Dr			
Jun 19	Executors of Rousseau: transfer					52,426	52,426 Cr
Jun 20	Cash: transfer		60	—	60		52,366 Cr

CASH ACCOUNT

Date	Details	Office account			Client account		
		Dr £	Cr £	Balance £	Dr £	Cr £	Balance £
1991							
Apr 24	Rousseau: bank loan				9,087		
	Rousseau: Inland Revenue					9,087	
	Rousseau: probate fees	80					
May 1	Rousseau: advertisement	23					
May 6	Rousseau: life policy				7,500		
	Rousseau: bank loan repaid					2,853	
May 12	Rousseau: sale of contents				4,978		
May 19	Rousseau: debts					850	
	Rousseau: funeral expenses					2,954	
May 23	Carlyle: Dumas	47					
Jun 6	Rousseau: sale				72,000		
	Rousseau: mortgage redemption					20,435	
	Rousseau: estate agent deposit				6,160		
Jun 13	Carlyle					9,854	
Jun 20	Rousseau: transfer	1,120				1,120	
	Carlyle: transfer	147				147	
	Shakespeare: transfer	60				60	
	Deposit cash: Shakespeare					52,366	

2   SHRIMP AND WHELK

PROFIT AND LOSS ACCOUNT FOR THE YEAR ENDED
30 JUNE 1991

	£	£	£
INCOME			
Profit costs		284,596	
Add: Closing work in progress		12,293	
		296,889	
Less: Opening work in progress		22,993	
		273,896	
Interest receivable		14,986	
Advisory fee		2,000	290,882
LESS: EXPENDITURE			
Administrative expenses	204,649		
Add: Accrued expenses	3,863		
	208,512		
Less: Transfer to Shrimp			
Current account		100	208,412
Bad debts		80	
Depreciation			
Furniture and library			
(10% of £8,400)	840		
Motor cars			
(20% of £18,750)	3,750	4,590	213,082
Net profit			77,800

APPROPRIATION ACCOUNT
1 July 1990 to 31 December 1990
Profit for 6 months to Shrimp   38,900

1 January 1991 to 30 June 1991
Profit for 6 months   38,900

INTEREST ON CAPITAL
Shrimp	3,000	
Whelk	1,500	4,500

SALARY
Whelk		6,000

PROFIT SHARE
Shrimp 3/5	17,040	
Whelk 2/5	11,360	28,400
		38,900

BALANCE SHEET AS AT 30 JUNE 1991

	£	£	£
CAPITAL EMPLOYED			
Capital accounts			
Shrimp capital at start	40,000		
Add revaluation of premises	20,000	60,000	
Whelk		30,000	90,000
Current accounts			
Shrimp		18,840	
Whelk		9,360	28,200
Long-term liabilities			
Bank loan			20,000
			138,200
EMPLOYMENT OF CAPITAL			
FIXED ASSETS			
Freehold premises		80,000	
Motor cats at costs	18,750		
Less: Accumulated depreciation	11,250	7,500	
Furniture and library at cost	8,400		
Less: Accumulated depreciation	3,360	5,040	92,540

CURRENT ASSETS

Work in progress		12,293	
Debtors	33,242		
Add: Sundry debtor	4,000	37,242	
Office account cash		8,885	
Petty cash		45	58,465

LESS: CURRENT LIABILITIES

Creditors		8,942	
Accrued expenses		3,863	12,805	45,660

CLIENT ACCOUNT

Deposit account	300,000	
Current account	47,586	347,586
Less: Due to clients		347,586
		138,200

MOVEMENT ON PARTNERS CURRENT ACCOUNTS

	Shrimp £	Whelk £
Interest on capital	3,000	1,500
Salary		6,000
Profit share	55,940	11,360
	58,940	18,860
Less: Drawings	40,100	9,500
	18,840	9,360

9.11   TEST SIX

1   Golden, Retriever & Co. are solicitors, and they deal with the
following events:

1991

2 December The designated deposit account opened by the firm re
Labrador, in respect of an amount of £5,000 held by
them for the period of four months, is closed, and a
cheque for the sum together with interest of £140
credited by the bank is sent to Labrador.

3 December Paid £20 plus VAT by cheque drawn on office account,
in respect of the reproduction of documents. This disbursement is to be treated as an input of the client (i.e.,
on the agency basis) Terrier, for whom the firm are acting
in a litigation matter.

5 December Retriever, a partner in the firm, hands over a cheque to
the firm's cashier for £3,500, being the deposit on a
cottage which he is purchasing. The firm is acting on his
behalf in this matter.

9 December Received the sum of £520 from Terrier on account of costs
generally.

11 December Banker's draft received for £63,000 on completion of the
sale of Alsatian's house, stake money of £7,000 being
transferred from stakeholder account. The mortgagee of
Alsatian's house (Kennel, a private lender) had already
instructed the firm to act on his behalf in the redemption of
his charge on that house, and redemption money of £22,675
is transferred to his account. It has been agreed that the
mortgagee's costs of £40 plus VAT will be borne by
Alsatian.

12 December The firm decides to write off the sum of £230 (inclusive
of VAT), which has been outstanding for some time, and
is owed by Bulldog who has been adjudicated bankrupt.

A bill of costs is rendered to Alsatian, showing profit
costs of £400 and commission on selling the house £700,
both amounts being exclusive of VAT. The amount due
to the mortgagee in respect of Alsatian's house is paid by
cheque.

17 December Paid fee of £345 (including VAT £45) to Collie, an expert witness who appeared on behalf of Terrier. The payment was made out of client account.

22 December Dalmatian requests that the firm send a cheque for £750 to one of his creditors, Spaniel. The firm sends the cheque, and later the same day, a cheque for £600 is received from Dalmatian in partial satisfaction.

Alsatian requests that the amount due to him, together with interest allowed by the firm of £120, should be transferred to a designated deposit account, costs and disbursements being transferred to office account the same day.

30 December Bill of costs in respect of litigation matter rendered to Terrier, showing profit costs of £800 plus VAT.

The bank notifies the firm that the cheque from Dalmatian has been returned unpaid by the paying bankers.

1992

5 January   A cheque for £730 is sent to English, Setter & Co., who had acted as agents on behalf of the firm, in connection with a litigation matter being pursued by Greyhound, a client of the firm. The bill showed profit costs of £800 less agency commission of £200 (both exclusive of VAT), and disbursements of £40 (no VAT). The firm now renders its own bill of costs to Greyhound, showing profit costs of £1,000 plus VAT and disbursements of £40 (no VAT). Both the profit costs and disbursements of the agent solicitors, are included in the foregoing amounts.

14 January   Cheque received drawn in favour of Whippet, a client, for £900. With the concurrence of Dalmation, the cheque is indorsed over to the firm in satisfaction of a debt due by Whippet to Dalmatian, the unpaid cheque for £600 made payable to the firm, consequently being cancelled.

21 January   Received from Terrier and Greyhound, the amounts due to the firm, their respective accounts then being closed.

You are required to show all the relevant entries in the accounts in the clients' ledger, recording the above transactions. It is important that the account in which the corresponding entry would be made, is clearly identified by the appropriate entry in the details column.

Ignore all forms of taxation, except VAT, which is to be taken as 17.5%.

50 marks
(Law Society Final Examination, updated)

2   Maize and Wheat are in partnership as solicitors. The partnership agreement shows the following relevant details:

(a)   Salaries of £10,000 per annum and £5,000 per annum are payable to Maize and Wheat respectively.

(b)   Interest is to be allowed on partners' capital at the rate of 10 per cent per annum.

(c)   Profits or losses remaining after partnership salaries and interest on capital have been charged, are to be divided as to Maize two-thirds and Wheat one-third.

The firm's bookkeeper has prepared a list of balances, which he has extracted from the firm's books, for the year ended 31 December 1991. They are as follows:

	£
Profit costs	241,657
Work in hand at 1 January 1991	22,243
Interest receivable	14,869
Rent received	5,500
Administrative and general expenses	183,489
Bad debts	600
Capital accounts	
Maize	40,000
Wheat	20,000
Current accounts	
Maize	1,678 (Credit)
Wheat	420 (Debit)
Drawings	
Maize	31,476
Wheat	24,566
Motor cars at cost	18,500
Furniture, library and equipment at cost	11,240

Provision for depreciation accounts at
1 January 1991

Motor cars	4,625
Furniture, library and equipment	5,058
Sundry creditors	8,564
Due to clients	164,675
Due from clients	13,034
Cash at bank — Clients' account	
Current account	34,675
Deposit account	130,000
Petty cash balance	141
Leasehold property at cost	35,000
Cash at bank — Office account	1,232

After reviewing the balances, the partners decide that the following adjustments are necessary:

(a)   Rent received includes the sum of £500, which has been paid in respect of the three months ending 31 March 1992.

(b)   Included in furniture, library and equipment is an amount (£400) which represents the cost price of some equipment which was scrapped on 1 January 1991. Depreciation charged on the scrapped equipment, and included in the depreciation account as at 1 January 1991, amounted to £180. No accounting entries have yet been made in respect of the scrapping of the equipment.

(c)   Each partner is to be charged with one third of the motor expenses he has incurred during the year. The amounts so incurred, and debited in the firm's administrative and general expenses account, are:

Maize	£2,466
Wheat	£1,818

(d)   There are bills outstanding at 31 December 1991, in respect of administrative and general expenses, which have not yet been accounted for, and these amount to £1,654.

(e)   Depreciation is to be charged (straight-line basis) at the following rates:

Motor cars	25 per cent per annum
Furniture, library and equipment	15 per cent per annum

(f)   Work in hand at 31 December 1991 was valued at £26,941.

(g)   An error in posting to the ledger accounts had been made, in that the sum of £400 which was to have been written off as a bad debt, had been inadvertently posted to the profit costs account, debit side.

From the foregoing information, prepare a profit and loss appropriation account for the year ended 31 December 1991, together with a balance sheet as at that date. (Use the vertical form of presentation.)

Movements on partners' current accounts must be shown in detail.

Taxation (including VAT) is to be ignored for the purpose of the preparation of these accounts.

50 marks
(Law Society Final Examination, updated)

9.12   SUGGESTED ANSWERS TO TEST SIX

1   GOLDEN RETRIEVER & CO.

CLIENT: LABRADOR

Designated deposit account
Opened August 1991 (£5,000)
Closed 2 December 1991

Date	Details	Office account			Client account		
		Dr £	Cr £	Balance £	Dr £	Cr £	Balance £
1991							
Dec 1	Balance b/d deposit						5,000 Cr
Dec 2	Cash: interest					140	
	Cash: you				5,140		–

STAKEHOLDER ACCOUNT

Date	Details	Office account			Client account		
		Dr £	Cr £	Balance £	Dr £	Cr £	Balance £
1991							
Dec 1	Balance b/d						7,000 Cr
Dec 11	Alsatian: transfer				7,000		–

CLIENT: KENNEL
MATTER: REDEMPTION OF CHARGE (ALSATIAN)

Date	Details	Office account			Client account		
		Dr £	Cr £	Balance £	Dr £	Cr £	Balance £
1991 Dec 11	Alsatian: transfer					22,675	22,675 Cr
	Costs	40					
	VAT	7		47 Dr			
	Alsatian: transfer costs		47	—			
Dec 12	Cash: you				22,675		—

CLIENT: TERRIER
MATTER: LITIGATION

Date	Details	Office account			Client account		
		Dr £	Cr £	Balance £	Dr £	Cr £	Balance £
1991 Dec 3	Cash: copying charges	23		23Dr			
Dec 9	Cash: you					520	520 Cr
Dec 17	Cash: Collie				345		175 Cr
Dec 30	Costs	800					
	VAT	140		963 Dr			
1992 Jan 21	Cash: you		788	175 Dr			
	Cash: transfer costs		175	—	175		—

CLIENT: DALMATION

Date	Details	Office account			Client account		
		Dr £	Cr £	Balance £	Dr £	Cr £	Balance £
1991							
Dec 22	Cash: Spaniel	750		750 Dr			
	Cash: you		600	150 Dr			
Dec 30	Cash: dishonoured cheque	600		750 Dr			
1992							
Jan 14	Cash: Whippet		750	–		150	150 Cr

Note:

An account could have been opened for Whippet and an entry made in that account by way of memorandum.

CLIENT: ALSATIAN   DESIGNATED DEPOSIT ACCOUNT
MATTER: SALE OF HOUSE   OPENED 22 DECEMBER 1991 (£46,134)

Date	Details	Office account			Client account		
		Dr £	Cr £	Balance £	Dr £	Cr £	Balance £
1991							
Dec 11	Cash: sale proceeds					63,000	63,000 Cr
	Stakeholder: transfer					7,000	70,000 Cr
	Kennel: transfer				22,675		47,325 Cr
	Kennel: transfer costs	47		47 Dr			
Dec 12	Costs	400					
	VAT	70					
	Sale commission	700					
	VAT	122.50		1,339.50 Dr			
Dec 22	Interest payable		120	1,219.50 Dr			
	Cash: transfer costs		1,219.50	–	1,219.50		46,105.50 Cr

CLIENT: GREYHOUND
MATTER: LITIGATION

Date	Details	Office account			Client account		
		Dr £	Cr £	Balance £	Dr £	Cr £	Balance £
1992							
Jan 5	Cash: agents' disbursements	40					
	Costs	1,000					
	VAT	175		1,215 Dr			
Jan 21	Cash: you		1,215	—			

CLIENT: BULLDOG

Date	Details	Office account			Client account		
		Dr £	Cr £	Balance £	Dr £	Cr £	Balance £
1991							
Dec 1	Balance b/d			230 Dr			
	Bad debts		200				
	Customs & Excise		30	—			

2   MAIZE AND WHEAT

PROFIT AND LOSS ACCOUNT FOR THE YEAR ENDED
31 DECEMBER 1991

	£	£	£
INCOME			
Profit costs		242,057	
Add: Closing work in progress		26,941	
		268,998	
Less: Opening work in progress		22,243	
		246,755	
Interest receivable		14,869	
Rent receivable		5,000	266,624
LESS EXPENDITURE			
Administrative and general expenses	183,489		
Add: Outstanding expenses	1,654		
	185,143		
Less: Partners' motor expenses	1,428	183,715	
Bad debts	600		
Add: Correction of error	400	1,000	
Depreciation:			
Motor cars	4,625		
Furniture and equipment	1,626		
Loss on disposal	220	6,471	191,186
NET PROFIT			75,438

APPROPRIATION ACCOUNT
SALARIES

Maize	10,000	
Wheat	5,000	15,000

INVESTMENT ON CAPITAL

Maize	4,000	
Wheat	2,000	6,000

PROFIT SHARE

Maize 2/3	36,292		
Wheat 1/3	18,146	54,438	75,438

BALANCE SHEET AS AT 31 DECEMBER 1991

	£	£	£
CAPITAL EMPLOYED			
Capital accounts			
Maize	40,000		
Wheat	20,000	60,000	
Current accounts			
Maize	19,672		
Wheat	(446)	19,226	79,226
EMPLOYMENT OF CAPITAL			
FIXED ASSETS			
Leasehold property		35,000	
Cars at cost	18,500		
Less: Accumulated depreciation	9,250	9,250	
Furniture, library and equipment at cost	10,840		
Less: Accumulated depreciation	6,504	4,336	48,586
CURRENT ASSETS			
Work in progress	26,941		
Debtors	13,034		
Office bank account	1,242		
Petty cash	141	41,358	

LESS: CURRENT LIABILITIES

Creditors	8,564		
Outstanding expenses	1,654		
Rent received in advance	500	10,718	30,640

CLIENT BALANCES

Cash at bank: deposit account		130,000
current account		34,675
		164,675
Less: Due to clients		164,675
		79,226

MOVEMENT ON PARTNERS' CURRENT ACCOUNTS

	Maize	Wheat
	£	£
Balance at start	1,678	(420)
Salary	10,000	5,000
Interest on capital	4,000	2,000
Profit share	36,292	18,146
	51,970	24,726
Less: Drawings	32,298	25,172
	19,672	(446)

9.13   TEST SEVEN

1 The following balances appeared in the relevant client's ledger accounts of Oak, Poplar & Co., Solicitors, as at 1 April 1991:

Larch	Office Account	£nil	Client Account	£600
Aspen	Office Account	£43	Client Account	£20,232
Willow	Office Account	£nil	Client Account	£1,500

The firm deals with the following events during the months of April and May 1991:

1 April	A designated deposit account is opened by the firm on behalf of Aspen, and the sum of £20,000 is transferred thereto, in accordance with his request.
6 April	Cheque received from Alder, being the deposit on the sale of a house by Aspen, the firm to hold the sum (£5,500) as stakeholders.
7 April	After receiving the agreement of Larch, the sum of £250 is transferred to the account of Maple Insurance Ltd from the amount held on behalf of Larch in client account, being an insurance premium due this day.
11 April	Exchanged contracts for the sale of Aspen's house, and paid disbursements of £14 (no VAT) on his behalf, out of petty cash the same day.
12 April	Poplar, a partner in the firm, is purchasing a cottage jointly with his wife and they have instructed the firm to act on their behalf in this matter. The firm pays the local land charges search fee (£14) re the cottage, from petty cash.
15 April	A bill of costs is received from Wych Elm & Co., a firm of solicitors acting as agents on behalf of the firm in connection with the affairs of Willow. The bill shows profit costs of £800 (excluding VAT) and disbursements of £100 (no VAT). The firm pays the agents' bill and renders its own bill of costs to Willow, showing disbursements of £100 (no VAT) and profit costs of £1,200 plus VAT. Both the profit costs and the disbursements of the agent solicitors, are included in the foregoing amounts.
18 April	Poplar hands over a cheque to the firm's cashier for £4,000, being the deposit on the cottage which he is purchasing jointly with his wife.
20 April	Paid by cheque to Willow, the amount outstanding in his client account, together with interest allowed by the firm of £42. The account is then closed.
25 April	Contracts are exchanged for the purchase of the Poplars' cottage, the deposit of £4,000 being paid to the vendor's solicitors as stakeholders.

27 April   Banker's draft (£49,500) received from Horse Chestnuts, solicitors, on completion of the sale of Aspen's house. Paid estate agents' fees (£700 plus VAT) the same day, the invoice being addressed to Aspen.

28 April   Aspen agrees with the bill of costs rendered by the firm, showing profit costs of £400 plus VAT and disbursements. The amount due to the firm is transferred to the office account, and Aspen's designated deposit account is closed, interest of £83 having been credited thereto.

The balance of monies now held on behalf of Aspen, including interest allowed by the firm of £106 (inclusive of interest on the deposit held by the firm as stakeholders) is paid over by one cheque, thereby closing the client's ledger account.

29 April   The net amount due to Maple Insurance Ltd is paid, being the gross premium received (£250) less commission of £37, the client (Larch) having agreed with the firm's retention of that amount. The account is then closed.

3 May   Larch requests that the firm send a cheque for £1,000 to Rowan, to whom he owes money. The firm sends the cheque, and later the same day, a cheque for £400 is received from Larch in partial satisfaction, together with a cheque for £250 drawn by Spruce (a debtor of Larch) payable to Larch. The latter cheque is indorsed over to Oak, Poplar & Co.

9 May   The bank notifies the firm that the cheque from Spruce has been returned unpaid by the paying bankers.

You are required to show all the relevant entries in the accounts in the clients' ledger (including a stakeholder account, if necessary), recording the above transactions. It is important that the account in which the corresponding entry would be made, is clearly identified by the appropriate entry in the details column. All accounts are to be balanced.

Ignore all forms of taxation, except VAT, which is to be taken as 17.5%.

55 marks
(Law Society Final Examination, updated)

2 The partnership agreement of Sherry and Brandy, who are practising solicitors, shows the following details which are relevant to the preparation of their annual accounts:

(a) Profits and losses are to be shared between the partners, as to Sherry three-quarters and Brandy one-quarter, after allowing a salary of £24,000 per annum for Brandy, and providing for interest on capital.

(b) Interest is to be allowed on capital at the rate of 10 per cent per annum.

(c) The sum of £4,000 per annum is to be transferred from Brandy's current account to his capital account, such transfer to cease once the balance on the latter account reaches the sum of £40,000.

The firm's accountant produces the following information, which he has extracted from the firm's books, for the year ended 30 April 1991:

	£
Freehold premises	80,000
Motor cars at cost	30,000
Furniture, library and equipment at cost	14,600
Computer and ancillary equipment at cost	8,400
Provision for depreciation accounts at 1 May 1990:	
Motor cars	18,000
Furniture, library and equipment	7,300
Computer and ancillary equipment	2,100
Amount due to clients	765,987
Cash at bank – clients' account	
Current account	65,987
Deposit account	700,000
Amount due from clients	53,567
Cash at bank – office account	7,617
Petty cash balance	123
Capital accounts	
Sherry	80,000
Brandy	30,000
Current accounts	
Sherry	8,342 (credit)
Brandy	654 (credit)

Drawings
  Sherry   47,326
  Brandy   22,768
Sundry creditors   11,890
Profit costs   367,875
Work in hand at 1 May 1990   21,426
Interest received   24,562
Administrative and general expenses   264,896

After reviewing the above balances, the partners decide that the following adjustments are necessary:

(a)   Depreciation is to be charged (straight-line basis) at the following rates:

Motor cars	20 per cent per annum
Furniture, library and equipment	10 per cent per annum
Computer and ancillary equipment	25 per cent per annum

(b)   Work in hand at 30 April 1991, was valued at £11,432.

(c)   There are bills outstanding at 30 April 1991, in respect of administrative and general expenses, which have not yet been accounted for, and these amount to £18,567.

(d)   It was agreed that the transfer of the sum of £4,000 from Brandy's current account to his capital account, should be effected on 30 April 1991, and that interest should not be allowed on that sum, in respect of the year ending on that date.

(e)   It was discovered that Sherry had drawn two cheques on the office bank account, on 29 April 1991, without reference having been made to the accounts department. Consequently, no entries had been made in the books of account as at 30 April 1991. One cheque was in respect of a private debt of £1,000, the other cheque being the repayment of a rebate (£420) which had been allowed to a client who had previously paid his bill in full. No entry has yet been made in the books in respect of the rebate, and any VAT is to be ignored.

(f)   The freehold premises had been revalued at £100,000 on 31 October 1990, but the necessary entries had not yet been recorded in the books.

From the foregoing information, you are asked to prepare a profit and loss appropriation account for the year ended 30 April 1991, together with a balance sheet as at that date. (Use the vertical form of presentation.)

Movements on partners' current accounts must be shown in detail.

Taxation (including VAT) is to be ignored, for the purpose of the preparation of these accounts.

45 marks

(Law Society Final Examination, updated)

9.14 SUGGESTED ANSWERS TO TEST SEVEN

1 OAK, POPLAR & CO.

CLIENT: ASPEN

Designated deposit account
Opened 1 April 1991 (£20,000)
Closed 28 April 1991

Date	Details	Office account			Client account		
		Dr £	Cr £	Balance £	Dr £	Cr £	Balance £
1991							
Apr 1	Balance b/d			43 Dr			20,232 Cr
Apr 11	Petty cash: disbursements	14		57 Dr			
Apr 27	Cash: sale proceeds					49,500	69,732 Cr
	Stakeholder: transfer					5,500	75,232 Cr
	Cash: estate agent				805		74,427 Cr
Apr 28	Costs	400					
	VAT	70		527 Dr			
	Cash: transfer		527	—	527		73,900 Cr
	Deposit cash: interest					83	73,983 Cr
	Cash: interest payable					106	74,089 Cr
	Cash: you				74,089		—

STAKEHOLDER ACCOUNT

Date	Details	Office account			Client account		
		Dr £	Cr £	Balance £	Dr £	Cr £	Balance £
1991							
Apr 6	Cash: Aspen: deposit					5,500	5,500 Cr
Apr 27	Aspen: transfer				5,500		–

CLIENT: LARCH

Date	Details	Office account			Client account		
		Dr £	Cr £	Balance £	Dr £	Cr £	Balance £
1991							
Apr 1	Balance b/d						600 Cr
Apr 7	Maple Insurance: premium due				250		350 Cr
May 3	Cash: Rowan	1,000		1,000 Dr			
	Cash: you (cheque £400; cheque £250 indorsed from Spruce)		650	350 Dr			
	Cash: transfer		350	–	350		–
May 19	Cash: dishonoured cheque	250		250 Dr			

CLIENT: WILLOW

Date	Details	Office account			Client account		
		Dr £	Cr £	Balance £	Dr £	Cr £	Balance £
1991							
Apr 1	Balance						1,500 Cr
Apr 15	Cash: agents' disbursements	100		100 Dr			
	Costs	1,200					
	VAT	210		1,510 Dr			
Apr 20	Cash: interest payable					42	1,542 Cr
	Cash: transfer		1,510	–	1,510		32 Cr
	Cash: you				32		–

CLIENT: MAPLE INSURANCE LTD

Date	Details	Office account			Client account		
		Dr £	Cr £	Balance £	Dr £	Cr £	Balance £
1991							
Apr 7	Larch: transfer premium					250	250 Cr
Apr 29	Commission	37		37 Dr			
	Cash: you				213		37 Cr
	Cash: transfer commission		37	–	37		–

MR & MRS POPLAR
RE: PURCHASE OF COTTAGE

Date	Details	Office account			Client account		
		Dr £	Cr £	Balance £	Dr £	Cr £	Balance £
1991							
Apr 12	Petty cash: search fee	14		14 Dr			
Apr 16	Cash: deposit received					4,000	4,000 Cr
Apr 25	Cash: deposit paid				4,000		

Note. Money treated as clients' money because purchase is in joint names and therefore received on behalf of Poplar and his wife. The Solicitors' Accounts Rules 1991 provide that a solicitor may not treat as client money, money to which *only* he or one of his partners is entitled.

2   SHERRY AND BRANDY

PROFIT AND LOSS ACCOUNT FOR THE YEAR ENDED
30 APRIL 1991

	£	£	£
INCOME			
Profit costs	367,875		
Less: Rebate	420	367,455	
Add: Closing work in progress		11,432	
		378,887	
Less: Opening work in progress		21,426	357,461
Add: Interest received			24,562
			382,023

LESS: EXPENDITURE

Administrative and general expenses	264,896	
Add: Outstanding	18,567	283,463

Depreciation			
Motor cars	6,000		
Furniture and library	1,460		
Computers	2,100	9,560	293,023

NET PROFIT		89,000

APPROPRIATION ACCOUNT
INTEREST ON CAPITAL

Sherry	8,750	
Brandy	3,250	12,000

SALARIES

Sherry	—	
Brandy	24,000	24,000

PROFIT SHARE

Sherry 3/4	39,750		
Brandy 1/4	13,250	53,000	89,000

BALANCE SHEET AS AT 30 APRIL 1991

	£	£	£
CAPITAL EMPLOYED			
Capital Accounts			
Sherry:			
Capital at start	80,000		
Add: Revaluation	15,000	95,000	
Brandy:			
Capital at start	30,000		
Add: Revaluation	5,000		
Add: Current account transfer	4,000	39,000	134,000
Current accounts			
Sherry		8,516	
Brandy		14,386	22,902
			156,902
EMPLOYMENT OF CAPITAL			
FIXED ASSETS			
Freehold premises		100,000	
Cars at cost	30,000		
Less: Depreciation	24,000	6,000	
Furniture at cost	14,600		
Less: Depreciation	8,760	5,840	
Computers at cost	8,400		
Less: Depreciation	4,200	4,200	116,040
CURRENT ASSETS			
Debtors		53,567	
Office bank account £7,617			
Less: £1,420		6,197	
Petty Cash		123	
Work in progress		11,432	71,319

LESS: CURRENT LIABILITIES

Creditors	11,890		
Outstanding expenses	18,567	30,457	
NET ASSETS			40,862

CLIENT BALANCES

Client current account		65,987
Client deposit account		700,000
		765,987
Less: Due to clients		765,987
		156,902

MOVEMENT ON PARTNERS' CURRENT ACCOUNTS

	Sherry £	Brandy £
Balance	8,342	654
Interest on capital	8,750	3,250
	17,092	3,904
Salary	–	24,000
	17,092	24,904
Profit share	39,750	13,250
	56,842	41,154
Less drawings	48,326	22,768
(Sherry: 47,326 + 1,000)		
	8,516	18,386
Transfer to capital		4,000
		14,386

Calculation of interest on capital:

	£
Sherry	
£80,000 @ 10%	8,000
£15,000 (revaluation) @ 10% = £1,500	
For 6 months: 1,500/2	750
	8,750
Brandy	
£30,000 @ 10%	3,000
£5,000 (revaluation) @ 10% = £500	
For 6 months: 500/2	250
	3,250

Index